INDIAN GAMING

INDIAN GAMING

TRIBAL SOVEREIGNTY AND AMERICAN POLITICS

By W. Dale Mason

University of Oklahoma Press : Norman

Library of Congress Cataloging-in-Publication Data

Mason, W. Dale (Walter Dale), 1951–
    Indian gaming : tribal sovereignty and American politics /
by W. Dale Mason.
      p. cm.
    Originally presented as the author's thesis (Ph.D.—
University of Oklahoma, 1996).
    Includes bibliographical references and index.
    ISBN 0–8061–3213–2 (cloth)
    ISBN 0–8061–3260–4 (paper)
    1. Indians of North America—Gambling—New Mexico.
2. Indians of North America—Gambling—Oklahoma.
3. Indian business enterprises—New Mexico.   4. Indian
business enterprises—Oklahoma.   5. Indians of North
America—New Mexico—Politics and government.
6. Indians of North America—Oklahoma—Politics and
government.   I. Title.

E78.N65 M39 2000
795'.089'97—dc21

               99–054880
                  CIP

The paper in this book meets the guidelines for permanence and durability of the Committee on Production Guidelines for Book Longevity of the Council on Library Resources, Inc. ∞

2 3 4 5 6 7 8 9 10

For Edwin and Christine Mason,
loving parents who emphasized education
and provided a moral compass.

Contents

Illustrations

National Indian Gaming Association director Tim Wapato
    speaking at a pro-gaming rally, Santa Fe, February 2, 1996
Employee of an Indian gaming facility at pro-gaming rally, state
    capitol, Santa Fe, February 2, 1996
Pro-gaming signs, state capitol, Santa Fe, February 2, 1996
Bumper stickers printed by Isleta Gaming Palace
Santa Ana Pueblo Star Casino, Bernalillo, New Mexico
Detail from a sample ballot for the 1997 gaming referendum
    at the Navajo Nation

Photographs from the author's collection

MAPS

Tables

Preface

What is past is prologue is palpably true in American Indian policy. In no other area of American public policy and law is the past given such expression in the present. The effects of past policies, congressional acts, and court decisions were ever-present during the research for this book. Past events have shaped Indian policy, Indian-white relations, the way Indians live their lives, and the sovereign status of tribal governments. For example, the history of Oklahoma tribes has helped to shape contemporary state politics and culture. That the Five Civilized Tribes are more successful in reaching agreements with the state on some issues is partly the result of their political development in Indian Territory.

In New Mexico the past is defined in terms of centuries; Indian-white relations extend back three hundred fifty years. I observed the continuing importance of past events on present realities when I interviewed the governor of Pojoaque Pueblo, Jake Viarrial. The pueblo itself had ceased to exist as a separate entity early in this century when its few remaining residents were urged to move elsewhere. However, the pueblo began to re-form in the 1930s. It had lost its religious societies and kivas, and its first governor was Hispanic. As I sat in Governor Viarrial's office, less than a mile from both the pueblo's casino and the pueblo's new kiva—paid for from casino profits—it struck me that these epitomized the continuity and the change in Indian life.

Indian gaming provided an opportunity to continue what has been a long personal and scholarly journey—to determine the status of Indian tribes in the American political system. The events in New Mexico over a period of three years alerted me to new data and caused me to contemplate future research possibilities. It was also fun, heady, and exciting to be so close to such momentous events.

I did not intend to write either a dissertation or a book about Indian gaming. When I began the doctoral program at the University of Oklahoma, a dissertation on Indian policy during the Johnson and Nixon administrations was my goal. I pursued this course of research for several years until my objectives became clearer: defining the place of Indian tribal governments in the contemporary American political system. While much could be learned about the topic from a study of the years 1964 to 1974, much had occurred in Indian policy since the concept of self-determination began to germinate during the Great Society. Among the many important changes was the growth of tribally owned and operated gambling establishments in Indian Country. As Indian gaming became more widespread, and as tribal-state conflict began to increase because of it, I changed the direction of my research and, with the support of my Ph.D. committee, chaired by Allen Hertzke, a dissertation on Indian gaming resulted—a dissertation that was in many ways outside the normal boundaries of the discipline.

Over the past ten years I have become acutely aware of the marginalized place of American Indian politics in political science. The literature review for my dissertation on Indian gaming demonstrated the dearth of studies by political scientists on American Indian policy and politics. Three separate personal encounters with prominent political scientists provided further evidence that American Indians are not generally seen as worthy of serious study by American political scientists. When

I first began my doctoral studies at the University of Oklahoma, I asked a professor in the department why Indians were not studied in the discipline. His reply was that they were not where the power lies.

The second conversation about Indians and the discipline took place with the groundbreaking political scientist Richard Fenno. I had been in touch with him about my research, and when he came to the university for a series of lectures sponsored by the Carl Albert Center for Congressional Studies, we talked at greater length. Fenno advised me to "put 'Indians' behind the colon" in the title of my dissertation. His reasoning was that the work would not be taken seriously if the title emphasized "Indians." Fenno's comment reveals a great deal about the relative significance the discipline gives Indian politics.

Perhaps that advice helped in my winning the American Political Science Association's (APSA's) William Anderson Award for "Best dissertation completed in 1996 or 1997 in the field of state and local politics, federalism, or intergovernmental relations." However, on the night I received the award neither the title nor the topic had been completely grasped by all members of the association. At a reception after the awards ceremony, Dr. Hertzke introduced me to the outgoing president of the APSA. He informed the president that my dissertation was about Indian gaming. This distinguished and widely published scholar said that there was someone I should meet and called over a graduate student to talk to me about his work, in game theory. He was from India. This somewhat humorous incident confirmed that American Indians are far from the frame of reference of most political scientists, even the most distinguished.

Although this book is based on my dissertation, in a larger sense it is the result of a winding and serendipitous journey of twenty-five years that began when I was a graduate student in political science at the University of Cincinnati. Like the late Harry Chapin, no straight lines have made up my life.

My involvement with Indian people and issues has been both academic and personal. My academic studies of the connection of American Indians to American politics began when, as a graduate research assistant, University of Cincinnati history professor Walter Williams and I investigated the connection between radical congressional Republicans of the Reconstruction period and their position on Indian issues. Soon after we completed our study I was accepted as a volunteer in Volunteers in Service to America (VISTA), a Great Society program commonly called the "domestic peace corps." I was sent to work as a paralegal with the Nebraska Indian Commission.

My work with the commission allowed me to apply my academic knowledge as well as the practical political experience I had gained in Cincinnati. More significantly, however, my education in Indian issues continued, and I met people who became lifelong friends and who changed my perspective on many things.

My work with the commission consisted of providing paralegal assistance to American Indian inmates in the Nebraska Penal Complex and investigating police brutality against Indian people in western Nebraska. In the former capacity I learned something about corrections and the horrors of life in maximum-security institutions. The inmate I worked most closely with, Enoch Robinson, a brilliant jailhouse lawyer from the Omaha reservation, was stabbed to death at an Indian Club meeting shortly before I left the state.

My education was most intense in western Nebraska, where Indian people were frequently harassed and brutalized by law enforcement officers. I interviewed people who had been on the receiving end of these abuses and listened to the explanations of public officials. The perceptions of the "problem" and exactly what the "problem" was were worlds apart.

One night in November 1975 I attended a Gordon City Council meeting with two of my VISTA colleagues to listen to local Indian residents present their grievances against the city and county police. The witnesses were late, and the white city council members bided their time with jokes about Indian names. Eventually a group of Indian people came into the council room. Leading them was a young Oglala Lakota man with a ponytail and wearing an old green army jacket. He was

Bob Yellow Bird, state coordinator of the American Indian Movement (AIM) and, with his family, a resident of Gordon.

This was my first encounter with a man who, along with his family's struggles, changed my life. Bob Yellow Bird was a man of immense passions and an unshakable belief that the rights of Indian people, especially the Lakota Sioux, were continuing to be trampled by white society. A trust developed between us that lasted until his passing in 1997. From him and his late wife, Joann, herself the victim of a savage attack by a white Gordon police officer, I learned that the pain resulting from genocidal policies and brutality did not take place on cold pieces of paper but on the bodies of human beings. Their memory is never far from me.

Bob and Joann's children, Clint, Wes, Charlie Brown, Wambli, Tatanka, Robin, Jennifer, and Sunset, keep their parents' flame alive. Bob's brother, Richard, fights the good fight, and his niece Toni is cut in the same mold. I am proud they are all my friends.

When I left Nebraska I knew I had been changed by what I had experienced there, but I could not have predicted that those experiences would return to me in continuing and unexpected ways. The first time my Nebraska experiences clearly influenced my life occurred when I was searching for a master's thesis topic. I had initially intended to write a thesis about Public Law 83-280, a federal statute that I had become familiar with in Nebraska. However, I could not settle on an acceptable approach.

One day I got a call from Norman Thomas, then head of the University of Cincinnati's Political Science Department. He suggested that I write my thesis on the American Indian Movement. AIM was, of course, the logical choice, and Dr. Thomas, political science professor Eric Wiese, and Dr. Williams served on my master's committee. The thesis in turn led to a 1984 article I was asked to write about AIM in Nebraska for a special edition of the *Journal of the West* edited by Williams. That article and Williams's generous offer have been important in subsequent years to opening doors and opportunities.

Dr. Thomas is one of the most influential people in my academic career. He mentored me through undergraduate school, understood my need to drop out of graduate school the first time, and readily welcomed me back. He chaired my master's committee and then wisely suggested the University of Oklahoma as a place to pursue my Ph.D. If I have accomplished anything in academics, it is because of the guidance of this wise and compassionate unreconstructed New Deal Democrat.

Along the way I have met some other very impressive, dedicated, and brilliant people. Two of those individuals, Gary Pitchlynn and Frank Chaves, continued to play important roles in providing information and guiding me in the right direction when I strayed. Gary was more than generous with his time and insightful comments. Frank Chaves was perhaps the most helpful person I met during the course of my journey up and down the Rio Grande. Frank opened the door that permitted me to see from the inside how the tribes were playing the political game. Frank is one of the most dignified and dedicated men I have ever known in public life.

Through Frank Chaves I was able to have fairly regular contact with the tribes' political consultant, Rex Hackler. Rex, a political pro, experienced a different kind of campaign, one in which more than winning at the polls was at stake. He now works in Washington, D.C., for the Bureau of Indian Affairs (BIA). Frank also introduced me to Odis Echols, a former state senator and perhaps the state's most influential lobbyist.

Along the way, serendipity sometimes seemed to be guiding the research. After chasing him for more than a year and a half, a last-chance encounter with attorney Kevin Gover in the Round House in Santa Fe led to an evening of political insight shared by him and his sister, Lisa Gover. It was an enjoyable evening and displayed the brilliance of the man who guided the tribes' political strategy and who now heads the BIA as assistant secretary of the Interior for Indian affairs.

Attorney Richard Hughes was consistently helpful with up-to-the-minute information and analysis of the legal difficulties the tribes found themselves in. I was also fortunate to interview several Pueblo governors and councilmen, including Governor Viarrial, the most colorful and volatile of the Pueblo leaders.

LaDonna Harris, president of Americans for Indian Opportunity, kindly opened her gaming files to me. Dr. Elizabeth Rosenthal generously provided a place to stay in Santa Fe and encouraged me at a crucial point in the research. In addition to Gary Pitchlynn, others in Oklahoma were helpful, including Ada attorney Jess Green and Tracy Burris, chair of the Oklahoma Indian Gaming Association. Chickasaw Nation governor Bill Anoatubby generously sat twice for interviews, including one that lasted well over three hours. Ph.D. committee member Rennard Strickland not only helped with the early thinking about this project, he also opened many doors to people across the state.

On an even more personal level, I want to thank all of the faculty members who served on my graduate committee at the University of Oklahoma: Allen Hertzke, chair, Rennard Strickland, Edwin Corr, David Ray, Phil Lujan, Susan Zlomke, Jon Hale, and Tom Hagan. No graduate student ever had committee members more supportive than these individuals. They provided both personal support and intellectual challenges. Hertzke was especially crucial in providing guidance and enthusiasm and in keeping me on track. He is a man of high personal and intellectual integrity. To each and every member of my committee I owe a debt of thanks.

I benefited from some remarkable teachers at the University of Oklahoma: Allen Hertzke, Ron Peters, Susan Zlomke, Betsy Gunn, Ed Corr, Al Trachtenberg, Tom Hagan, and Rennard Strickland. Each helped to shape the way I think about, write about, and approach problems. Arguably no one can receive a Ph.D. in political science from the University of Oklahoma without the cooperation and support of Geri Rowden. She was for six years a supporter, a butt kicker, a facilitator, and a friend. She too is one whose support I cannot begin to repay. Department staff Mickey Ward and Mary France were always patient and helpful.

University of Oklahoma Political Science Department Chair Ron Peters facilitated my research, including unexpected but very needed financial support. Professor Stephen Sloan became a friend and supporter. His good-humored encouragement helped during rough times. Professor Cindy Simon-Rosenthal was a friend when I needed one.

Others over the years have provided personal encouragement and friendship, including Angie Vaught, Susan Gray, Bruce Poolaw, Larry Carter, Erich and Tammy Frankland, Gayle Lawn-Day, Eric Shabuya, Deb St. John, Angela Jones, Terry Garrett, and Michele Privette in Oklahoma; Ryan Sandoval, Charles Hustito, Vernon Laughlin, Felicia Begay, Jo McKenzie, Lavinia Sam, Lee Zouhannie-Russell (and Ashleigh and Connerie), Martin Panteah, and Ruth Rhoad in New Mexico; and Mike and Alyce Rieck and Jeanne Harris in Cincinnati.

My sister, Linda Rinear, has given me her love and moral support over the years and was a source of endless encouragement and advice during my moves to Norman and Gallup. Her attendance, with my niece Melanie, at my commencement made it a joyous time.

I owe thanks to my spring 1995 "American Politics and Indian Cultures" students at the University of Oklahoma. They helped me to achieve a fundamental breakthrough in understanding Indian policy from a different perspective. It was a very special class.

I also owe thanks to the chairman of the APSA committee that granted me the Anderson Award, Professor Daniel Elazar of Temple University. He has been instrumental in getting my work recognized. He recommended that I write an article for *Publius* about tribal-state governments, which was published in 1998, and served as one of the not-so-anonymous reviewers of the manuscript for this book. I especially want to acknowledge his appreciation of the importance of Indian tribal governments in the American federal system.

In my three years at the University of New Mexico–Gallup (UNM–G) I have been befriended and supported by numerous people. I have appreciated the support of Behavioral and Social Sciences chair Helen Zongolowicz. Anthropology professor Teresa Wilkins has been a close friend, colleague, collaborator, and critic. Professor Liz Gilbert is a friend and strong advocate for the UNM-G faculty. Professor Jack Crowl helped me get the manuscript in the mail by editing the preface. I owe Joan Sheski a large debt of gratitude for her prompt and thorough proofing of the dissertation manuscript. Erlinda Torres, department administrative secretary, is my friend, confidante, and com-batant—nobody else tolerates my hillbilly ways like she does.

I wish that my mom and dad were alive to see their son achieve what they so long wanted and encouraged him to do. Momma always wanted me to be a doctor; I think she would accept the fact that I didn't get the title from a medical school. She did not live long enough to see me begin this journey. My dad did. For my first three years at the University of Oklahoma, Dad was my friend and confidant. I lost them much too soon.

This book would not be possible without the University of Oklahoma Press. I want to thank the three reviewers and the editorial board for their comments, criticisms, and suggestions. Kimberly Wiar was an early and enthusiastic supporter of this effort, and it would not have gone this far without her dedica-tion. Karen Weider filled in during Kim's recovery from an acci-dent and guided the selection of photographs and maps. Sheila Berg did an outstanding job of editing the manuscript, a job I couldn't be paid enough to do. In-house editor Jo Ann Reece and Aimee Ellis, sales manager, have done excellent work. I am grateful for their hard work and patience with a first-time author who must have been born weeks after he was due since he can't seem to meet a deadline.

Many people have helped me get here, but there would have been no graduate school, no dissertation, and no book without the encouragement, support, insight, patience, and at times impatience of Barbara Flanagan. I am forever grateful and in her debt for the sacrifices she made in getting me here. I wish her a long life of love, peace, and happiness.

INDIAN GAMING

Introduction

The status of American Indian tribes is unlike that of any other participant seeking to achieve its goals within the American political system. Their anomalous status flows from their having retained vestiges of aboriginal sovereignty and from their constitutionally established relationship with the federal government. For some purposes, tribes act as sovereign entities similar to states; for others, they act as interest groups; and for still others, they act as both simultaneously.[1] But no definition is fully explanatory because tribes can act in ways that states and interest groups (or states as interest groups) cannot.

More than two hundred years after the Founding and one hundred twenty-five years after the end of the treaty-making process, the political status of Indian tribes continues to evolve. Over the past thirty years Indians have played an increasingly active role in shaping and implementing Indian policy. The ability of tribes to perform the functions of governance has been strengthened, and there are a large number of active Indian organizations that support tribal sovereignty. The historic concerns of Indians, such as health care, education, religious freedom, law enforcement, and taxation, remain significant issues for tribes and Indian organizations.

There are new concerns as well. Economic development, hazardous waste storage, and gaming, among other issues, have emerged in the last decade and a half as new areas of policy requiring the attention of tribal governments. Of these, gaming has become possibly the most visible and contentious issue in Indian Country. Since the 1987 *Cabazon* decision by the United States Supreme Court and the passage of the 1988 Indian Gaming Regulatory Act (IGRA), Indian gaming has become the focus of many tribes in efforts to assert their sovereign status and achieve economic independence.

For those tribes engaged in this activity, gaming is both a means to an end and an end in itself. The revenue raised from gaming operations can help tribes to gain new political and economic independence and provide funds for long-neglected tribal needs. Gaming also represents a stand for political independence as tribes assert their sovereign right to determine for themselves what they can control on tribal lands. It is an issue that is helping to define the limits of state involvement in Indian affairs and the shape of American federalism generally, from law enforcement to taxation. Finally, gaming provides the financial resources for tribes to achieve their policy goals through the political process.

New Mexico presents an opportunity to view in all its complexity how Indians have used their anomalous political status to protect tribal gaming. Using their sovereign status following *Cabazon* and passage of the IGRA, a number of Pueblo tribes and two Apache tribes are operating gaming establishments. Having been blocked in these efforts earlier, tribes followed two paths. The first, which included filing suit in federal court under the IGRA and lobbying the state legislature for a change in the state's gaming laws, is in accordance with their sovereign status. The second, active involvement in New Mexico political campaigns, follows the path of interest groups. For example, several Pueblo tribal councils and the Mescalero Apache Tribe formally endorsed and made campaign contributions to candidates in the 1994 gubernatorial election based solely on the candidates' position on Indian gaming.

Oklahoma provides an interesting counterpoint to the gaming-related political activities of New Mexico tribes. Barred from the kinds of gaming operations permitted in New Mexico, Oklahoma Indian tribes have not had the same opportunities under federal and state law to expand games of chance. However, although there has been political opposition to expanded Indian gaming in Oklahoma, seven gaming compacts have been successfully negotiated as of April 1998. Another difference between Oklahoma and New Mexico is the much lower level of political activity by Indian tribes in the former.

Indian gaming, then, is clearly an issue ripe for research by political scientists and for scrutiny by both policy makers and the general public. By attempting to discover the status of Indian tribes in the political system, it is also possible to inform the discipline's understanding about federalism and interest group activity. Both are fundamental to the American political system. Thus, by focusing on Indian gaming, I hope to begin to answer the question, What is the status of Indian tribes in the American political system?

The lack of attention to the role of tribal governments in the area of intergovernmental relations is glaring in light of the federal Indian policy of self-determination. The increasing sophistication of Indian tribal governments and Indian organizations generally is occurring at a time of increasing tribal-state conflict and a national political movement to devolve power to the states.

Tribal governments have a large stake in broader federalism concerns. Being included in legislation on a par with state governments raises the same concerns for them about competitive and coercive federalism that states have. Scope of conflict and benefit coalitions would seem to be appropriate frameworks for analyzing the place of tribal governments in federalism, particularly on issues involving economic competition between tribes and states.

Analysis of Indians and federalism permits a further investigation into the significance of tribal sovereignty as a motivating factor in Indians' political participation. Federalism provides a way to determine if the interests of tribal governments are indeed the same as other nontribal governmental organizations.

The sovereign yet amorphous status of Indian tribes appears to place tribes somewhere between states and interest groups. For some purposes and under some conditions tribes resemble state governments. This sovereignty is acknowledged in law and is exercised by federally recognized Indian tribes. Tribal governments perform functions similar and parallel to those of all other governments in the American federal system, subject only to voluntarily agreed limits or limits imposed by federal law. The federal trust status of tribes also provides an obligation on the part of the federal government owed to no other group of citizens or level of government.

Like other levels of government that engage in typical interest group activities, tribes testify before Congress and attempt to achieve their individual and common tribal goals by presenting issues directly to elected officials. Tribes also attempt to directly affect the electoral process through tribal endorsements of and contributions to candidates for elective office. In the case of Indian gaming, tribally owned enterprises also donate to candidates who indicate their support of this tribal activity.

There is no example of this kind of duality in the political science interest group or federalism literature. The singular sovereign status that has developed for tribes has resulted in political entities that have a legal standing and pragmatic flexibility unlike any other in the American political system. This status of tribes as something more than either a government or an interest group raises questions relative to the normative arguments about the good or evil of interest groups. For example, what is the role of sovereign tribes in a society based on pluralism? Does the sovereign status of tribes provide constitutional and political protection to individual Indians that members of traditional interest groups lack?

Indian gaming provides a unique opportunity to observe tribes acting in their dual roles. It appears that tribes are making use of this duality and are seeking the most opportune arena available to protect their ability to control Indian gaming.

Gaming also provides an opportunity to observe the actions of nontribal Indian organizations and lawyers in support of tribal efforts in this area. To what degree, for example, are the goals of these organizations linked to sovereignty, and how are they able to use this to achieve their own ends?

Tribes have attempted to influence a variety of policy makers and political processes at several levels. In advancing their gaming interests, tribes and tribal representatives have been involved in tribal-state negotiations, lawsuits, congressional lobbying, presidential consultation, and political campaigns. In many instances they have been joined by nontribal Indian organizations. Gaming may also bring into sharper focus the policy agenda–setting process. Arguably federal court decisions regarding Indian gaming in the early and mid-1980s were the catalyst for congressional action leading to the Indian Gaming Regulatory Act in 1988.

Indian policy and politics are of vital concern to Indian people. That is obvious. But for most Americans and even most elected officials, what happens in Indian Country might as well be happening in Antarctica. For these Americans, Indian people are both out of sight and out of mind. This fact has at least two consequences. First, because most elected officials are not from Indian Country and do not have Indian constituents, they are ripe for education. In the past policy educators have been non-Indians, either "friends of the Indians," who sought to enact their vision of what was best for Indians, or adherents of interests opposed to those of Indians. This has been changing as Indian tribal leaders and leaders of other Indian-led organizations have become active, sophisticated, and well-funded lobbyists.

Second, Indian policy is often caught up in the current political zeitgeist. The broader currents and trends of American politics often carry Indian politics along. Often the political zeitgeist coincides with the interests of those opposed to Indian interests. For example, the current trend in American federalism toward devolution—the return of power to the states—is being used by state officials and members of Congress who want to curtail Indian sovereignty and extend state sovereignty into Indian Country. These two closely related facts of American politics must be the backdrop against which any effort to understand the place of tribes in the political system takes place.

CHAPTER ONE

Indian Policy and Conflict in the American Political System

The roots of U.S. Indian policy lie deep in the conflicting worldviews of two peoples: one reared in the European tradition of liberal democratic society; the other, in tribal-based communal societies. This fundamental conflict was present before the creation of the American republic and still exists today, setting the boundaries for debate over the direction of Indian policy generally. Whether a given policy is "anti-Indian"—removal, termination—or "reform"—Indian New Deal, self-determination—each era of Indian policy is set within this ideological battleground. The practical application of liberal principles to Indian policy has in turn been guided by the U.S. Constitution and the American political system.

Regarding the many eras of Indian history, policy, and law, Charles F. Wilkinson has observed that "each . . . needs to be reconciled with the egalitarian and libertarian laws and traditions of the majority of society."[1] Put simply, the policies that drove Indian nations from their homelands and deprived them of their communal liberty had to be reconciled with the principles of individual liberty, equality, and government by consent that were at the heart of the United States' republican form of government. The justification could be found in the

belief that the "uncivilized" natives were not qualified for
equal treatment under the law while their treatment must
nonetheless conform to the law. Applying the law opportun-
istically[2] has often meant that policy was in reality "genocide-
at-law."[3]

The original inhabitants of the "New World" had a wide
variety of cultures. Some tribes were nomadic, others sedentary; some were hierarchically organized, with a recognized
central authority, others loosely organized and widely dis-
persed geographically, with a shifting locus of authority. But as
diverse as they were, they all differed in fundamental ways
from Europeans in their personal, political, spiritual, and
property relationships.

American Indian nations, tribes, and bands were largely self-
governing, communal, and tribally based. According to Sharon
O'Brien, "To be a member of a tribe meant sharing a common
bond of ancestry, kinship, language, and a political authority
with other members."[4] These interpersonal and kinship relationships were part of a worldview quite different from that of
the European "discoverers" and their descendants. Indian
conceptions of the sacred and time itself were very different
from those held by non-Indians. Vine Deloria, Jr., has noted,
"Western European peoples have never learned to consider the
nature of the world discerned from a spatial point of view. . . .
The very essence of Western European identity involves the
assumption that time proceeds in a linear fashion."[5]

Perhaps the most significant difference between Indians and
Euro-Americans was their relationship to land and property
ownership. The difference was significant both in substance
and in what it meant for subsequent policies. Individual Indians
were generally recognized by their societies as having a right to
some personal property. As William T. Hagan has noted, personal
property rights did not generally include land.

> Private property rights in such items as cooking and eating
> utensils, weapons, and jewelry were respected among the
> Indians. Private property in land, as we understand the

concept, was not known. Springs, cultivated fields, and particular hunting or gathering grounds in some instance might be considered the exclusive property of certain families, bands, or tribes. However, the members of that family, band or tribe would all share equally in the property concerned.[6]

Similarly, the Jemez Pueblo scholar Joe S. Sando has written,

Concepts of land ownership, and its use, have always differed between aboriginal Americans and European invaders. While the Europeans' main purpose has been commercial exploitation, Native Americans have always practiced alternative uses of their land; for example, certain areas were mainly for religious significance.[7]

To a people whose culture, economy, and governance were based on ideas of the Enlightenment and what has come to be known as liberal democracy, the ways and worldviews of the Indians were anomalous at best, threatening at worst. A society that valued and protected the individual's pursuit of property and that relied on a government of written laws, popular consent, and ordered processes could not long accept in its midst a people so vastly different. Reconciling the differences in worldviews was made both more difficult and imperative by the desire of the Americans for Indian resources, chiefly land at first and raw materials in later years. The values implicit in the American political system established the framework for the dominant society's relationships with American Indians. Individual ownership of land exemplified the values of individualism and served as the basis for Wilcomb E. Washburn's observation that "the principal point of dispute between white and Indian historically has been land."[8]

According to Theodore J. Lowi, the British philosopher John Locke "was the proximate source" of the founding of the American republic.[9] According to Lowi, the Founders' "Constitution made the United States the first and probably only polity to be formed self-consciously according to Locke's blueprint."[10] This "blueprint" not only provided the basis for the principles of natural rights and consent of the governed enunciated in the Declaration of Independence; it also provided the ideology of individualism and private property inextricably linked to liberal society.[11]

If Locke is the blueprint for the American republic, native America, or at least his understanding of it, was the blueprint for much of Locke's own conceptions of the state of nature and the nature of property. In a phrase reminiscent of the Book of Genesis, Locke wrote in the *Second Treatise of Government,* "Thus in the beginning all the world was *America.*"[12] According to Locke, Indians were in the first stage of human development; they were without either money or private property.[13]

The legal scholar Robert A. Williams, a Lumbee, contends that Locke "legitimated the appropriation of the American wilderness as a right, and even as an imperative, under natural law."[14] This is consistent with Michael Paul Rogin's observation that liberal society is "the unchallenged primacy of propertied individualism across the political spectrum. . . . Liberalism insisted on the independence of men, each from the other and from cultural, traditional, and communal attachments."[15] American Indian policy has been formulated and implemented in a political system founded on this ideological imperative.

WHOSE SOVEREIGNTY?

From before the founding of the republic, the nation dealt with Indian tribes as it dealt with all foreign sovereigns—through negotiated treaties. The Founders made Indian affairs a national concern in Article I, section 8, of the Constitution. Congress, in the Indian Commerce Clause, was given power to regulate trade with the Indian tribes, the basis for that institution's "plenary power" in Indian affairs.

In a fundamental way the parameters of continuing disputes over the status of Indian tribes in the American political system were best articulated in the era of Jacksonian democracy. The sovereignty of tribes and the power of national and state governments to decide questions of Indian policy were significant political and constitutional issues during the 1820s and 1830s. On one side was the strong states' rights position advocated by state officials, especially in the Southeast, and strongly supported by President Andrew Jackson. This view held that Indians as individuals could and should be subject to state jurisdiction. It followed that Indian political institutions inside a state were illegitimate. This view interpreted the Indian Commerce Clause so narrowly as to make it nearly inoperative within state borders.

On the other side was the view that tribes were sovereign. The extent of sovereignty was in dispute, however. Indian tribes and nations claimed to hold all of the rights and powers of self-governance that they held before the arrival of Europeans. They claimed power over their own people and the right to make decisions on a par with non-Indian governments. The treaty relationship seemed to confirm this belief. When tribes ceded land or authority over their land or individuals, they claimed to do so voluntarily through negotiations.

Others, notably Chief Justice John Marshall, recognized a diminished sovereignty vested in Indian tribes and nations based on their aboriginal status. The extent of this sovereignty and under what conditions and against what authority it could be exercised were questions of historical and constitutional interpretation and political expediency.

Echoes of these strongly held views have been heard ever since in debates over Indian policy. Advocates of a particular policy in a given era often fall back on these early arguments modified in form, if not in tone. Although Andrew Jackson's often-incendiary views on Indian sovereignty are rarely cited as support for a particular policy, his underlying assumptions have often determined acts of Congress and court decisions. Marshall's description of tribes as "domestic dependent nations" has been used to justify policies that have both strengthened and weakened tribal sovereignty. Almost all Indian policy is the progeny of the conflicting views of Jackson and Marshall.

One point not in dispute among policy makers, however, was the view that the Euro-American way of life was superior in all forms to the Indians' communal tribalism. Neither Jackson nor Marshall questioned the assumptions of liberal democratic political institutions, the importance of individually owned private property, or the righteousness of Christianity. All agreed this was the proper course for Indians to follow.

THE MARSHALL TRILOGY AND JACKSONIAN STATES' RIGHTS

Three opinions written by Chief Justice Marshall provide the ideological and legal basis for Indian law and policy. In the so-called Marshall Trilogy, the chief justice's articulation of the nature of Indian land title and his descriptions of federal-state-tribal political relations established the parameters for the essential relationship among federal and state governments and Indian tribes. The latter two cases of the trilogy also provide an insight into federal-state relations generally and the relationships among the three presumably coequal branches of the federal government.

The liberal concern with the formalities of law and the primacy of property rights was given doctrinal support in Indian policy by Marshall's interpretation and application of the Doctrine of Discovery in an early 1820s property dispute. Tracing its roots to the "discovery" of the New World by European explorers, Marshall, in *Johnson & Graham's Lessees v. McIntosh*, established the limits of Indian land title.[16] In resolving the title of a single piece of property that had been transferred separately to different parties by both an Indian tribe and the U.S. government, Marshall and the Court held that the Indian title was inferior to that of the United States.

The chief justice was faced with a conundrum: the Indians were obviously on the land before the Europeans, but the Europeans, and subsequently Americans, had taken possession of much of the New World. How could this be legal? To answer that question, Marshall engaged in an anthropological and Lockean analysis of the nature of the "heathens" and their use of the land. According to Marshall, those "inhabiting this country were fierce savages, whose occupation was war, and whose subsistence was drawn chiefly from the forest. To leave them in possession of their country was to leave the country a wilderness. " The aboriginal people therefore did not have a title to the land that could be transferred to others.

The act of "discovery" gave the European power an ownership title in the land good against Indians and other European powers alike. As Marshall stated it,

> This principle was that discovery gave title to the government by whose subjects or by whose authority, it was made against all other European governments, which title might be consummated by possession. The exclusion of all other Europeans, necessarily gave to the nation making the discovery the sole right of acquiring the soil from the natives and establishing settlements upon it.

This right was assumed by the United States when it gained independence.

According to Deloria, as originally conceived, "the doctrine was to apply to uninhabited countries only."[17] However, Marshall had to resolve the problem of landownership in an inhabited country. He acknowledged that the aboriginal peoples had some kind of land title, but it was of a lesser kind. Marshall claimed that "the rights of the original inhabitants were, in no instance entirely disregarded; but were necessarily impaired."

> They were admitted to be the rightful occupants of the soil with a legal as well as just claim to retain possession of it, and to use it according to their discretion. Conquest gives a title which the courts of the conqueror cannot deny. . . .
>
> . . . The Indian inhabitants are to be considered merely as occupants, to be protected, indeed, while in peace in

the possession of their lands, but to be deemed incapable of transferring the absolute title to others.

Marshall thus provided the legal justification for continued American expansion into the western frontier. Indians could exercise their right to occupy the land so long as the original conquerors' successors did not need it, but they could not transfer that right to anyone but the United States. When the land was needed and ready to be put to a better use, the United States could extinguish the aboriginal title of occupancy. Deloria and Clifford Lytle argue that "every legal doctrine that today separates and distinguishes American Indians from other Americans traces its conceptual roots back to the Doctrine of Discovery and the subsequent moral and legal rights and responsibilities of the United States with respect to Indians."[18]

Having dispensed with the question of land title in *McIntosh,* Marshall and the Court were soon drawn into one of the major political controversies of the age: the continuing presence of unassimilated Indian tribes in the southeastern United States. Three cases in the early 1830s, together referred to as the Cherokee Cases, involved not only the sovereign status of Indian tribes but also questions touching on the very meaning of the constitutional relationship between national and state governments and among the branches of the national government itself.

The stakes were high for all parties. For the Cherokee Nation, and by extension all Indian tribes and nations, it was political, economic, and cultural sovereignty. For the states, it was the right to exercise sovereign power within their borders without interference from the national government. For the national government generally, it was the power to assert its authority under the Supremacy Clause. The Kiowa legal scholar Kirke Kickingbird wrote, "The Union was in fragile condition from the tug of war between the powers of the state government and the power of the federal government. Federal control of Indian affairs was merely one part of this struggle."[19]

Within the national government the stakes for each branch were, by the nature of the Constitution, different and conflicting. For the president, a political promise and a political philosophy clashed with a differing political philosophy and constitutional interpretation enunciated by the chief justice of the United States Supreme Court. Congress was pulled between the political demands of the president and his allies and those who opposed the president politically or who supported the moral position of the Cherokees.

The Cherokee Cases were precipitated by the state of Georgia's unwillingness to continue to tolerate the presence of an organized sovereign Indian nation within its borders. In 1802 Georgia and the United States signed a compact providing that Georgia give up its claims to western lands in return for the federal government extinguishing Indian land title in the state. A quarter century passed, and the federal government had done nothing to fulfill its part of the deal. Giving urgency to Georgia's desire to terminate the Cherokees' separate status was the discovery of gold on Cherokee lands.

The Georgia legislature unilaterally extended its sovereignty over the Cherokee Nation. In a series of laws Georgia incorporated the territory of the Cherokee Nation into several counties, extended Georgia laws to Cherokee land, annulled Cherokee law, and forbade non-Indians from entering Cherokee lands without receiving permission from the state. According to Jill Norgren, "The Georgia politicians' ultimate hope was that these laws would make it impossible for the Cherokees to resist a treaty of removal."[20]

The Cherokee Nation's Principal Chief, John Ross, and their tribal attorneys sought a legal test of Georgia's law. They appeared to have one when a Cherokee named George Tassels was tried and convicted in Georgia court for the murder of a Cherokee man on Cherokee land.[21] Cherokee Nation attorney William Writ appealed Tassels's conviction to the Supreme Court. However, Georgia officials ignored the Court's order to appear before it and proceeded to hang Tassels. As Norgren notes, "The state would not submit to federal judicial reviews of its laws."[22]

The next opportunity for a test arose when the Cherokee Nation sought to sue the state of Georgia in a case of original jurisdiction in the Supreme Court in 1831, *Cherokee Nation v. Georgia.*[23] Article 3, section 2, clause 2, of the U.S. Constitution gives the Supreme Court original jurisdiction in cases "in which a State shall be a party." The Cherokee Nation sought to prohibit Georgia from enforcing its laws within the Nation's borders, arguing that the Nation was "a foreign state, not owing allegiance to the United States, nor to any State of the Union, nor to any prince, potentate or State, other than their own." The question for the Court was, "Is the Cherokee Nation a 'State' within the meaning of Article III?"

In possibly the most significant Indian law decision in history, Chief Justice Marshall answered no. While claiming sympathy for Indian people, Marshall found that tribes were neither states in the Union nor foreign nations, writing that "the Indian Territory is admitted to compose a part of the United States" and that Indians "acknowledge themselves in their treaties to be under the protection of the United States." Marshall found a unique place for Indian tribes:

> They may, more correctly, perhaps, be denominated domestic dependent nations. They occupy a territory to which we assert a title independent of their will, which must take effect in point of possession when their right of possession ceases. Meanwhile they are in a state of pupilage.

He went on to describe Indians in dicta that would have a profound effect on the future of Indian-government relations:

> Their relation to the United States resembles that of a ward to his guardian. They look to our government for protection; they rely upon its kindness and its power; appeal to it for relief of their wants; and address the President as their great father.

Because the Court decided *Cherokee Nation* on the narrow jurisdictional question, the substantive question of the power of Georgia to assert its sovereignty over the Cherokee Nation was not addressed. That would occur, however, in the last of the Cherokee Cases, *Worcester v. Georgia.*[24] Samuel Worcester was one of several missionaries arrested for violating Georgia law by entering Cherokee lands without first obtaining a state license and signing a loyalty oath to the state. Worcester and Rev. Elizur Butler were tried, convicted, and sentenced to four years at hard labor. They appealed their conviction to the Supreme Court.

There was no jurisdictional issue in *Worcester;* the Court considered the legality of the Georgia laws. In ultimately finding Georgia's acts unconstitutional, Marshall also backed away from his strong language in *Cherokee Nation.* In reviewing treaties between the United States and the Cherokee Nation, Marshall found that the latter had acknowledged itself to "be under the protection of the United States of America." However, he wrote, "protection does not imply the destruction of the protected." The treaty relationship between the United States and the Cherokee "was that of a nation claiming and receiving the protection of one more powerful, not that of individuals abandoning their national character, and submitting as subjects to the laws of a master." All of the treaties and laws "manifestly consider the several Indian nations as distinct political communities, having territorial boundaries, within which their authority is exclusive, and having a right to all the lands within those boundaries, which is not only acknowledged, but granted by the United States."

As to Georgia's assertion of authority over Cherokee lands, Marshall looked to Congress's power under Article I, section 8, clause 3, "to regulate Commerce with foreign Nations, among the several States, and with the Indian tribes." He continued, "The treaties and laws of the United States contemplate the Indian territory as completely separated from that of the States; and provide that all intercourse with them shall be carried on exclusively by the government of the Union."

Linking the political status of the Cherokee Nation and the constitutional power of the U.S. government, Marshall wrote,

> The Cherokee nation, then, is a distinct community, occupying its own territory, with boundaries accurately described, in which the laws of Georgia can have no force, and which, the citizens of Georgia have no right to enter but with the assent of the Cherokees themselves or in conformity with treaties and with the acts of Congress. The whole intercourse between the United States and this nation is, by our Constitution and laws, vested in the government of the United States.

The missionaries and the Cherokee Nation won a clear legal victory in the Supreme Court. However, the prevailing political climate was not in agreement with the Court. The Jackson administration's policy of removal continued to gain momentum, and the president's states' rights ideology supported Georgia's refusal to acknowledge the Court's decision. Indeed, as in the two previous Cherokee Cases, the state had not bothered to enter an appearance before the Court in *Worcester*. On hearing of the *Worcester* decision, Jackson is said to have remarked, "John Marshall has made his decision, now let him enforce it." Whether or not he actually said this, Jackson's inaction sent a clear signal to the states and the Indian tribes.

Jackson's response to *Worcester* is not surprising. He combined a strong sense of nationalism and belief in the expansionist destiny of the United States with an equally strong conviction that the Constitution recognized a significant degree of sovereignty in the individual states. Jackson's most recent biographer, Robert V. Remini, notes his commitment to republicanism, individual liberty, limited government, and national expansionism. Jackson, however, "was never dogmatic. . . . [H]e was a pragmatic politician, not an ideologue."[25] He believed that "protecting state sovereignty was to guarantee individual liberty."[26]

Indian removal furthered Jackson's political agenda and ideology. Remini notes, "The policy of removal formed an important part of Jackson's overall program of limiting federal authority and supporting states' rights. Despite the accusation of increased executive authority, Jackson successfully buttressed state sovereignty and jurisdiction over all inhabitants within state boundaries."[27]

Indian policy consistent with broader political goals and philosophy was not unique to Jackson; it has generally followed that a president's Indian policy is driven by, or at least consistent with, the broader goals he has established for his administration. This is also generally true of congressional Indian policy. What is politically possible often drives Indian-government relations. This in turn can operate to defeat the political and policy goals of Indians.

The Cherokees, while proclaiming their sovereignty, had fought to preserve it within the boundaries of the American Constitution and political system. In the end, however, neither the laws and institutions nor the processes of the United States provided the Cherokee Nation with the recognition and protection it sought. Rennard Strickland notes the poignancy of the Cherokees' efforts to withstand Georgia's onslaught.

> They turned first to the Executive and were told to move west. They next turned to Congress and were again told to move west. They finally turned to the Supreme Court and were told that their rights would be protected. This may have been the cruelest of all the answers given, for the Court had neither the power nor the will to grant this protection.[28]

In the presidential campaign of 1832 the Cherokees found a supporter in Henry Clay, but Jackson's overwhelming victory meant a political defeat for the Cherokee Nation. The Cherokee Nation was removed west along the Trail of Tears in 1838.

MARSHALL, JACKSON, AND
THEIR INDIAN POLICY PROGENY

The opposing views of Indian sovereignty, the relationship among tribal, state, and federal governments, and the place of individual Indians in American society provide a framework for understanding the ebbs and flows of Indian policy. Indian policy can be summarized chronologically or by era, but another way to review and evaluate the permutations of Indian affairs is to divide policy initiatives by their emphasis on tribal, state, or federal authority. This framework not only demonstrates the alternating policy of termination and recognition of tribal self-governance; it also demonstrates how closely cultural assimilationist policies are related to the political status of tribal governing entities.

"Dependent"

Evidence of the dependent status of tribes is most clearly seen in the "trust relationship" maintained by the federal government with tribal governments, assets, and members. Expanding on Chief Justice Marshall's notion of the United States as guardian of its tribal wards, Congress has created bureaucratic structures to oversee even the most minute details of life on Indian land. An entire section of the United States Code, Title 25, deals solely with Indian affairs; a sizable and largely inefficient bureaucracy, the Bureau of Indian Affairs, is responsible for carrying out the government's trust responsibilities. Created as the Office of Indian Affairs by Secretary of War John C. Calhoun in 1824, Congress formally established the agency in the War Department in 1832 and transferred it to the newly created Interior Department in 1849.

Two specialized areas of concern to the federal government have historically been Indian education and health. The BIA continues to operate day schools and a limited number of boarding schools. The Indian Health Service, created as part of the Public Health Service by Congress in 1954,[29] is responsible for providing health care to Indians living on or near Indian land. A number of departments and agencies have offices whose purpose it is to deliver their services to Indians, including the Department of Housing and Urban Development and the Farmers Home Administration.

The early development of the federal Indian bureaucracy had less to do with carrying out a trust responsibility than it did with efforts to civilize and assimilate Indians. As reservations were created throughout the West in the latter half of the 1800s, bureaucrats in the Office of Indian Affairs, from the commissioner to reservation agents, implemented policies designed to transform individual "pagan" tribal Indians into individual Christian liberal farming Americans. To this end, administrative directives and regulations were issued to implement congressional policy and treaty provisions. The ultimate goals, according to Donald L. Parman, were to destroy "tribal authority, eradicat[e] native religions, and chang[e] Indians into farmers," especially after passage of the General Allotment Act in 1887.[30]

The reservation was where regulations could be enforced and Indians could begin the transformation desired by government officials and "reformers" who believed they knew what was best for Indians. Because the successful transformation of Indians from "savagery" and "paganism" was thought to lie in changing their behavior, many of the regulations were directed at curbing traditional Indian cultural and spiritual practices as well as other activities viewed as immoral.

Massachusetts Republican senator Henry Dawes was perhaps the most influential public official in Indian policy in the last quarter of the nineteenth century. As congressman, senator, chairman of the Senate Committee on Indian Affairs, and chairman of the Dawes Commission, Dawes led the efforts that resulted in the loss of much of the western Indian landholdings. Dawes's public statements reflected the sentiments of many "friends of the Indians" that Indians must emerge from communal tribalism into propertied individualism. In 1883 Dawes related an experience with some Indians still in their primitive communal state.

The head chief told us there was not a family in that whole Nation that had not a home of its own. There was not a pauper in that nation and the nation did not owe a dollar. It built its own capitol . . . and it built its schools and its hospitals. Yet the defect of the system was apparent. They have got as far as they can go, because they own their land in common, . . . and under that there is no enterprise to make your home any better than that of your neighbors. There is no selfishness, which is at the bottom of civilization. Till this people will consent to give up their lands, and their citizens so that each can own the land he cultivates, they will not make much more progress.[31]

The role of reservations in teaching Indians the benefits of civilization was nowhere more clearly stated than in the opinion of an Oregon federal district court judge. Upholding the secretary of the interior's power to promulgate rules for the courts in dealing with Indian offenses, the judge described these courts as "mere educational and disciplinary instrumentalities." "In fact," he continued, "the reservation itself is in the nature of a school, and the Indians are gathered there, under the charge of an agent, for the purpose of acquiring the habits, ideas, and aspirations which distinguish the civilized from the uncivilized man."[32]

Even with the late-twentieth-century policies of self-determination and self-governance stressing tribal sovereignty, the dependency bureaucracy is still in place. Not only does the BIA act as trustee for Indian resources, it also determines what people are entitled to be given "recognition" as a legitimate sovereign Indian tribe. Absent a determination by either the BIA administratively or Congress legislatively, a group claiming to constitute an Indian tribe receives no federal benefits or protections, nor does it have a sovereign government-to-government relationship with the United States.

In 1978 the BIA published criteria for groups seeking legal acknowledgment as an Indian tribe. The bureau created the Federal Acknowledgment Branch to review the applications of such groups and determine if they meet the criteria. Congress can also acknowledge a tribe's existence by passing legislation granting it recognition. In October 1993 the BIA Division of Tribal Services, as required by law, published in the Federal Register a list of 555 recognized tribes and Alaska Native villages.[33]

As trustee for Indian resources, the BIA has responsibility for protecting individual and tribal holdings. The BIA's incompetence in this area is well documented and continues to the present day. The 1989 *Final Report and Legislative Recommendations* of the Special Committee on Investigations of the Senate Select Committee on Indian Affairs declared that the committee had "found fraud, corruption and mismanagement pervading the institutions that are supposed to serve American Indians."[34] Paternalistic federal control over American Indians had created a federal bureaucracy ensnarled in red tape and riddled with fraud, mismanagement, and waste. The committee found, for example, that BIA hiring practices had failed to weed out convicted child molesters as teachers at BIA schools and that tribal natural resources, such as oil and gas in Oklahoma, had been stolen. Worse, the committee found that federal officials in every agency knew of the abuses but did little or nothing to stop them.[35]

The BIA's breach of its fiduciary responsibilities to Indian people is nowhere more apparent than in its mismanagement of trust funds. Since the 1830s the BIA has held individual and tribal Indian assets in trust. The BIA has responsibility for more than fifteen hundred tribal accounts belonging to more than two hundred tribes, amounting to $2.1 billion; another $453 million is held in the Individual Indian Money (IIM) accounts of 390,000 tribal members.[36] This money belongs to tribes and individuals and is derived from mineral resource royalties, land settlements, leases, and other assets unrelated to federal program expenditures. Beginning in the late 1980s, a series of congressional and General Accounting Office (GAO) investigations documented the mismanagement of tribal assets by the federal government.

A May 1996 GAO report charged that the BIA could not "reconcile" $2.4 billion in transactions involving trust funds because of missing records and the lack of an audit trail.[37] The magnitude of the trust fund loss led Native American Rights Fund (NARF) executive director John Echohawk to call it "the largest and longest-lasting financial scandal ever involving the federal government,"[38] and Jeff Barker of the *Arizona Republic* has called it "one of the quietest scandals in American history."[39] In 1994 Congress passed the American Indian Trust Fund Management Reform Act and created the Office of Special Trustee for the American Indians to be responsible for the BIA's financial trust services. Although the new office has made progress in reconciling some accounts, it has been unable to resolve the ongoing administrative problems. Other efforts to make sense of the problem include the Intertribal Monitoring Association and the Task Force on Trust Fund Management of the House Resources Committee.

Dependence on the federal government becomes painfully clear during times of national budgetary constraints. In the early 1980s and then again following the 1994 congressional elections, financial support for Indian programs was jeopardized by the prevailing political currents calling for cutbacks in federal domestic expenditures. Since the days of John F. Kennedy's New Frontier, federal support for Indian programs had been gradually expanded. New programs created during the Great Society that were designed to alleviate poverty nationwide included Indians as a target group. The Nixon administration continued to expand Indian programs as well and included Indian tribes in such administrative policies as "New Federalism" and revenue sharing.

The election of Ronald Reagan in 1980 brought a decided shift in national spending priorities, and Indian programs were not exempt from the budgetary realignment. C. Patrick Morris and many Indian leaders saw the Reagan cutbacks as pointedly anti-Indian—as "termination by accountants."[40] Other observers pointed out that Indians were merely caught in the administration's larger policy goals. For example, Hazel W. Hertzberg wrote that these cuts were "simply being applied mechanically to Indians, for whom they are even less appropriate than for the rest of the population."[41] Deloria similarly observed in 1985 that "the present posture of Indian policy is not distinguishable from other domestic objectives."[42]

This was also true of the cuts made in Indian program funding by Congress after the 1994 midterm elections. As the new Republican majority went about enacting the Contract with America, cutting domestic spending was high on the agenda of those determined to balance the federal budget. Senate Interior Appropriations Subcommittee chairman Slade Gorton of Washington concisely placed Indian budgets in the context of the Republican agenda:

> The dynamics of debate about spending have changed since the 104th Congress began. Instead of racing to get more money for this program and that program, we are— at the American people's behest—putting ourselves on the road to a balanced budget and reversing the trend of explosive government growth. Again, no one can or should expect to be exempt from the inevitable cuts which ensue from balancing the budget.[43]

The Indian program cuts were consistent with Republican ideology, but they were also the result of congressional power politics. The Senate Committee on Indian Affairs and the Senate Appropriations Committee were chaired by men generally sympathetic to Indian issues—John McCain of Arizona and Pete Domenici of New Mexico, respectively. The subcommittee on Interior Department appropriations, however, was chaired by longtime tribal antagonist Gorton. In 1978, as attorney general for the state of Washington, Gorton had successfully argued *Oliphant v. Suquamish Indian Tribe* before the U.S. Supreme Court, a decision that eliminated tribal criminal jurisdiction over non-Indians.[44] In the 1995 budget debate Gorton presented senators with the choice of supporting the funding of Indian programs or other worthwhile Interior projects, many having more relevance to their constituents than did BIA expenditures.[45] Efforts by Domenici and former Senate Indian Affairs Committee chairman Daniel Inouye (D-Hawaii) to restore money to the BIA met with resounding defeat on a 61 to 36 vote.[46] Such liberals and generally pro-Indian senators as Edward Kennedy (D-Mass.), Barbara Boxer (D-Calif.), and Minority Leader Tom Daschle (D-S.Dak.) voted with the majority.

Although the Supreme Court has occasionally reaffirmed and even strengthened tribal sovereignty, it has also reinforced dependency and supported states' rights at the expense of tribal self-governance. Two such decisions, in 1886 and 1903, respectively, were *U.S. v. Kagama* and *Lone Wolf v. Hitchcock.*[47] In 1881 Brule Lakota chief Spotted Tail was shot to death by Crow Dog, an opponent of Spotted Tail's policy of accommodation with the federal government. Justice was dispensed according to traditional Brule law but not to the satisfaction of federal authorities.[48] Crow Dog was arrested, charged with murder, and convicted in a Dakota territorial court. In *Ex parte Crow Dog,* the Supreme Court overturned Crow Dog's conviction on the basis of treaty guarantees and a policy of allowing Indians to govern their internal affairs according to tribal law.[49] Neither territorial nor federal law made it an offense for one Indian to murder another Indian on Indian land.

According to Sidney Harring, "Crow Dog's case is important because it is a bridge between the ambiguous and ineffective sovereignty language of *Worcester* and the complete subjugation of tribal sovereignty during the late nineteenth century."[50] *Crow Dog* demonstrated what many non-Indians believed to be a loophole in the law. The outcry against the Court's ruling led Congress to pass the Major Crimes Act in 1885, making seven offenses perpetrated by one Indian on another violations of federal law.[51] The constitutionality of the act was decided by the Supreme Court in *United States v. Kagama,* when it upheld the murder conviction of a Klamath Indian in northern California. In enunciating the "the Supreme Court's first statement of the plenary power doctrine," Justice Samuel Miller echoed John Marshall's language:

> These Indian tribes are the wards of the nation. They are communities dependent on the United States. Dependent largely for their daily food. Dependent for their political rights. . . . The power of the General Government over these remnants of a race once powerful, now weak and diminished in numbers is necessary for their protection, as well as to the safety of those among them whom they dwell.

Further evidence of the diminished political standing of tribes and the extraordinary reach of congressional plenary powers in Indian affairs came in 1903. The Court, in *Lone Wolf v. Hitchcock,* upheld the right of Congress to alter the Treaty of Medicine Lodge with the Kiowa by approving an agreement allotting the reservation without the requisite valid signatures of adult male tribal members. Harring notes that *Lone Wolf* "shifted the method of weighing tribal sovereignty from a complex balancing function in the federal courts to Congress's plenary power to simply do with the tribes whatever it chose."[52] Congress used its vast plenary powers to enact policies conducive to state assumption of jurisdiction over Indian lands. The decision reaffirmed and reinforced congressional power over Indians. The Court not only supported congressional authority in Indian affairs, it did so in a case that placed the interests of non-Indian state residents over those of Indian state residents.

"States' Rights"

Of immediate concern to frontier states during the early days of the republic was achieving peace so their citizens could pursue the pastimes of civilization. This at first required a military presence or a negotiating team. As peace was achieved through warfare or treaty, state officials began to demand that the remaining natives be sent somewhere else. The resulting federal policy provided two alternative solutions that were implemented in different ways during different eras: removal or assimilation.

Removal of individual Indians from the presence of whites could be achieved by a literal removal of the people en masse from their homeland to a distant land out of the way of white settlement; or it could be achieved by breaking up communal landholdings, issuance of individual allotments of private land, and subsequent "opening" of the "surplus" land to white settlement. Both strategies effectively disrupted the cultural, spiritual, and political life of the affected peoples. Both effectively extended state jurisdiction over the former Indian lands, if not the people themselves.

The removal policy came to fruition under President Jackson, although Thomas Jefferson was the first to propose it as a way to resolve the Indian question. Initially tribes in the Southeast were targeted for removal to an unorganized territory beyond the Mississippi River. Later tribes west of the Mississippi were also forced to relocate in what had come to be called "Indian Territory." Removal did put tribal Indians out of the way of white settlement, but, Francis Paul Prucha argues,

> in some respects the policy and the process brought increased rather than lessened interference in domestic Indian affairs on the part of the Great Father. And when the emigrant Indians were settled in their western homes, the drive for education, civilizing, and Christianizing them took on new vigor.[53]

As the treaty-making process continued and tribes ceded more and more land, the government established the reservation system. As each tribe or group of tribes received land for their exclusive use and as the authority of the Great Father was exercised directly by reservation agents, the intrusion of the federal government became greater. Reservations meant that Indian landholdings were reduced and room was made for white settlement. This was a crucial step to statehood for newly created territories.

The Dawes Severalty Act, or General Allotment Act of 1887,[54] "represented a comprehensive attempt to create a new role for the Indian in American society."[55] While demonstrating the dependency of Indians, it also ultimately strengthened state sovereignty by extending the reach of state law over former Indian lands and, eventually, over "citizen" Indians themselves. In addition to its political consequence, the Dawes Act also was a clear demonstration of assimilationist policies of the federal government in the final decades of the nineteenth century.

The Dawes Act authorized the president to allot tribal lands. Each tribal member would receive a specified number of acres, with the head of the household getting the largest allotment. "Surplus" land left over after each tribal member received his or her allotment was opened for white settlement. The allotments would be held in trust by the secretary of the interior for a period of twenty-five years; at the end of the trust period the individual would be given title to the land in fee simple. An Indian would become a U.S. citizen on receiving his or her allotment. In 1906 the Burke Act[56] postponed citizenship for an allotted Indian until the end of the trust period and gave the secretary of the interior the power to issue a patent in fee before the end of the trust period if the Indian allottee could be shown to be competent.

The loss of land under the allotment policy was dramatic. In 1881 Indians held more than 155 million acres; by 1890, 104 million acres; and by 1900, 77 million acres.[57] The Burke Act sped up the process; 60 percent of the more than 2,600 allottees receiving competency certificates gave up their land.[58] Allotment continued until 1934 when Congress passed the Indian Reorganization Act (IRA).

The IRA brought reform to Indian policy and slowed the incursion of non-Indians and state law into Indian land, but it was a relatively short-lived era. Indian policy went through one of its most dramatic changes after World War II. Notwithstanding the emphasis of the IRA and Indian New Deal on tribal revitalization, from the mid-1940s until at least the late 1950s Indian cultural and political sovereignty was threatened by a renewed emphasis on getting the federal government out of the Indian business. Individual Indians, tribal governments, and Indian lands were made vulnerable to state jurisdiction. Assimilation, eliminating the Indian land base, and the end of tribal political sovereignty once again were the goals of policy makers. Congress passed a series of bills to achieve these ends, the most significant being the Indian Claims Commission Act, House Concurrent Resolution 108, Public Law (P.L.) 83–280, and a series of "termination acts."

A continuing problem for state and federal officials was the growing number of land claims being pressed by tribes alleging that the government had cheated them or otherwise violated the law. To bring an orderly end to this mountain of litigation Congress passed the Indian Claims Commission Act in 1946,[59] creating a three-person commission to hear tribal claims against the United States.[60] The commission could hear only those claims filed before to August 13, 1951. If the commission found against the United States in a particular claim, it could award only monetary damages; no land could be returned to a tribe. By the time the commission went out of business in 1978, it had awarded more than $818 million.[61] The process of settling claims "appeared to be not a bold stroke to correct all past injustices, but simply a necessary preliminary step toward termination."[62]

The policy pronouncement setting out the goals of termination was House Concurrent Resolution 108, passed in 1953:

> Whereas it is the policy of Congress, as rapidly as possible, to make the Indians within the territorial limits of the United States subject to the same laws and entitled to the same privileges and responsibilities as are applicable to other citizens of the United States, and to end their status as wards of the United States, and to grant them all of the rights an prerogatives pertaining to American citizenship.[63]

The resolution divided tribes into categories of readiness for being the objects of the policy. All of the tribes located within California, Florida, New York, and Texas were slated for termination "at the earliest possible time." Selected tribes in several other states were also targeted for early termination.[64]

Termination, endorsed by the Hoover Commission, was achieved through individual termination acts withdrawing federal recognition and protection one tribe at a time. Between 1954 and 1962 Congress passed fourteen termination acts affecting more than one hundred tribes in eight states.[65] As the *Handbook of Federal Indian Law* notes, these "acts ended the special federal-tribal relationship in most, but not all respects for the terminated tribes."[66]

The impact of these laws on individuals and tribal sovereignty was sweeping. The trust relationship between the tribe and the federal government came to an end; most federal Indian services were no longer available to members of terminated tribes; Indians living on former tribal land would henceforth be subject to state jurisdiction; tribal rolls were closed; and "tribal sovereignty and tribal jurisdictional prerogatives were effectively, though not technically ended."[67]

Terminating individual tribes provided one way of getting the federal government out of the Indian business; another was turning responsibility for the remaining reservations over to the states. Congress took this pro–states' rights step in 1953 when it passed P.L. 83-280.[68] Donald Lee Fixico has termed P.L. 83-280 "a reform measure that called for liberating the tribes from federal trust dependence and placing them under state jurisdiction," a goal consistent with termination.[69]

One of the most far-reaching pieces of legislation passed during the termination era, P.L. 83-280 transferred criminal and civil jurisdiction over Indian Country to California, Nebraska, Minnesota (except for the Red Lake Chippewa Reservation), Oregon (except for the Warm Springs Reservation), and Wisconsin (except for the Menominee Reservation).[70] Sections 6 and 7 of the law made it possible for any other state to assume either type of jurisdiction if it chose. States with provisions in their constitutions or enabling acts limiting jurisdiction over Indians would have to first amend them.[71]

Tribes were given no opportunity to approve or reject state assumption until Congress passed the Indian Civil Rights Act of 1968.[72] Thereafter, tribal consent was required before a state could assert its jurisdiction. States already exercising P.L. 83-280 jurisdiction were also given the opportunity to "retrocede" it back to the federal government.

Consistent with the general thrust of termination was the "relocation" program of the 1950s and 1960s. Described by Prucha as "a corollary of termination," relocation was designed to move individuals and families from rural reservations to cities.[73] There they could receive the benefits of an increasingly urbanized America while being freed from dependence on the federal government. The program began among the Navajo and Hopi in the late 1940s and became a major activity of the BIA by the mid-1950s. For many relocated Indians, urban life was alien. The promises of BIA employees were often unfulfilled. Coping with urban pressures and disconnected from culture, land, and family, the outcome of relocation was often unemployment, alcohol and drug abuse, and contact with the criminal justice system. Rather than lessen the reach of the BIA, relocation ultimately required the federal government to provide additional services to a growing urban Indian population. Another unanticipated result of relocation was its catalytic effect in providing a pool of young activists who would have a profound impact on Indian life in the late 1960s and 1970s.

Termination and relocation came to an effective end in the 1960s. In 1962 the Poncas of Nebraska became the last tribe terminated by Congress.[74] In his 1970 Special Message, President Richard Nixon asked Congress to repeal House Concurrent Resolution 108. However, it was not until 1988 that Congress did so: "The Congress hereby repudiates and rejects House Concurrent Resolution 108 of the 83rd Congress and any policy of unilateral termination of Federal relations with any Indian Nation."[75] A number of terminated tribes were restored to their previous status, including the three terminated Oklahoma tribes, the Wyandot, Peoria, and Ottawa, in 1977.[76]

Thirty years after House Concurrent Resolution 108 was passed, when removal was no longer possible and assimilation was no longer the overriding policy of the federal government, state officials have found new ways to assert claims on Indians and their land. These most often have involved state attempts to "shrink Indian country . . . as a way of divesting or voiding tribal sovereignty."[77] Shrinking Indian trust land coincides with state attempts to tax individual Indians or business ventures on Indian land.

Robert N. Clinton argues that the Supreme Court has increasingly ruled against tribes in disputes with states. According to statistics compiled by the Iowa College of Law professor, between 1986 and 1990 tribes won 20 percent of the time in cases decided by the Court and only 14 percent of the time between 1990 and 1995. This failure rate is even more dramatic when compared to the 60 to 70 percent *success* rate enjoyed by tribes between 1959 and 1986.[78] According to Clinton, "The Supreme Court's historic sympathy for enforcing tribal claims against hostile state and other non-Indian interests collapsed in 1986."[79] As Richard A. Monette has pointed out, the Court's reinterpretation of federalism under the influence of Chief Justice William Rehnquist and Justice Sandra Day O'Connor has had a sometimes negative impact on tribal sovereignty.[80]

While Court support for states' rights has reasserted itself in recent years, it has been a factor in the past, particularly in the area of criminal and civil jurisdiction in Indian Country. In 1881, in *U.S. v. McBratney*, the Court ruled that state courts have jurisdiction over a crime in Indian Country involving only non-Indians.[81] In 1978, in a decision that seems somewhat inconsistent with others handed down the same year, the Court held in *Oliphant v. Suquamish Indian Tribe* that tribal courts have no jurisdiction over non-Indians charged with a tribal criminal offense because it was "inconsistent with their status."[82] Further limiting tribal jurisdiction and sovereignty was the Court's finding in *Montana v. United States* that the Crow Tribe had no authority to regulate fishing by non-Indians on non-Indian portions of its reservation.[83]

Recent cases consistent with these assertions of state authority of tribal authority include *Duro v. Reina*, which held that a tribal court has no jurisdiction over Indians who are not members of the tribe but are charged with violating a tribal criminal ordinance; and *Brendale v. Confederated Tribes and Bands of the Yakima Indian Nation,* where the Court ruled that the Yakima Nation could not regulate business activities of non-Indians on non-Indian land located on the reservation.[84]

"NATION"

In a tacit recognition of an aboriginal sovereign status, the United States conducted treaty relations with Indian tribes from shortly after independence from Britain was declared until 1871. According to Prucha, 367 treaties were ratified by the U.S. government between 1778 and 1868; a large number of treaties negotiated between representatives of the United States and Indian tribes and submitted to the Senate were never ratified, especially those with California tribes.[85]

The very act of treaty making was a recognition that tribes had at least "a measure of autonomy."[86] Washburn notes that "the treaty system . . . explicitly recognizes the fact that the United States government formerly acknowledged the independent and national character of the Indian peoples with whom they dealt."[87] A treaty, in Deloria's view, "is nothing more than a construct to describe the relationship of political entities."[88] But, as he also notes, the significance of treaties varied over time, and in 1871 Congress ended the treaty-making process with the tribes.[89] In a constitutional and political conflict, the House of Representatives objected to the continuation of a process that required it to fund treaty obligations but prevented it from participating in decisions about what its obligations should be. This battle reflected not only interinstitutional prerogatives; ending the treaty-making process tacitly recognized the rapidly diminishing independent status of tribes.

Not until the Indian Reorganization Act was passed in 1934 did the federal government begin to take steps to recognize an independent political voice for Indians.[90] The IRA was the vision of John Collier, reformer, social worker, and Franklin D. Roosevelt's commissioner of Indian affairs. It "was part of Collier's attempt to encourage economic development, self-determination, cultural plurality, and the revival of tribalism."[91] Reversing fifty years of policy, the IRA stopped the allotment process and halted the loss of Indian landholdings. The legislation also extended the trust periods indefinitely. Unallotted surplus lands could be returned to the tribe.

Tribes were given the opportunity to organize under a constitution adopted by tribal members. The tribal governments could hire legal counsel; prevent the sale, lease, or encumbrance of tribal land and assets; and negotiate with other units of government. Tribes could incorporate business councils to manage tribal property.

A tribe could exempt itself from the act by a vote of its members. The BIA conducted local tribal elections over the next few years and encouraged tribes to organize under the IRA. A unique aspect of these elections was that a nonvote was counted as a yes vote. Many tribes thus organized under the IRA's provision notwithstanding the fact that a majority of those voting had rejected the proposal. On many reservations the more traditional Indians led the opposition to incorporation. The most important tribe to reject the IRA was the Navajo Nation. While, as Prucha notes, "the vote to accept the Indian Reorganization Act did no more than identify tribes to which the legislation could be applied," the tribal governments established under the IRA "became the basis for later developments in tribal autonomy."[92]

Beginning with initiatives in the Kennedy administration, the 1960s brought about another dramatic change in Indian policy. By de facto ending termination and turning responsibility for federal programs over to the tribes, Presidents Lyndon Johnson and Richard Nixon set in motion a process that by the 1990s resulted in dynamic, thriving tribal governments. The bipartisan continuity of "self-determination" was the result of a consensus among Democrats and Republicans that the policy was consistent with the broader domestic goals of the two presidents responsible for its development. Both presidents demonstrated the significance of self-determination by sending special messages on Indians to Congress, Johnson in 1968 and Nixon in 1970.

Tribes were treated as other governmental units in many Great Society programs, such as the Office of Economic Opportunity. A significant advance for tribes in the Johnson administration was the BIA initiative permitting them to contract to operate BIA programs free of local bureau control.[93] Nixon expanded the emphasis on tribal control of federal programs and proposed legislation that became the Indian Self-Determination and Education Act of 1975.[94] The act gave legislative sanction to the contracting procedures that had begun under Johnson and provided greater tribal control over the education of Indian children.

Other advances in tribal governance occurred in the 1970s. In a move with significant implications for tribal sovereignty and the future of Indian children, Congress passed the Indian Child Welfare Act in 1978.[95] For decades Indian children had been removed from their parents and reservations by private and public social services agencies in the belief that they would be better off in a "stable" home, which usually meant one with white parents. Congress acted to halt this practice by recognizing a tribal interest in the future of children born to tribal members. Tribal courts were given a role in custody questions involving Indian children, and tribes and individual Indians could intervene in such matters.

Although federal Indian programs suffered severe cutbacks during the 1980s, Presidents Ronald Reagan and George Bush reaffirmed the policy of self-determination and the term of art became "government-to-government relations." In 1991, at the urging of several tribes, Congress took the policy of self-determination contracting procedures to a new level. It amended the Indian Education and Self-Determination Act to provide for a "Self-Governance Demonstration Project."[96] The seven tribes initially participating in the project would be able to assume the delivery of specific BIA services, eliminating much of the local BIA bureaucracy.[97] Over the next few years additional tribes took part and Indian Health Services programs were made eligible for contracting. In 1994 Congress passed legislation making the Self-Governance Demonstration Project permanent.[98] By 1998, 206 tribes were participating in the project overseen by the BIA's Office of Self-Governance;[99] 254 tribes were participating in the Indian Health Service Self-Governance program.[100]

Just as the Supreme Court had played a significant role in diminishing tribal sovereignty and increasing tribal dependence on the federal government, it eventually supported the reassertion of tribal rights. The new era of judicial support for tribal sovereignty began in 1959 with *Williams v. Lee*.[101] In the matter of a lawsuit filed in state court by a non-Indian against a Navajo to recover losses on goods sold in the Navajo Nation, the Court held that the Arizona court lacked jurisdiction; the matter belonged exclusively in Navajo court. The Court held that "absent governing Acts of Congress, the question has always been whether the state action infringed on the right of reservation Indians to make their own laws and be governed by them."

Three cases decided in the 1970s further strengthened tribal sovereignty. In 1973, in *McClanahan v. Arizona State Tax Commission,* the Supreme Court held that Arizona's income tax could not be imposed on Indians earning their income on Indian land.[102] In a lawsuit emerging from litigation over the Indian Civil Rights Act of 1968, the Court ruled against a Santa Clara Pueblo woman who sued her tribe over its denial of membership to her daughter by a Navajo man. The Court held that the suit was barred by tribal sovereign immunity in *Santa Clara Pueblo v. Martinez*.[103] A second case decided in 1978, *United States v. Wheeler,* strongly asserted an independent inherent tribal sovereignty in holding that convictions for the same offense in tribal and federal courts did not violate double jeopardy.[104]

INDIAN POLITICAL ACTIVISM

Given the often-drastic consequences of government policy for Indian people, there is a tendency to overlook the significant attempts by many Indian leaders to shape those policies. The reality is that Indian leaders have always addressed the policies being perpetrated on and for them. The Indian Wars were fought by tribes protecting their sovereignty. It is often lost sight of in popular culture that the great Indian-cavalry battles were fought by a people resisting the imposition of foreign values and an alien political system. Indian leaders such as Crazy Horse, Sitting Bull, Chief Joseph, Tecumseh, and Geronimo were, to use Alvin Josephy's term, "patriot chiefs."[105]

Warfare was not the only way Indians attempted to influence policy. As indicated by the nearly one hundred years of treaty making, diplomacy was an avenue many tribal leaders traveled to protect their people's interest. Some tribes also attempted strategies that would today be viewed as inside and outside lobbying efforts to achieve their policy goals. Herman J. Viola documents in colorful detail the numerous delegations of Indian leaders that visited Washington to meet with administration and congressional officials.[106] Often Indian leaders made direct appeals to the American people. As noted above, the Cherokees launched a sophisticated public relations campaign to defeat removal. Other later Indian leaders such as the Oglala Lakota warrior Red Cloud toured eastern American cities to arouse popular support for Indian issues.

One limitation on Indian participation in the political process was the denial of citizenship and the right to vote. Indians as a group did not become citizens of the United States until the passage of the Indian Citizenship Act in 1924.[107] Before that time, Indians could become citizens only under certain circumstances, such as special acts of Congress. In 1884 the Supreme Court held in *Elk v. Wilkins* that John Elk, an Omaha Indian who had severed his tribal connections, was not a U.S. citizen under the Fourteenth Amendment.[108] The Indian Citizenship Act, while overturning *Elk*, also protected the continuing tribal status of individual Indians. Citizenship did not necessarily grant the right to vote, but it did enable "reservation Indians to participate in state programs, and such participation [made] state laws applicable to them in certain instances."[109]

Organized activities by Indian organizations to influence federal policy became increasingly important in the second half of the twentieth century. The National Congress of American Indians (NCAI), founded in 1944, is the most prominent inter-tribal organization in the nation and mounts effective lobbying efforts on Capitol Hill. The National Indian Gaming Association (NIGA) has become a significant factor in gaming issues (see chap. 2). Other organizations deal specifically with such issues as health, education, and natural resources.

While all of these organizations attempt to influence policy with traditional inside-politics tactics, the 1960s and 1970s saw a different kind of organized Indian activism. This activism was more confrontational and more public than that engaged in by such organizations as the NCAI. Beginning with the "fish-in" protests on the Northwest Coast in 1965, young Indians, many the products of the relocation process, began demanding that treaty rights and other guarantees be enforced by the federal government. Confrontations between young "militants" and law enforcement personnel intensified. In November 1969, in a dramatic display of activism, a number of Indians "occupied" Alcatraz Island.

The organization that became the focus for Indian activism was the American Indian Movement (AIM), founded in 1968 in the Twin Cities to monitor alleged police brutality against Indians living there. Within a few years AIM chapters were founded in a number of other cities and on reservations. In 1972 AIM leaders organized the Trail of Broken Treaties, a caravan across the country to highlight Indian grievances. Along the way a list of demands was drawn up for presentation to officials in Washington, D.C. These Twenty Points called for a return to the treaty-making process and a stop to state incursion on Indian lands. While in Washington, members of the caravan occupied the headquarters of the BIA for several days before agreeing to leave town. The government ultimately rejected the Twenty Points.

AIM's most serious action occurred in February 1973 when several of its leaders joined some members of the Oglala Sioux

Tribe at the Pine Ridge Reservation in South Dakota to protest the rule of the tribal chairman. The result was a seventy-one-day occupation of the village of Wounded Knee, site of the 1890 massacre of nearly three hundred Lakotas. In the 1973 armed standoff between AIM and federal and tribal law enforcement, two Indians were killed by gunfire and a U.S. marshal was paralyzed by a bullet.

CURRENT TRENDS

Echoes of Jacksonian states' rights continue to reverberate in Indian policy formulation, making state governments one of the significant new arenas of political activity by Indians. Made possible in large measure by gaming-generated revenue, Indian tribes in several states have the resources to become significant forces in state politics. This is occurring at another potential turning point in American politics and Indian policy. The movement toward devolution of federal programs to state governments and significant federal budgetary constraints are once again threatening not only Indian programs but also tribal sovereignty itself. Unlike similar national currents of previous decades, Indians now have a large and sophisticated network of political leaders and organizations capable of effectively mounting opposition to these trends in Washington, D.C. However, tribes in many states have not yet developed similar capabilities to challenge actions inimical to their interests in state capitols. The story of Indian gaming parallels many of these concerns.

CHAPTER TWO

Indian Gaming

THE LAW, THE INTERESTS,
AND THE SCOPE OF CONFLICT

Government-sponsored gambling has become the
revenue-raising activity of choice among governments in the
United States. To counter continuing federal budget cutbacks
in the past decade, state, local, and tribal governments have
turned to public, legal games of chance to fund services. Every
state in the nation except Hawaii and Utah permits some form
of gambling, as do the District of Columbia and Puerto Rico.
Thirty-six states and the District of Columbia operate lotteries.
According to the gambling critic Robert Goodman, "Politicians
often adopt a hold-your-nose-and-legalize-it position. Frustrated
by their failure to find other solutions to stimulate economic
growth, city and state legislators have turned to gambling companies to create an economic development policy of last resort."[1]
In 1995 Nevada, New Jersey, Illinois, and Louisiana each collected
more than $200 million in gaming tax revenue; Mississippi,
Connecticut, and Missouri each collected more than $100
million; and gambling tax revenue for all states was $1.9 billion.[2]

Americans have not been hesitant about supporting the new
gaming establishments. In 1984 Americans wagered approxi-
mately $117 billion on all forms of legalized gaming;[3] by 1994
that amount had increased to $482 billion.[4] Since 1976, when

New Jersey became the second state after Nevada to legalize casino gambling, eleven states have taken similar action. Since 1991 six states have approved riverboat casinos; nearly sixty riverboats now operate out of cities in Illinois, Iowa, Mississippi, Missouri, Louisiana, and Indiana.[5] According to Harrah's Survey of Casino Entertainment, there were 154 million visits to casinos in the United States in 1995, a 23 percent increase over 1994.[6]

Arguably, Indian tribes have led the movement of governments to gaming as a source of revenue. As federal support for tribal activities continued to diminish and alternative economic development activities in Indian Country remained minimal, tribal governments turned first to high-stakes bingo and then to other forms of gaming to provide revenue for tribal services. NCAI president Gaiashkibos observed, "The harsh reality is that the financial world has not historically looked towards locating business on Indian reservations."[7]

The dollar figures for Indian gaming are as dramatic as those for non-Indian gaming. Total revenues from tribal gaming activities in 1988, mostly from bingo, were estimated at $121,000.[8] Class III gaming—lotteries, casinos, pari-mutuel racing—has been responsible for the subsequent increase. Bingo revenue increased from $380,200 in 1989 to $435,300 in 1993, and Class III revenues increased from $100,300 to $2,594,000.[9] By 1994 total Indian gaming revenue was $4.4 billion.[10] A 1996 GAO study of financial statements for 178 of the 281 Indian gaming facilities documented revenues of $4.5 billion. Tribes earned an additional $300 million from hotels and food services.[11]

These figures indicate the tremendous increase in the number of tribes offering Class III gaming after Congress passed the Indian Gaming Regulatory Act in 1988. In 1990, 14 tribes in four states offered some form of Class III gaming. By 1993, 102 tribes in nineteen states did so;[12] and in March 1998, 148 tribes in twenty-four states had Class III gaming.

Only about one-third of the nation's tribes operate Class III gaming establishments; at least two-thirds offer bingo. Eight tribal gaming operations account for 40 percent of total Indian gaming revenues.[13] Some tribes are located in parts of the country that make a profitable gaming venture unlikely. Others have decided not to engage in this kind of economic enterprise for tribal-specific reasons. Since passage of the IGRA tribes are permitted to spend their gaming profits only on services to members, on charitable contributions, or on a per capita distribution to members. This revenue has allowed tribes with profitable gaming to replace or supplement federal funds.

THE CLASH OF INTERESTS AND IDEOLOGIES

Congress passed the IGRA in an attempt to balance the competing economic and ideological interests raised by the emergence of Indian gaming. The economic interests involved in the spread of various kinds of gambling in Indian Country were fairly straightforward: the tribes, which saw gaming as a source of revenue independent of government control; the states, which were increasingly turning to state-run gaming endeavors; and non-Indian gaming enterprises. The economic conflict was also straightforward: who would control or share in the financial benefits resulting from the money wagered and lost in games operated by Indian tribes? Both the conflict and the interests are consistent with E. E. Schattschneider's classic "scope of conflict" arrangement wherein parties with an economic interest in an issue seek the level or arena of government most likely to award them victory.[14]

There were also ideological conflicts involving fundamental questions of federalism, states' rights, and Indian sovereignty. These questions, as old as the Republic, found new saliency in the war to control Indian gaming. The political environment for this aspect of the gaming conflict was, first, the quarter-century federal policy of Indian self-determination and, second, the shift away from a federalism dominated by the state governments to one dominated by the national government.

How the IGRA came to be passed is a fascinating study in both of these areas of conflict. It also highlights a significant

and overlooked institution of agenda setting in American politics, the federal courts. John W. Kingdon's important study of
how issues get placed on the policy agenda overlooks the role
of the courts.[15] He cites neither the courts as institutions nor
the judicial system as a process in one of the "two categories of
factors" affecting "agenda setting and the specification of alternatives: the participants who are active, and the processes by
which agenda items and alternatives come into prominence."[16]
As Beth M. Henschen and Edward I. Sidlow observe, the judiciary is "noticeably absent from his list" of agenda setters.[17]

Kingdon also fails to acknowledge the importance of fundamental constitutional questions in the process of agenda
setting. Although it is true that battles over such grand ideas as
federalism often cover more basic (and baser) conflicts, such
notions are crucial to how the American political system functions. Samuel Beer has noted that American federalism is both
an "idea" and a "structure."[18] As has been pointed out, Indian
policy has often been driven by conflict over who controls
Indian Country—the federal government, state governments,
or the tribes themselves. The "structure" of the policy arrangement at any point in history has been driven by the "idea"
behind that policy. This battle has been engaged again in the
issue of Indian gaming, for, as Sidney M. Wolf observed, "the
semisovereign status of Indian tribes is at the heart of the
Indian gaming controversy."[19]

INDIAN GAMING AND THE COURTS

The first significant case establishing the right of tribes to
conduct games of chance involved attempts by Florida law
enforcement officials to subject Indian bingo to state law. The
Seminole Tribe operated bingo games six days a week and
awarded prizes in excess of $100, both above limits set by state
law. Broward County Sheriff Robert Butterfield informed the
tribe that he was prepared to make arrests at the bingo hall on
the reservation near downtown Fort Lauderdale. The tribe was

granted a preliminary injunction by a federal judge for the Southern District of Florida in December 1979.

The following May the district court held that Florida's gambling laws were civil/regulatory, not criminal/prohibitory. Therefore, notwithstanding the state's assumption of criminal jurisdiction over Indians on Florida reservations under P.L. 83-280, the state limits on bingo did not apply to the Seminole games.[20] The district court's decision was upheld the following year by the Fifth Circuit Court of Appeals.[21] Both courts looked to the 1976 Supreme Court decision in *Bryan v. Itasca County* to determine the extent of state jurisdiction granted P.L. 83-280 states.[22]

In *Bryan* the Court had developed the civil/regulatory, criminal/prohibitory test for P.L. 83-280 states. If a state statute regarding an activity conducted in the state was merely civil and regulatory in nature, it was not enforceable against Indian tribes within the state. The Court held that Congress had intended civil jurisdiction in P.L. 83-280 states to apply only in private disputes between Indians and between Indians and non-Indians in Indian Country. If the activity in question was criminal, the state had jurisdiction over it when conducted in Indian Country.

In *Seminole v. Butterfield* the district and circuit courts found that while the Florida constitution prohibited "lotteries, other than the types of parimutuel pools authorized by law," the overall public gaming policy of the state was regulatory. The circuit court found, "It is clear from the provisions of the bingo statute in question and the statutory scheme of the Florida gambling provisions considered as a whole that the playing of bingo and operation of bingo halls is not contrary to the public policy of the state." The Seminole Tribe could continue its high-stakes bingo games.

Federal courts across the country heard similar disputes as more tribes opened bingo halls operating outside state limits. Federal court decisions dealing with attempts by P.L. 83-280 states to regulate Indian gaming continued to follow the *Bryan* and *Butterfield* reasoning.[23] The most significant challenge to state authority over tribal gambling activities came in California, where the state attempted to halt bingo games offered by the Cabazon and Morongo bands of Mission Indians.

California law permits several kinds of gambling. Like many states, it has legalized bingo games operated by certain charitable organizations, with prizes limited to no more than $250. Pari-mutuel horse race betting is legal, and the state operates a lottery. Card games are not illegal under state law, although they can be outlawed locally, and "card rooms" can be found throughout the state. California was also one of the original mandated P.L. 83-280 states.

By the early 1980s a number of California's Indian tribes had opened or were planning to open bingo halls or card clubs.[24] Tribal bingo halls uniformly offered prizes in excess of the state limit. California law enforcement officers just as uniformly considered these actions a violation of the state law they were sworn to uphold. Seeing their duty, several county sheriffs either threatened to close tribal bingo games or actually attempted to do so by executing raids. The imminent action by San Diego County Sheriff John Duffy led to the Ninth Circuit's 1982 ruling in *Barona* that California's gaming policy was permissive/regulatory and the tribe's bingo beyond Sheriff Duffy's jurisdiction.

The General Council of the Cabazon Band of Mission Indians passed tribal ordinances in February and May 1980 authorizing bingo games and the establishment of card clubs offering draw poker.[25] The Cabazon's card club opened in Riverside County on October 16, 1980. Two days later the Indio City Police Department raided the club and "arrested over 100 officers, members, employees and non-members of the Cabazon Band, and ordered the card club closed, for allegedly violating a local ordinance of the City of Indio which prohibited poker games."[26] The tribe filed suit in the Federal District Court for the Central District of California, which held in favor of the City of Indio in May 1981. The Ninth Circuit Court of Appeals reversed the district court on December 14, 1982.[27] The court held that Indio's attempted annexation of Cabazon lands was void and its gaming laws therefore did not apply to the tribe.

Although the Ninth Circuit had now nullified two different state jurisdictions' attempts to stop Indian gaming, other jurisdictions continued to maintain that their gambling laws were controlling in Indian Country. On February 15, 1983, sixteen Riverside County sheriff's officers issued citations to more than thirty individuals, including the tribal officers, for violating the county ordinance prohibiting the card games being played in Cabazon's card club.[28] The officers confiscated $3,000 in cash, files, records, playing cards, and poker chips.

At about the same time Cabazon was engaged in its ongoing conflict with various law enforcement agencies, the nearby Morongo Band of Mission Indians found itself in a similar predicament. On April 23, 1983, the Morongo Band authorized bingo games that would operate contrary to state and county regulations governing bingo. Unlike the Cabazon Band, the Morongo did not authorize a card club.

The Cabazon and Morongo bands sued Riverside County in the Federal District Court for the Central District of California. The tribes sought a declaratory judgment that the county's ordinances did not apply on tribal lands and asked for an injunction preventing Riverside from enforcing them. The state of California intervened on the side of the county. Judge Laughlin E. Waters ruled in favor of the tribes. The Ninth Circuit Court of Appeals affirmed Waters's ruling, concluding that "the federal and tribal interests at stake here outweigh the State's interest."[29] The court of appeals found "that California's bingo statute is civil/regulatory in nature and does not apply, under Public Law 280, on the Indian reservations." California's argument that the Federal Organized Crime Control Act[30] barred the tribes' gaming activities was rejected by the court because "bingo games are not contrary to the public policy" of the state.

California appealed, and the Supreme Court granted a writ of certiorari on June 21, 1987. In its brief California contended that "the State has a vital interest in prohibiting the tribal bingo games here" and that the Court should apply a balancing test recognizing the state's interest in regulating gambling activities on Indian land.

> First, State gambling policy is frustrated if Indian tribes can market an exemption from State gambling laws to non-Indians. Second, the tribal bingo games create a serious risk of organized crime infiltration. . . . The federal interest is, at most, neutral in this case.[31]

Attorneys for the state also argued that P.L. 83-280 gave California civil and criminal jurisdiction over Indian tribes located within the state. The brief urged the Court to reject "the *Bryan* dictum that state 'civil regulatory' laws do not apply." But even within the scheme established by *Bryan,* the state argued, "California's gambling laws are 'criminal prohibitory' and hence are included under Public Law 280 in any event."[32] The state also sought to apply the Organized Crime Control Act to Indian gaming in California as the act authorizes the application of state and local gambling laws to Indian lands. Twenty-five states (including New Mexico and Oklahoma) joined in three separate amicus curiae briefs in support of California's position.

Attorneys for the Cabazon and Morongo bands rejected California's contention that a common law balancing test gave the state jurisdiction over Indian gaming. The brief for the tribes argued, "The analysis of this case must begin with the well-established principle that absent express congressional authorization, states have no jurisdiction over Indian tribes on the reservations."[33] According to tribal lawyers, P.L. 83-280 conferred no jurisdiction on California that would allow the state to regulate Indian gaming. The tribes also rejected the application of the Organized Crime Control Act to tribal gambling because the statute "does not give appellants jurisdiction to enforce their civil regulatory laws on the reservation."[34] The brief specifically rejected the application of county ordinances to the Cabazon card club, asserting, "That enterprise is identical in all respects to hundreds of other card rooms operating elsewhere in California, including at least five others in Riverside County."[35] Eighteen tribes and two Indian organizations joined in three amicus briefs in support of the California tribes.

The Supreme Court handed down its ruling in *Cabazon* on February 25, 1987.[36] The 6 to 3 decision, written by Justice Byron White, rejected California's position and handed Indian tribes a significant victory in the face of strong states' rights arguments. White reiterated the Court's long-held position that tribes have "attributes of sovereignty over both their members and their territory" and that "tribal sovereignty is dependent on, and subordinate to, only the Federal Governments, not the States." White also acknowledged congressional power to confer states with jurisdiction if it "has expressly so provided."

To determine whether P.L. 83-280 gives states jurisdiction over a certain activity on Indian lands, the Court said that "the shorthand test is whether the conduct at issue violates the State's public policy." In reviewing California's gaming laws, White wrote, "We must conclude that California regulates rather than prohibits gambling in general and bingo in particular. . . . [W]e conclude that Pub.L. 280 does not authorize California to enforce" the California penal code regarding gambling on the Cabazon and Morongo lands. In rejecting state jurisdiction under the Organized Crime Control Act (OCCA), the Court noted that "there is nothing in OCCA indicating that the States are to have any part in enforcing federal criminal laws or are authorized to make arrests on Indian reservations that in the absence of OCCA they could not affect."

The justices reviewed the competing interests at stake in the case before it. Recognizing that the state has an interest in regulating gambling within its borders, the Court also considered whether Congress had preempted state jurisdiction. "The inquiry," wrote Justice White, "is to proceed in light of traditional notions of Indian sovereignty and the congressional goal of Indian self-government, including its 'overriding goal' of encouraging tribal self-sufficiency and economic development."

White noted that President Reagan had reaffirmed the federal interest in these goals in his 1983 Statement on Indian Policy. Noting congressional acts promoting economic development, the Court found,

> These policies and actions, which demonstrate the Government's approval and active promotion of tribal bingo enterprises, are of particular relevance in this case. . . . The tribes interests obviously parallel the federal interests. . . .
>
> We conclude that the State's interest in preventing the infiltration of the tribal bingo enterprises by organized crime does not justify state regulation of the tribal bingo enterprises in light of the compelling federal and tribal interests supporting them. State regulation would impermissibly infringe on tribal government, and this conclusion applies equally to the county's attempted regulation of the Cabazon card club.

Justice John Paul Stevens wrote a dissent in which Justices Antonin Scalia and Sandra Day O'Connor joined. Justice Stevens rejected the majority's holding that Congress had preempted the issue and wrote that "Congress has permitted the State to apply its prohibitions against commercial gambling to Indian tribes," although he cited no statute providing for that jurisdiction. Stevens contended that the state's economic and safety interests were legitimate; when tribal gambling is beyond the reach of state regulation, the state loses revenue. Stevens was not as sanguine about the ability of tribal gaming enterprises to remain corruption-free: "I am unwilling to dismiss as readily as the Court does the State's concern that these unregulated high-stakes bingo games may attract organized criminal infiltration."

Cabazon and the lengthy controversy in California mirror other tribal-state gaming disputes around the country. While the civil/criminal question had been laid to rest by *Cabazon,* the issues of criminal involvement in Indian gaming, economic competition, and the fundamental question of state versus tribal regulation in Indian Country continued to frame the debate.

CONGRESS ENTERS THE GAME

It was the cumulative effect of federal court rulings ending in the *Cabazon* decision that finally spurred Congress to action. The federal courts had added import to the increasing pressures of state officials and the non-Indian gaming industry. As Henschen and Sidlow point out, it is not unusual for court decisions to place an issue on the congressional agenda.

> While courts are not the most important actors in the agenda-setting process of Congress, in some significant instances a court decision or series of decisions will provide an impetus for congressional action—or reaction. Moreover, court rulings and interpretations of the law, especially those handed down by the United States Supreme Court, may spur interest groups or other actors to urge Congress to enact new statutes or to amend existing ones in response to judicial policymaking.[37]

"Interest groups or other actors" were clearly involved in pressuring Congress to address the growing concerns emerging from the spread of Indian gaming made possible in large part by the federal courts.

I. Nelson Rose of the Whittier College School of Law observed in 1990, "Ever since the Seminole Tribe of Florida won the right in 1979 to run high-stakes bingo games free from government control, the controversy has been fought in legislatures, the press, and cases going all the way to the United States Supreme Court."[38] Until Congress reacted to the increasing demands for action and passed the IGRA, the boundaries and limits of state and tribal authority in Indian gaming were set largely by federal court decisions. These decisions expanded the boundaries of tribal control and limited the extent of state jurisdiction over gambling in Indian Country.

As tribes won in court the states widened their efforts to gain control of the issue by turning to Congress. Former Secretary of the Interior Stewart Udall observed, "States and state governments simply said, let's stop Indians, let's make them conform to our law and let's not let them have the freedom to introduce other forms of gaming. Let's stop Indian gaming in its tracks before it gains momentum and enlarges the status quo."[39] But, as Roland J. Santoni points out, the tribes and non-Indian gaming interests also "desired legislation that would protect their respective interest."[40]

According to Franklin Ducheneaux, former House Committee on Interior and Insular Affairs counsel, the impetus for congressional action came from the federal court decisions. As he told the Senate Committee on Indian Affairs in May 1996,

> The result of the these early cases, particularly the *Barona* and *Seminole* cases, was two-fold: first, as awareness of the holdings filtered trough Indian country, more tribes began to turn to gaming as a source of tribal revenue, and, second, an anti-Indian gaming backlash began to develop. These two developments raised the issue of Indian gaming in the Congress.[41]

This interpretation is echoed by Sen. Harry Reid (D-Nev.): "Following the Supreme Court's ruling in the *Cabazon* case, though, there was little choice except for Congress to enact laws regulating gaming on Indian lands."[42]

The search for a legislative response to Indian gaming began its five-year odyssey in November 1983 when Rep. Morris Udall (D-Ariz.) introduced the first bill proposing gaming regulation in Indian Country, H.R. 4566. In introducing his bill, co-sponsored by Rep. John McCain (R-Ariz.), Udall noted the "concern about the attraction of organized crime and other undesirable elements" to Indian-operated gaming. The Arizona congressman emphasized that the intent of the legislation was to neither support nor oppose gaming and noted that the federal courts had determined that Indian tribes had the right "under certain circumstances" to conduct gaming.[43] The following year Rep. Norman David Shumway (R-Calif.) introduced a bill to prohibit Indian gaming that was not legal within the state where the tribe was located or that was contrary to the state's public policy.[44] The first Senate bill to regulate Indian gaming was Sen. Dennis DeConcini's (D-Ariz.) Indian Gaming Control Act, S. 902, introduced in April 1985.[45]

In the five years following the introduction of H.R. 4566, Senate and House committees conducted a number of hearings on tribally operated gambling, the first held by Udall's Committee on Interior and Insular Affairs on June 19, 1984. All sides in the controversy staked out their positions; the scope of the tribal-state intergovernmental conflict and the position of the non-Indian gaming interests were established.

Representatives of state and local governments argued that states should regulate Indian gaming. They made four main points: (1) the need to control criminal activity associated with gambling and the alleged inability of tribes to deal with such crime; (2) the loss of state revenue if tribes or the federal government regulated Indian gaming instead of the states; (3) tribal governments' inexperience in regulating gaming; and (4) a lack of faith in the federal government's ability to regulate Indian gaming.

Tribes argued that the regulation of Indian gaming was an attribute of their sovereignty. Those tribes that acknowledged that some order had to be brought to Indian gaming preferred that it be done at the federal rather than the state level. The tribes also argued that they alone were entitled to the revenue generated by the games. They answered the law enforcement argument by pointing out that those tribes that had gaming had not had any serious law and order difficulties. Finally, the tribes argued that gaming was a legitimate way to implement self-determination and economic development policies.

The respective arguments of the states and tribes reflect Schattschneider's observations about conflict: "The attempt to control the scope of conflict has a bearing on federal-state-local relations, for one way to restrict the scope of conflict is to *localize* it, while one way to expand it is to nationalize it."[46] In the tribal-state conflict over gaming, the states and some tribes wanted to localize the issue and maintain control over what they each viewed as their sovereign sphere. Some tribes, realizing complete tribal control was not possible, sought to nationalize the issue and have the federal government intervene to protect tribal interests.

During House and Senate hearings on proposed legislation, the scope of the intergovernmental and federalism conflict was most often indirectly stated. However, explicit definition of the conflict as a federalism issue sometimes emerged. Brian McKay, attorney general of Nevada, told the House Committee on Interior and Insular Affairs,

> Excluding high-stakes gaming from state regulation is imprudent law enforcement. State agencies can best police gaming operations, a traditional function performed by these agencies. . . . In our system of Federalism, state agencies are the most appropriate entities to provide regulatory oversight of high-stakes gaming operations.[47]

John Duffy, chairman of the National Sheriff's Association's Law and Legislative Committee, echoed these sentiments in a letter to Mark Andrews (R-N.Dak.), chairman of the Senate Select Committee on Indian Affairs. He wrote that his association believed "that each state has the right to regulate gambling for all its citizens—Indian and non-Indian alike. It is a question of states rights."[48]

Indian tribes saw the question of federalism from a different perspective. Repeatedly tribal leaders and representatives of Indian organizations stressed the need to protect their sovereignty. Alvino Lucero, chairman of the Southern Pueblos Governors Council, told the Senate committee, "State assumption of civil and/or criminal jurisdiction over Indian reservations has serious implications for erosion of tribal sovereignty."[49]

Jim Hena, governor of Tesuque Pueblo, representing the Gaming Pueblos of New Mexico, told the House Committee on Interior and Insular Affairs, "I want to point out to you that the United States Constitution envisions a federal system which has as its component parts federal, state and tribal governments."[50]

State-elected officials saw the conflict as threatening to their own sovereignty. Sen. Chic Hecht (R-Nev.) told the House Interior and Insular Affairs Committee, "Legal gaming on Indian Lands should be subject to the same rules and regulations which non-Indian games must abide. Indian gaming should also be taxed the same way."[51] An accompanying document expanding on his remarks was titled "Law Enforcement, Not Indian Sovereignty, Is Key to Legal Wagering on Indian Lands."[52]

This view was supported by representatives of the gaming industry. In a prepared statement for the Senate Select Committee on Indian Affairs, the counsel for the American Greyhound Track Operators' Association wrote, "A State's laws and regulations relating to gambling represent a consensus of views as to standards of conduct allowable in that State as a whole."[53]

There was support for the Indian perspective on sovereignty among some members of Congress. Representative McCain told the House Committee, "Imposing State jurisdiction on tribes, I believe, I am convinced, violates" congressional responsibility to Indian tribes and "cuts across the grain of past Congressional policies, encouraging self-determination and self-government."[54] Representative Udall repeatedly asserted that, while seeking ways to regulate Indian gaming and accommodating competing interests, he would allow nothing to diminish tribal sovereignty.

THE REAGAN ADMINISTRATION'S POSITION

The Reagan administration generally reacted to congressional activity rather than take the lead on the increasingly controversial issue of Indian gaming. In 1983 the BIA established a task force on bingo that was later expanded to include tribal representatives. Hazel Elbert, BIA deputy director of the Office of Indian Services, said at the Annual Federal Bar Association Indian Law Conference, "Our position was that prohibiting tribes from engaging in such [bingo] operations would be inconsistent with the announced Indian policy of President Reagan."[55]

The Reagan administration's position became clearer as officials raised questions about potential organized crime infiltration as well as about which level of government should be responsible for regulating what types of Indian gaming. Interior Deputy Assistant Secretary John Fritz voiced concern at an August 1983 meeting of the BIA Task Force about possible organized crime connections. He also raised concerns about the high percentage many tribes were paying non-Indian management firms to operate their gaming enterprises.[56]

In 1984 Fritz testified before the House Committee on Interior and Insular Affairs in support of Udall's H.R. 4566 but urged that action on the bill be deferred. Although he commented on the administrative difficulties the Interior Department was having in approving bingo management contracts, his major concern was law enforcement. Fritz told the committee, "The opportunities for skimming and laundering are enormous."[57] He also had doubts about federal regulatory capabilities. According to Fritz, neither the Justice Department nor the Interior Department was in a position to regulate Indian gaming.[58]

Ross Swimmer, an assistant secretary of the interior for Indian Affairs under Reagan and former principal chief of the Cherokee Nation of Oklahoma, indicated his displeasure with tribal bingo operations. In December 1985 Swimmer said that bingo "tells you you don't have to work you can just get it by gambling" and that it "sends the wrong signal."[59] As assistant secretary, Swimmer sought tighter regulation of Indian bingo but opposed state regulation. He maintained that bingo should only be a "stepping stone" to more diversified reservation economies.[60] He was more concerned about what he called "hard-core gaming."[61] "Our preference as to the so-called class III [gaming]," he told a House committee in 1987, was that it "either not be allowed in Indian country, or that if it is allowed in Indian country, it should be regulated by the State that has the appropriate regulatory body already in place to do it."[62]

In commenting on pending legislation, including S. 555, the bill eventually amended and passed as the Indian Gaming Regulatory Act, the Justice Department stated its "overriding goals." Legislation passed by Congress should "provide a set of 'bright line' rules that set out the extent to which State gambling laws, both regulatory and prohibitory, apply in Indian country and provide that such rules apply in all States containing Indian country, not just in P.L. 280 States."[63] Any Indian gaming legislation should also "balance law enforcement concerns raised by commercial gaming with the understandable desire of the tribes to obtain revenue from this activity, and, consistent with the interests of federalism, must pay due regard to the authority of the States to regulate activities within their borders."[64]

Thus, to the extent that the Reagan administration had a position on Indian gaming, it involved regulatory concerns balancing state, federal, and Indian interests, promotion of Indian gaming as part of its overall Indian policy emphasizing economic development, and the elimination or reduction of possible criminal activity.

CONGRESS ACTS

While public hearings were under way private negotiations were being conducted among members of Congress, their staffs, and the competing interests. The positions of the tribes and the states were clear. Senator Reid observed,

> Following *Cabazon* there were two basic positions in regard to Indian gaming. On the one hand many tribes believed that the *Cabazon* decision and the concept of Indian sovereignty meant that gaming on Indian lands should be controlled exclusively by the tribes, with little or no oversight by the federal government. On the other hand,

many lawmakers and state and local government officials
believed that the states should have to directly regulate
gaming on Indian lands. . . . We were going to have to find
some realistic middle ground or face the consequences of
continued inaction in this area.[65]

And as Ducheneaux explained, "The problem for the negotiators was how to permit the state to have a role in regulation of
Indian class III gaming, which *Cabazon* precluded, through the
requirement for a compact without placing tribes at the mercy
of a state which would not act in good faith."[66]

The Supreme Court's action in *Cabazon* altered the course
of gaming legislation. "The practical effect" of the Supreme
Court agreeing to hear *Cabazon*, according to Ducheneaux,
"was to substantially weaken the position of the tribes and their
supporters, and greatly enhance the bargaining power of the
anti-Indian gaming forces." While the Indians were confident
that the Court would uphold the Ninth Circuit, "the anti-Indian
gaming forces were equally sure that the eventual decision of the
Court would be a 'slam-dunk' for them." The states demanded
"full jurisdiction over all Indian gaming and the right to tax all
tribal proceeds."[67]

The report accompanying S. 555 had a somewhat different
interpretation of the tribes' reaction to the Court's review of
Cabazon.

Tribes, concerned that the Court's ruling might adversely
affect their position on the legislation, became more willing
to compromise. Other parties, believing the Court would
rule in favor of State regulation, became more adamant
about furthering the position in favor of transferring jurisdiction over Indian gaming activities to the States.[68]

The House passed H.R. 1920, Udall's latest effort at resolving
the increasingly difficult issue, on April 21, 1986, three days
before the Supreme Court docketed *Cabazon*.[69] The bill, Udall
said, "accepts the state of law."[70] Three classes of gaming and

the National Indian Gaming Commission were established. A five-year moratorium was set on new Class III gaming, and the GAO was slated to conduct a study to determine what kind of regulatory scheme would be appropriate for Class III Indian gaming. The moratorium provision was a compromise worked out by Congressmen Bill Richardson (D-New Mex.) and Tony Coelho (D-Calif.). Representative John McCain called H.R. 1920 "an honest attempt to join the conflicting interests of the state and the Indian tribes."[71]

The Senate Select Committee on Indian Affairs reported an amended version of H.R. 1920 in September 1986, but no further action was taken before the beginning of the next Congress. It would not be until after the Supreme Court upheld *Cabazon* that Congress finally enacted legislation regulating Indian gaming.

Two events involving leading members of Congress on Indian issues were probably significant in achieving a resolution to the gaming issue. In 1986 the Democrats regained control of the Senate. Inouye replaced Andrews as chairman of the Select Committee on Indian Affairs. In October 1986 Senator Andrews had introduced an amendment in the nature of a substitute to H.R. 1920, the bill passed by the House earlier in the year. Andrews called his amendment "a tough law and order bill" giving the states greater authority over Class III games.[72] Inouye became one of the strongest advocates for Indian sovereignty in Senate history and sought to protect tribal interests in gaming and other issues.

The second important event was the increasingly poor health of Congressman Udall. In the middle of 1988, faced with the intransigence of those opposing Indian gaming and "in failing health, Mr. Udall advised his staff that he did not think he could hold his position in the Committee, and even less in the House. In light of that conclusion, it was his decision to cease action on the bill rather than risk the consequences."[73]

Senator Inouye introduced S. 555 on February 19, 1987, six days before *Cabazon* was decided by the Supreme Court. In floor debate on the bill, Inouye concisely summarized the fundamental issue involved in Indian gaming.

We should be candid about the interests surrounding this particular piece of legislation. The issue has never really been one of crime control, morality, or economic fairness. . . . At issue is economics. At present Indian tribes may have a competitive economic advantage. . . . Ironically, the strongest opponents of tribal authority over gaming on Indian lands are from States whose liberal gaming policies would allow them to compete on an equal basis with the tribes.[74]

He added, "We must not impose greater moral restraints on Indians than we do on the rest of our citizenry."[75]

Senator Daschle spoke for many tribes in announcing his opposition to the bill after provisions were added permitting a larger role for the states.

My reason for opposing this bill is that those Indian tribes from South Dakota whom I represent have informed me that this bill is unacceptable. The tribes strongly object to any form of direct or indirect State jurisdiction over tribal matters. . . . As the Friends Committee on National Legislation has pointed out, S. 555 represents the first time a State would have jurisdiction over tribal affairs rather than over individuals.[76]

Daschle was referring to provisions in S. 555 modifying *Cabazon* to the extent that tribes could conduct Class III gaming only if such games were legal in the state and if a tribal-state compact permitting such games had been concluded. This was included in S. 555 because of demands by state officials that they have some regulatory say over Class III games. It is clear that the legislation was not intended to give states more than limited regulatory authority in Indian gaming and was not meant to be used by states to thwart tribes in their legitimate interests in conducting legal Class III games.

Inouye told the Senate,

The compacts are not intended to impose de facto State regulation. Rather the idea is to create a consensual agreement between sovereign governments and it is up to those entities to determine what provisions will be in the compacts. . . . I do want to publicly state that I hope that States will be fair and respectful of the authority of the tribes in negotiating these compacts and not take unnecessary advantage of the requirement of a compact.[77]

Sen. Daniel Evans (R-Wash.) said, "We intend that the two sovereigns—the tribes and the States—will sit down together in negotiations on equal terms and come up with a recommended methodology for regulating class III gaming on Indian lands." Furthermore, "compacts should not be used as subterfuge for the imposition of State jurisdiction on tribes."[78]

McCain echoed Evans's statement when he announced,

If the States take advantage of this relationship, the so-called compacts, then I would be one of the first to appear before my colleagues and seek to repeal this legislation because we must ensure that the Indians are given a level playing field in order to install gaming operations that are the same as the States in which they reside and will not be prevented from doing so because of the self-interest of the States in which they reside.[79]

The Senate passed S. 555 on a voice vote on September 15, 1988. The House took up the bill eleven days later, even though it had not been considered in committee. Representative Udall informed the House that "certain members and committee staff did participate very actively in the negotiations in the Senate which gave rise to the compromise S. 555."[80] He termed the bill a "delicately balanced compromise" and said that he sympathized with the "anger and frustration" of the tribes but felt "that this bill is probably the most acceptable legislation that could be obtained given the circumstances."[81] The House passed S. 555 on September 27 by a vote of 323 to 84.[82] President Reagan signed S. 555 into law on October 17, 1988.

The IGRA was, according to Santoni, "an amalgamation of ideas presented in bills introduced in Congress from 1983 to 1987."[83] The *Congressional Quarterly* called the law "a compromise between the tribes, which are extremely leery of any diminution of their sovereignty, and the states, which adamantly oppose any gambling operations within their borders unless they have regulatory authority over them."[84] According to Reid, the IGRA, a "fragile compromise," was passed for two reasons.

> First, the bill was as fair as we could make it, and it provided protection to states without violating either the *Cabazon* decision or the concept of Indian sovereignty. Second, although nobody agreed with every provision of the legislation, it was the only bill that could pass, and there were no alternatives that could become law.[85]

National Congress of American Indians executive director W. Ron Allen (Jamestown S'Klallam) noted, "To the extent IGRA diminished tribal sovereignty over gaming, it reflected a compromise. The act transferred to the states authority previously reserved to the federal and tribal governments."[86] The National Indian Gaming Association's chairman, Rick Hill, said in 1996 that the association could "not locate a single Indian Nation who formally supported the inclusion of states in the compacting provision."[87]

The major provisions of the IGRA are as follows:

- a declaration of congressional policy that includes "promoting tribal economic development, self-sufficiency, and strong tribal governments"; the protection of tribes from organized crime; and ensuring that "the Indian tribe is the primary beneficiary of gaming." The policy declaration asserts that the regulation of Indian gaming by the National Indian Gaming Commission is necessary for the protection of Indian gaming (25 USC 2701 (3)).

- establishment of three classes of Indian gaming: Class I, traditional Indian social gaming with minimal prizes that would be under the sole jurisdiction of the tribe where they are played (25 USC 2703(6), 2710(a)(1)); Class II, bingo, pull tabs, punch boards, tip jars, instant bingo, nonbanking card games that would be regulated by the tribes and the newly created National Indian Commission (25 USC 2703(7), 2710(a)(2),(b)); and Class III, all other gaming, including horse racing, casino gambling, dog racing, slot machines, jai alai, which would be permitted in Indian Country only if legal in the state and if agreed to in a compact negotiated between the state and tribe (25 USC 2703(8), 2710(d)(1)).

The IGRA sets out a procedure for tribes to follow when, in their view, states have failed to negotiate Class III compacts in good faith. A tribe wishing to conduct Class III gaming must request that the state begin negotiations on a tribal-state compact (25 USC 2710(d)(3)(A)). If after 180 days from the day the tribe requested negotiations a compact has not been concluded, or if the state has not responded to the tribe's request (25 USC 2710(7)(B)(i)), the tribe may sue in federal district court alleging the state has failed to negotiate in good faith (25 USC 2710(7)(A)(i)). The burden of proof lies with the state (25 USC 2710(7)(B)(ii)(II)). If the court finds that the state failed to negotiate in good faith, it then orders both parties to conclude a compact within 60 days (25 USC 2710(B)(iii)). If after 30 days no compact has been concluded, the court will have the tribe and the state submit compacts to a mediator who will select from the one that best conforms to federal law and submit it to both parties (25 USC 2710(B)(iv) and (v)). If the state agrees to the compact within 60 days of its submission by the mediator, the compact is considered valid (25 USC 2710(B)(vi)). If the state does not consent to the compact submitted by the mediator within 60 days, the mediator notifies the secretary of the interior, who will then prescribe procedures under which the tribe may conduct Class III gaming (25 USC 2710(B)(vii)).

Neither the tribes nor the states were satisfied with the new law. While tribes were free of state regulation of bingo and other Class II games, they were prohibited from Class III gaming unless the states agreed to a compact permitting it. As a 1996 Senate Committee on Indian Affairs report noted, "In IGRA, Congress provided State governments with an unprecedented opportunity to participate in the regulation of Indian gaming on Indian lands pursuant to Tribal-State compacts."[88] Advocates of tribal sovereignty believed any diminution of tribal authority was a loss for the tribes. That the ultimate regulator was a federal commission did not lessen their dislike of non-tribal regulation.

Although states were given "an unprecedented opportunity" to assert some regulatory role in Indian Country in the area of Class III gaming, they lost in three significant ways. First, they were prohibited from exercising any regulatory control over Class II gaming in Indian Country. Second, as states were barred from exercising regulatory power, they were also prevented from sharing in any economic benefits accruing to the tribes from their gaming operations. Third, they were required by the IGRA to enter into negotiations with those tribes wishing to conduct Class III casino-style games and could be sued by a tribe alleging failure to negotiate in good faith. State officials argued that this violated *their* sovereignty by violating their Tenth Amendment rights and abrogating their Eleventh Amendment immunity from lawsuits.

Nor was the gaming industry entirely pleased with the congressional solution. Organizations representing various kinds of gaming enterprises had made it clear that they wanted state rather than tribal or federal regulation. Furthermore, many saw the real possibility of serious competition from tribal gaming.

The scope of the conflict over Indian gaming had not been narrowed by the IGRA; rather, the opportunity for expanded conflict had been created. Tribal-state conflict was intensified by the reluctance or refusal of some states to negotiate Class III compacts in good faith. Two central issues became the source of ongoing and escalating tensions involving tribal and state governments and members of Congress. First, tribes and states continued to battle over the scope of gaming permitted under the IGRA. Whereas state officials argued that only those games specifically authorized under state law were available to tribes within their borders, Indian leaders argued that the *Cabazon* standard of general state gaming policy should be interpreted broadly in light of the IGRA. Second, notwithstanding state support for compacting provisions, a number of tribes were compelled to file suit against states and their governors for failing to negotiate Class III compacts in good faith. This was a classic intergovernmental confrontation, sovereign against sovereign on an issue of fundamental import: which government—federal, state, or tribal—had the greater authority in deciding what occurs within their respective borders. The answer would be determined by the federal structure and in turn further refine understandings of American federalism. The federal circuit courts of appeal split on the constitutionality of IGRA, the immediate issue on which this arrangement would be interpreted. Three circuits, the eighth, ninth, and tenth, rejected state contentions that the IGRA violated their sovereign immunity.[89] The Eleventh Circuit Court of Appeal held otherwise.[90]

To continue the fight for control of Indian gaming, states and tribes relied not only on their individual efforts in specific intergovernmental conflicts; each side used national organizations to press their interests at the national level. The National Governors Association (NGA) and the National Association of Attorneys General were the most active and visible groups presenting the states' position on Indian gaming. The governors developed a nearly unanimous policy on Indian gaming in 1993 and reaffirmed it in 1995.

While asserting support for "the efforts of Native Americans to create better and more prosperous lives" and stating that they "[did] not seek to prevent Native Americans from pursuing any opportunity available to other citizens of their states," the governors proposed amendments to the IGRA enlarging their regulatory role in Indian gaming.[91] The governors wanted to limit the scope of gaming to include "only those games expressly authorized by state law," and they wanted clarification of the meaning of "good faith" and how it applied to tribes. In their view, "a state's adherence to its own laws and constitution should not be regarded as bad faith." Finally, the governors sought clarification of the IGRA's provisions allowing tribes to acquire trust land for gaming purposes.[92]

The organized effort of gaming tribes was led by the National Indian Gaming Association, founded in 1985. Reflecting the status of tribal governments and the unique role of gaming in tribal affairs, NIGA and its activities do not meet the usual descriptions of intergovernmental associations. NIGA is neither a "generalist" nor a "specialist" organization according to the definition of those terms by Beverly A. Cigler.[93] NIGA resembles a generalist organization in that it represents tribes carrying on gaming activities but differs from such an organization in its focus on one issue while formally representing the tribes. It is also not really a "specialist" organization for the same reason. According to Cigler, these groups comprise "the professionals who staff government bureaucracies at all levels."[94] NIGA's members are gaming tribes and "other non-voting associate members representing organizations, tribes and businesses engaged in tribal gaming enterprises."[95]

> NIGA's mission is to protect and preserve the general welfare of tribes striving for self-sufficiency through gaming enterprises in Indian Country. To fulfill its mission, NIGA works with the Federal government to develop sound policies and practices and to provide technical assistance and advocacy on gaming-related issues. In addition, NIGA seeks to maintain and protect Indian sovereign governmental authority in Indian Country.[96]

Working closely with NIGA on gaming and sovereignty issues is the National Congress of American Indians, founded in 1944.[97]

NIGA and NCAI joined forces in a task force that was a "vehicle for imparting information in person to Tribal leaders and for getting unified consensus direction from the Indian Nations on legislative or policy issues."[98] The Attorneys' Work Group comprising tribal lawyers reviews legislation and court decisions. This group is responsible for preparing the analysis for distribution to tribal leaders and for leading the later discussion of the analysis with the tribal leaders as NIGA or the NIGA/NCAI Task Force moves to decision on the various issues.[99] According to Ponca Tribe attorney Gary Pitchlynn (Choctaw), these and other more "fluid" groups of elected tribal leaders and lawyers perform a wide range of activities, including advising and accompanying Task Force members who negotiate with congressional and state officials.[100] In August 1993, as pressure on Indian gaming increased, the association hired the Washington, D.C., public relations firm of Dorf and Staton at a cost of $20,000 per month.

CHAPTER THREE

New Mexico

GAMING AND HARDBALL POLITICS

Following *California v. Cabazon Band of Mission Indians* and passage of the Indian Gaming Regulatory Act, a state's public policy concerning legalized gambling establishes the parameters for Indian gaming. It is within these boundaries that tribes must pursue their own gaming policies. Their success is affected by at least two other variables: the extent of tribal cohesion within a particular state and the degree of cooperation or antagonism with which a state's political and governmental institutions greet tribal efforts.

Tribes may engage in one or all of three strategies to achieve their gaming goals: litigation, lobbying—both inside and outside—and electoral pressure. New Mexico's Indian tribes aggressively pursued all three strategies. They litigated their position in federal court; attempted to follow the IGRA and negotiate compacts with the governor on a sovereign-to-sovereign basis; appealed to the general public; and became involved in the electoral process. This multifront battle was fought by tribes individually and in concert through the New Mexico Indian Gaming Association.

NEW MEXICO AND INDIAN TRIBES

New Mexico lays claim to a unique cultural heritage. Within its borders are some of the oldest continuously occupied communities in North America. It is also the birthplace of the most modern of technologies, atomic power, as well as home to Spanish-speaking people who are descendants of the conquistadors and thus have more in common with Spain than Mexico.[1] The description of the state written in 1940 for the Work Projects Administration (WPA) Writers' Program's Guide to New Mexico is just as apt today: "New Mexico today represents a blend of the three cultures—Indian, Spanish, and American—each of which has had its time upon the stage and dominated the scene."[2]

Politically, New Mexico is also unusual among American states. Daniel Elazar classifies the dominant political culture of the state as traditional-individualistic, a designation it shares with Oklahoma, Texas, Florida, Kentucky, and West Virginia. According to Elazar, "The traditionalistic political culture is the most tolerant of out-and-out political corruption, yet it has also provided the framework for the integration of diverse groups into the mainstream of American life."[3] However, it also "contributes to the search for continuity in a society whose major characteristic is change, yet in the name of continuity, its representatives have denied blacks (or Indians, or Hispanic-Americans) their civil rights."[4]

Ronald J. Hrebenar describes New Mexico as belonging to the "Mountain West," distinguishing it from the "Pacific West" of the coastal states, Alaska, and Hawaii.[5] Among the factors that make this region unique is "its lack of water and its enormous size in comparison to its small population."[6] Economically, the region also has a "tradition of absentee ownership of factories and natural resources" and weak labor unions.[7]

New Mexico has also been described as a "borderland," "that zone in the Western Hemisphere where the sharply contrasting Latin and Anglo cultures overlap."[8] The WPA Guide noted,

In the migratory annals of the United States, the direction of movement has been from east to west; in new
Mexico (meaning in this instance all the southwestern
states originally embraced in the old Spanish province of
Nuevo Mejico) that direction did not hold. For three
centuries preceding the United States occupation, the
trend of settlement here was all from the south."[9]

While migration of Spanish and Anglo settlers is important
to the political and cultural heritage of the state, so is the
aboriginal and continued presence of American Indians. Frank
Waters's 1950 observation holds true nearly a half century later:
"The only Indians left as integral groups today exist within the
immemorial boundaries of their ancient homeland. The village
Pueblos and semi-nomadic Navahos, fringed by the mountain
Utes and desert Apaches—these are the last remnants of what
we call the Vanishing Americans."[10]

Today there are twenty-two nonvanished federally recognized tribes in New Mexico, all of whom can indeed trace a long
historic presence within the present state boundaries. The
Indians of New Mexico are categorized in two major groups:
the nomadic Athabascan tribes and the pueblo tribes. The
Navajo, Mescalero Apache, and Jicarilla Apache make up the
first group; nineteen tribes separated by three language families
make up the Pueblo people.(See table 1.) According to the
1990 U.S. Census, New Mexico had an Indian population of
134,355, the fourth-largest in the United States.

The post-Columbian political history of New Mexico tribes
has been shaped by the governance of three sovereigns: Spain,
Mexico, and the United States. The first Europeans to see what
would become the state of New Mexico were four Spanish ship-
wreck survivors who wandered from Texas to the Gulf of
California between 1527 and 1536. An expedition seeking the
"Seven Cities of Gold" reached the Zuñi Pueblo of Hawikuh in
1539. The next year a major expedition under Francisco
Vásquez de Coronado began its entrada into the unexplored
country along the Rio Grande, visiting the pueblos along the

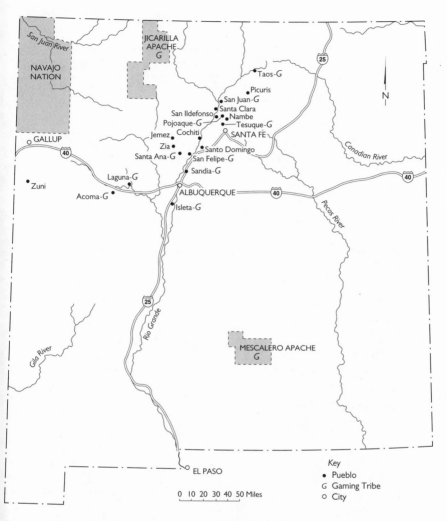

Map 1. New Mexico Tribes and Pueblos. Adapted from Warren A. Beck and Ynez D. Haase, *Historical Atlas of New Mexico* (Norman: University of Oklahoma Press, 1969).

TABLE 1
New Mexico Indian Tribes

TRIBE	1990 INDIAN POPULATION
Navajo Nation	143,405
New Mexico	50,563
Arizona	92,842
Alamo Navajo Reservation	1,228[a]
Canoncito Navajo Reservation	1,177[a]
Ramah Navajo Community	191[a]
Jicarilla Apache Tribe	2,375
Mescalero Apache Tribe	2,516
Acoma Pueblo	2,551
Cochiti Pueblo	666
Isleta Pueblo	2,699
Jemez Pueblo	1,738
Laguna Pueblo	3,634
Nambe Pueblo	329
Picuris Pueblo	147
Pojoaque Pueblo	2,134
Sandia Pueblo	358
San Felipe Pueblo	1,859
San Ildefonso Pueblo	347
San Juan Pueblo	1,276
Santa Ana Pueblo	481
Santa Clara Pueblo	1,246
Santo Domingo Pueblo	2,947
Taos Pueblo	1,212
Tesuque Pueblo	232
Zia Pueblo	637
Zuni Pueblo	7,073

[a] Navajo tribal land separated from the major portion of the Navajo Nation.

SOURCE: U.S. Bureau of the Census, *1990 Census of Population: General Population Characteristics: American Indian and Alaska Native Areas.*

river and eventually going as far as modern-day Oklahoma and Kansas.

In 1598 Don Juan de Oñate established the first permanent Spanish outpost in New Mexico, making the Pueblo of San Juan the capital of the province. The Spanish Crown ruled this country almost continuously until 1821, when Mexico declared its independence and took control. Mexico lost the territory north of the Rio Grande in the Mexican-American War and ceded control to the United States in the Treaty of Guadalupe Hidalgo in 1848.

In 1850 the U.S. Congress passed the New Mexico Organic Act that created the territory of New Mexico. The territory included most of what today are the states of New Mexico and Arizona as well as parts of Nevada and Colorado. The size of the territory was diminished in 1861 and 1864 when the territories of Colorado and Arizona were established. In 1910 Congress passed the Enabling Act, paving the way for Arizona and New Mexico to be admitted to the Union. The New Mexico legislature adopted a constitution in 1911, and New Mexico was declared the forty-seventh state by President William Howard Taft on January 6, 1912.

The Enabling Act made several references to the territory's Indian people and lands. In addition to requiring the new state to prevent the "introduction of liquors into Indian country," the act had the state "disclaim all right and title" to Indian lands "the right or title to which shall have been acquired through or from the United States or any prior sovereignty." These lands were also exempted from state taxes for as long as they maintained their status. Taxes on Indians living off reservations and Indian-owned land not part of a reservation were permitted unless prohibited by Congress.[11]

THE TRIBES

The singular history of New Mexico tribes has meant that federal Indian policy has often been singularly applied to them. This has been especially true of the Pueblo tribes, given the unique status of their culture and landholdings. In his classic and authoritative *Handbook of Federal Indian Law,* Felix Cohen described the people encountered by Spanish explorers.

> When the Spaniards entered the Rio Grande Valley in the sixteenth century they found certain Indian groups or communities living in villages and these Indians they designated "Indios Naturales" or "Indios de los Pueblos" to distinguish them from the "Indios Bárbaros," by which term the nomadic and warlike Indians of the region were designated. The Indians who were called Pueblo Indians were not of a single tribe and they had no common organization or language. Each village maintained its own government, its own irrigation system, and its own closely integrated community life.[12]

Sando writes that "the Pueblos are an ancient people whose history goes back into the farthest reaches of time."[13] The Acoma Pueblo in west central New Mexico and the Hopi village of Oraibi in Arizona are the two oldest, continuously occupied communities in North America. A sedentary farming people, the Pueblo Indians have an intricately developed ceremonial life that is jealously guarded by the people. Most Pueblo governments combine elements of democracy and theocracy.

Most of the modern Pueblos live on land they have occupied for nearly one thousand years. They are unique among American Indian tribes in that they hold fee title to most of their land "under grants of the Spanish, the Mexican or the United States Government, or by reason of purchases made by the Pueblo."[14] Other Pueblo landholdings are the result of acts of Congress or purchase by the federal government.

The character of Pueblo culture and landholdings has often led to the denial of their status as Indians under federal law. In 1876 the Supreme Court held that provisions of the 1834 Trade and Intercourse Act relating to trespass on Indian lands did not apply to the Pueblo people. In *United States v. Joseph,* a case involving Taos Pueblo, the Court held that Pueblo Indians "if, indeed, they can be called Indians," were different in fact and in law from other Indians. Finding that there were no other Indians like the Pueblo people within the United States when the 1834 law was passed, the Court differentiated the Pueblos from the "nomadic Apaches, Comanches, Navajoes [sic], and other tribes whose incapacity for self-government required both for themselves and for the citizens of the country this guardian care of the general government."[15] In effect, Pueblo people were not Indians.

Thirty-seven years later the Court reversed both its anthropological and legal understandings of the Pueblos in a case involving the application of federal law barring the introduction of alcohol into Indian Country. In *United States v. Sandoval* Justice Willis Van Devanter found that "the people of the pueblos, although sedentary rather than nomadic in their inclinations, and disposed to peace and industry, are nevertheless Indians in race, customs, and domestic government."[16] He continued:

> Always living in separate and isolated communities, adhering to primitive modes of life, largely influenced by superstition and fetishism, and chiefly governed according to the crude customs inherited from their ancestors, they are essentially a simple, uninformed and inferior people. . . . With one accord the reports of the superintendents charged with guarding their interests show that they are dependent upon the fostering care and protection of the Government, like reservation Indians in general; that although industrially superior, they are intellectually and morally inferior to many of them; and that they are easy victims to the evils and debasing influence of intoxicants.[17]

The Court thus found that the Pueblo people *were* indeed Indians, "and considering their Indian lineage, isolated and communal life, primitive customs and limited civilization, this assertion of guardianship over them cannot be said to be arbitrary but must be regarded as both authoritative and controlling."[18] Ironically, the holding in *Sandoval* has provided the Pueblos protection from state efforts to extend its jurisdiction over them.

Sando has written that "only the vigilance of the Pueblo people has made it possible for them to protect their land and preserve it from destruction."[19] An obvious historic example is the Pueblo Revolt of 1680 that temporarily drove Spanish settlers from New Mexico. It has also been evident in at least three twentieth-century instances when the Pueblos, well organized and with the support of non-Indians nationwide, influenced congressional action.

The first occurred in 1922 when New Mexico's U.S. senator Holm O. Bursom introduced legislation that would have led to the loss of the Pueblo land base by placing the burden of proof of ownership on the government against the claim of non-Indians. The Pueblos organized to fight the Bursom Bill and, joined by such groups as the Federation of Women's Clubs and the Indian Rights Association, saw it defeated. Instead, Congress passed the Pueblo Lands Act in 1924 in an attempt to bring order out of the confusion of landownership in New Mexico. The Pueblo Land Board was created to determine the boundaries of Pueblo holdings and the status of the land within those boundaries. The act was amended in 1933 to provide for settlement awards to Indians and non-Indians as a result of the findings of the board.[20]

Nearly fifty years later, at the urging of President Nixon, Congress passed legislation returning the sacred Blue Lake to Taos Pueblo. The lake had been taken from the pueblo during the administration of Theodore Roosevelt and made a part of the Carson National Forest under the control of the Department of Agriculture. Taos residents had fought continuously for the lake's return in the face of strong opposition from such New Mexico politicians as Democratic senator and former Secretary of Agriculture Clinton Anderson. However, the effort was given strong impetus in 1970 when President Nixon included a call for the return of the Lake in his Special Message to Congress on American Indians. After a highly organized and visible campaign by the Pueblos and their supporters, Congress passed legislation in 1971 returning Blue Lake to Taos Pueblo.[21]

In 1968 Congress considered legislation introduced by Sen. Sam Ervin (D-N.C.) applying the Bill of Rights to Indian tribes. The Pueblos became concerned because they feared a strict application of the First Amendment's wall of separation of church and state threatened their theocratic form of government. After strong testimony by Pueblo representatives before Congress, the legislation was amended to delete this provision from what ultimately passed as the Indian Civil Rights Act of 1968.[22]

The Indian status of the Navajo has never been in question. Their seminomadic culture and periodic warlike ways more clearly met the stereotypical view of "wild Indians." They, along with the Jicarilla and Mescalero Apaches, had experiences with the U.S. government similar to many tribes outside New Mexico. All three tribes were at one time or another removed from their homelands, and all three, unlike the Pueblos, signed treaties with the United States.

After signing a treaty in 1868 the Navajos returned to their native lands from their exile at Bosque Rodondo (along with the Mescalero). The Navajo Nation has become the largest Indian tribe in both population and land base. Most of the Navajo Nation's population lives in Arizona, and its capital is in Window Rock. Nevertheless, the Navajo presence is strongly felt in New Mexico, politically and economically. Navajos have a major impact on the economies of reservation border towns such as Gallup and Farmington. As noted below, Navajo voters can dramatically affect New Mexico state and local elections, and five of the current six Indian members of the New Mexico legislature are Navajo.

The two immediate past presidents of the Navajo Nation have been identified with state and national political parties. Peter McDonald, elected tribal chairman four times (nonconsecutively) before being forced out of office, was a vocal Republican. His successor and bitter political rival, Peterson Zah, has close ties to the Democratic party.[23]

The Navajo Nation has no written constitution; its government is divided into three branches, with a popularly elected tribal council and president. The Tribal Council was first organized in 1923 by the BIA as a means of facilitating mineral leases to non-Indians seeking to extract the Nation's rich natural resource reserve.

Unlike the Navajo Nation, the Jicarilla and Mescalero Apache tribes are organized under the Indian Reorganization Act. The Jicarilla Reservation in northwestern New Mexico was established in 1887 by executive order. It today consists of 742,315 acres. The 460,000-acre Mescalero Reservation was established by executive orders in 1873 and 1883. The current longtime Mescalero tribal chairman, Wendell Chino, is one of the most prominent Indian leaders in the country.

CONFLICTS OF INTEREST

In the years since statehood, the interests of Indians and the state government have often collided. Three major areas of Indian/state conflict in New Mexico are noteworthy: water, taxation, and voting rights. Each of these issues involves the ongoing struggle of tribes, states, and the federal government to define the limits and extent of the political status of Indian tribes and individuals. While the immediate parameters of each issue are defined by the New Mexico context in which they are fought, they are similar in kind and significance to others played out wherever there are competing tribal/state interests.

Water

Sando has observed that "while the loss of water has been a threat since the advent of the Europeans, it has become the gravest of dangers now that New Mexico has experienced a vast expansion of its population."[24] The 1908 Supreme Court decision in *Winters v. United States* protected tribal reserved water rights,[25] but the demand for water in the high desert

of New Mexico has led the state and the Army Corps of
Engineers to develop creative mechanisms for sharing this
valuable resource.

One such device was the creation in 1925 of the Middle Rio
Grande Conservancy District. A political subdivision of state
government, the district "was designed to plan, construct and
operate a coordinated modern irrigation and flood control
project."[26] The effects of the district, whose establishment a
number of pueblos were party to, have included a redefinition
of "reclaimed lands" for purposes of cultivation, diversion of
water for non-tribal-related uses, and a great deal of ongoing
litigation.

In 1966 New Mexico filed suit in federal court to determine
the rights to water use of the Nambe-Pojoaque River System, a
tributary of the Rio Grande. The Tenth Circuit Court of
Appeals reversed the district court's decision and denied the
applicability of state law to reservation water in New Mexico.
The appeals court held that "the United States has not relin-
quished jurisdiction and control over Pueblos and has not
placed their water rights under New Mexico law."[27]

Taxation

In the last two decades the federal policy of self-determination has encouraged tribal governments to assume more
governing responsibility, including the levying of tribal taxes.
These taxes have often met resistance both from those subject
to them and from state governments. The conflict is exacerbated when state taxes and tribal taxes fall on the same party.
These kinds of economic-based conflicts between sovereigns
have occurred in New Mexico.

In the mid-1970s the Jicarilla Apache Tribal Council voted
to impose a severance tax on oil and gas production on the
reservation. The tax amounted to, at the wellhead, five cents
per million BTUs of gas produced and twenty-nine cents per
barrel of crude oil or condensate. Over the years mineral leases
had been granted on 69 percent of tribal land. Leaseholders

who produced oil and gas were already subject to New Mexico's oil and gas severance tax as well as a tax on oil and gas production equipment.

Several leaseholders sought to have the tribal severance tax overturned in federal court. The state of New Mexico sided with the leaseholders in an amicus curiae brief filed with the Supreme Court. The Court, however, upheld the right of the tribe to impose these taxes.[28]

In the late 1980s a non-Indian oil and gas producer on the Jicarilla Reservation, Cotton Petroleum Corporation, sought a refund of the oil and gas severance taxes it had paid to the state. The Jicarilla Apache Tribe supported Cotton Petroleum in its efforts, believing that double taxation by state and tribal governments would tend to dissuade companies from doing business on tribal lands. The Navajo Nation and the housing authorities of the Mescalero Apache Tribe and Laguna Pueblo also filed amicus briefs in support of the company's position. However, the Supreme Court held in a 1988 decision that companies doing business on tribal land and subject to tribal taxes are not exempt from state taxes.[29]

A related issue is the attempt by the state to require hunting and fishing licenses of non-Indian sportspersons on reservation land. The Mescalero Apache Tribe has developed a thriving tourist industry that includes hunting and fishing. The tribe has adopted ordinances requiring anyone hunting or fishing on the reservation to purchase a license from the tribe. It has also worked closely with the federal government to develop reservation wildlife resources.

The state, however, attempted to force non-Indian hunters and sportfishermen on the reservation to purchase state game licenses. In 1977 the tribe sought to prevent the state from arresting non-Indians who were hunting and fishing on the reservation with a license from the tribe but not from the state. In a 1983 decision the Supreme Court held that, at least as far as the Mescalero Apache Tribe was concerned, the federal government had preempted this area of law and the state could not enforce its licensing requirements on the reservation.[30]

VOTING RIGHTS

Indians in New Mexico were not permitted to vote in state elections until 1948. Article 7, section 1, of the state's 1912 constitution denied the right to vote to "Indians not taxed." In 1948 an Isleta Pueblo man named Miguel Trujillo attempted to register to vote and was not permitted to do so because he did not pay state property taxes.[31] A three-judge federal district court panel held in *Trujillo v. Garley* that New Mexico's constitutional voting prohibition violated the Fourteenth Amendment of the U.S. Constitution.[32] On the same day that *Trujillo* was decided, a federal district court judge ordered in *Bowman v. Lopez* that the McKinley county clerk register to vote all Navajos in the county and "not exclude them by reason of being residents on the Navajo Reservation."[33] Neither of these decisions was appealed. In 1953 the legislature eliminated the words "Indians not taxed" from New Mexico law as it applied to voting requirements, but they remained in the state constitution.

New Mexico courts did not rule on the right of Indians to vote in state elections until 1962, when a defeated candidate for lieutenant governor contested the election in court based on 2,202 votes cast on the Navajo Reservation in San Juan and McKinley counties.[34] Eliminating the 2,202 ballots would turn a 279-vote statewide loss into a 63-vote victory. Reviewing the 1868 treaty with the Navajo as well as state and federal statutes and case law, the court rejected the unhappy candidate's arguments and concluded,

> It is obvious that the Navajo Indian Reservation is not a completely separate entity existing outside of the political and governmental jurisdiction of the State of New Mexico. . . . We are convinced that, for voting purposes, there is nothing in our constitution or in the statutes which prohibits an Indian from voting in a proper election, provided he fulfills the statutory requirements required of any other voter.[35]

In a 1967 special election the voters of New Mexico, after several failed attempts, finally removed the phrase "Indians not taxed" from the state constitution. The same measure also removed the word "male" before the word "citizen," thus making the New Mexico constitution consistent with the Nineteenth Amendment to the U.S. Constitution. The vote was overwhelmingly in favor of the proposed changes, 42,101 to 9,757.

There was one final challenge to the right of Indians to vote in New Mexico, however. In 1975 some residents of the Central Consolidated Independent School District No. 22 in northern New Mexico sought to set aside a school board election and to have the court declare that votes were illegally cast in the defeat of a school bond issue. The school district encompasses both Navajo and non-Navajo land, and two-thirds of the district's pupils were Indians who lived on the reservation. As the state supreme court noted, the residents who brought suit argued "that the Indian citizens who reside on this nontaxable land should not have been allowed to vote in the District bond election since they do not share the burden of repayment of the indebtedness created by the issuance of the bonds. In effect, they contend that there should be no representation without taxation."[36] Citing the Equal Protection Clause of the Fourteenth Amendment and U.S. Supreme Court decisions, the court affirmed the trial court and rejected Prince et al.'s claim.

Although the court in *Montoya v. Bolack* had in effect upheld the right of an Indian living on a reservation to vote in New Mexico, it indicated at the same time some discomfort with the situation. The court's views on voting rights and citizenship responsibilities for Indians are worth quoting at length, for it is an argument often heard in debates over whether Indians should be allowed to vote in state elections. It is an argument that also resonates in other tribal/state conflicts.

> The anomalous situation here existing places the Navajo in a more favored position than other legal residents of the state. They have the right to participate in the choice of officials, but, under many circumstances, cannot be

governed by or be subject to the control of the officials so elected. Whether this should be allowed to continue is a matter to be determined by the legislature, after it has considered all of the facts including the wishes of the Indians involved. Just as the constitution does not sanction first or second class citizens, neither does it provide that any one group, large or small, should have greater rights or responsibilities than others.[37]

This concern was echoed twenty-six years later in the amicus curiae brief filed by the state of New Mexico in *Cotton Petroleum v. New Mexico*. Referring to a "double standard," the state attorney general argued that "the nub of the issue is a single question: Is the reservation part of the state or is it not?"

When it comes to taxing on the reservation, the answer by Cotton and several amici is no, the reservation is not part of the state. But when it comes to spending for the reservation, to providing schools, roads and health care, as well as access to universities, parks, courts and all other government services tribal members use, the answer is most emphatically yes, the reservation is part of the state and tribal members are citizens entitled under the 14th Amendment to all state services and benefits.

The more reservations are considered to be separate jurisdictions outside state taxing power, the more the underlying rationale for Indians' state citizenship and consequent entitlement to state services and financial benefits weakens. The political consequences will be that financially strapped legislatures, already prohibited from taxing Indian property and income, will hardly be encouraged to increase state funding for services and benefits on the reservation.[38]

The "anomalous status" and "double standard" of Indians in the political arena means that Indians as citizens and as tribal entities are both threatened and presented with opportunities not available to other American citizens. Although this has been true throughout the history of Indian-government relations, it is nowhere truer today than in the area of Indian gaming. The perspective of the attorney general in the *Cotton Petroleum* brief is essentially the states' rights position that is at the heart of disputes over Indian gaming.

THE BATTLE FOR GAMING

As the Supreme Court's 1986 *Cabazon* decision held, a state's public policy vis-à-vis gaming in general provides the broad parameters for the kind of gaming an Indian tribe can operate. The IGRA establishes the criteria for Class II and Class III gaming in which tribes are permitted to engage and links them to those games legally permitted in the states where a tribe is located.[39] Table 2 lists those games of chance that are legal in New Mexico.

The Permissive Lottery Law allows charities to conduct gambling that is "an enterprise wherein, for consideration, the participants are given an opportunity to win a prize the award of which is determined by chance. . . . Consideration means anything of pecuniary value."[40] This statute provides charities in New Mexico with the legal rationale for conducting "Las Vegas

TABLE 2
Legal Gaming in New Mexico

CLASS II
bingo, raffle (60-2B-1, NMSA)

CLASS III
Pari-mutuel live horse races (60-1-10, NMSA)
Pari-mutuel simulcast horse races (60-1-25, NMSA)
Pari-mutuel bicycle racing (60-2D-1, NMSA)
Permissive Lottery Law for charities (30-19-6, NMSA)

Nights" offering patrons blackjack, keno, poker, craps, roulette, and slot machines. In March 1995 Gov. Gary Johnson estimated that charitable organizations in New Mexico were operating more than fifteen hundred video slot machines, which are technically illegal under New Mexico law, although authorities have generally permitted their continued operation. A New Mexico appeals court ruling that charities may legally use electronic pull tabs withstood a challenge in the state supreme court when in October 1994 it refused to review the appeals court decision. Reviewing the scope of legal gaming in the state, the New Mexico Indian Gaming Association contended that "with such expansive gaming in New Mexico the Governor of the State cannot take the moral high ground opposing gaming."[41]

In the early 1970s and then in again in the early 1980s, at least two pueblos considered opening dog racing tracks. The efforts by Santa Ana Pueblo were strongly opposed by New Mexico's attorney general, Paul Bardacke, and Secretary of the Interior Donald Hodel in 1985. Santa Ana contended that because pari-mutuel betting on horse races was legal under state law, it should also be legal for dog racing. Bardacke held that because pari-mutuel betting on dog races was *not legal,* it would be *illegal* for the tribes to establish such an enterprise. Hodel endorsed this argument, basing his opinion on the federal Assimilative Crimes Act, which makes it a federal crime to commit an act in Indian Country otherwise illegal under state law. This view, that the only gaming allowed in Indian Country is that which is legal under state law, was a central point of debate before passage of the Indian Gaming Regulatory Act and remained a point of controversy in subsequent years.

High-stakes Indian bingo began in New Mexico in 1983 when Acoma Pueblo opened its bingo hall four miles south of Interstate 40, some fifty-five miles west of Albuquerque.[42] Sandia Pueblo, on the north edge of Albuquerque, opened its thirty-thousand-square-foot bingo hall just off Interstate 25 a few months later, in January 1984.[43] Within a year Santa Ana and Tesuque pueblos had also opened bingo facilities.

The Acoma and Sandia bingo operations soon demonstrated the economic benefits of such enterprises. Acoma's
unemployment rate of 78 percent was reduced by 15 percent,
with 35 people finding work with the gaming operation, 8 with
food concessions, and 2 with child care services. By August 31,
1986, gross sales had reached a total of more than $700,000.
The games were conducted in a building constructed with
funds from the Economic Development Administration.[44]

Sandia Pueblo's bingo produced similar results. Unemployment was reduced from 11.7 percent in February 1983 to 4
percent in February 1985. The 35 tribal members employed at
the bingo made up 29 percent of the pueblo's total labor force.
In addition to the Sandia tribal members employed at bingo, 19
non-Sandia Indians and 73 non-Indians also worked for the
facility in June 1986. Between its opening in January 1984 and
July 31, 1986, Sandia bingo revenues amounted to more than
$1.6 million.[45]

In November 1988, following passage of the IGRA, Sandia
Pueblo notified the state of its desire to enter into negotiations for Class III gaming compacts.[46] Because the IGRA is
silent as to whom notification should be delivered, Sandia officials sent their request to the New Mexico Office of Indian
Affairs, designated by state law as the coordinating agency for
tribal affairs.[47] The director, Regis Pecos, of Cochiti Pueblo,
accepted notice on behalf of the state, an act Frank Chaves
describes as "courageous."[48]

Four months later, in March 1989, Gov. Garrey Carruthers
informed Pecos that only the governor's office had authority
to negotiate gaming compacts with the tribes and requested
that all records be sent to his office.[49] Carruthers then named
Ray Shollenbarger, director of the New Mexico Regulation and
Licensing Department, as his gaming negotiator.

There was a lack of clarity about the operation of the IGRA
in the first two years after it became law, and no Class III
compacts were approved for any tribe until 1991. No serious
negotiations took place in the last two years of Carruthers's
administration. In November 1990 the former Democratic

governor, Bruce King, was elected to another term. Negotiations resumed in January 1991 after King took office.

By May 1991 Sandia and Tesuque Pueblos and the Mescalero Apaches had expanded their gaming operations to include video gambling devices, a move that raised serious questions about the scope of gaming defined as Class II and Class III. The tribes contended that the Permissive Lottery Law opened up all types of Class III gaming to negotiation. It was the position of both U.S. Attorney William Lutz and Governor King that such gambling devices were illegal under both federal and state law. However, negotiations between the state and Sandia Pueblo and the Mescalero Apache Tribe began in summer 1991. In September Mescalero tribal president Wendell Chino, commenting on the progress of negotiations, said, "We're getting pretty close."[50]

King appointed an interagency team to review the proposed compacts and existing tribal gaming operations. Representatives of the state attorney general, the Public Safety Department, the Crime Commission, the Alcohol Beverage Control Division, Taxation and Revenue Department, the Office of Indian Affairs, and the governor's office made up the team.[51] They visited the Sandia and Isleta gaming operations to review the tribes' regulatory schemes and security arrangements. According to Pecos, "For the most part all of us were overwhelmed with [their] complexity."[52] The findings of the review team and a December 9, 1991, letter from the state's attorney general, Tom Udall, to King laid the foundation for Class III compacts. Udall pointed to the Mutual Aid Act and the Joint Powers Agreement[53] as authorization for tribal-state gaming compacts.[54]

Negotiations between Sandia Pueblo and the Mescaleros and King's representative, regulation and licensing superintendent Jerry Manzagol, had resulted in compacts by December. In October Sandia had in fact sent King a signed compact.[55] In what was the beginning a tortuous path through the political minefield of Indian gaming, King delayed signing the compacts, saying that he would not do so until the public had an opportunity to see what they contained. He charged, "[The compacts had] gotten into other types of equipment I don't agree with. . . . I don't want to sign something they [New Mexicans] don't want."[56]

Having thus far followed the terms of the IGRA and negotiated with the state to no avail, Sandia Pueblo and the Mescalero Apache Tribe continued to follow the law by taking Governor King and the state of New Mexico to federal court. The Mescaleros filed suit in New Mexico federal district court in January 1992 charging that King and the state had failed to negotiate in good faith as required by the IGRA. Sandia Pueblo filed a similar suit six months later.[57] As the lawsuits were filed and the legislature debated expanding gaming, King announced his opposition to any additional nonreservation video gaming. He did, however, indicate a willingness to consider a statewide lottery.

While the lawsuits were pending in federal court, state and federal authorities in New Mexico presented unified opposition to "illegal" video gaming machines on and off tribal land. U.S. Attorney Svet said, "Without an agreement with the state, tribes don't have the right to use them and they're illegal. . . . I'm going to talk to those tribal leaders about the fact that they're illegal, and take the appropriate legal action."[58] However, he said that he would take no immediate action against the tribes pending an investigation.

The state of New Mexico was more forceful in confronting those non-Indian organizations and establishments operating video gaming machines. In a letter to fifteen hundred liquor licensees, Mary Ann Hughes, director of the Alcohol and Gaming Division, warned that they must dispose of any video gambling machines in their possession. Recipients included nonprofit fraternal organizations as well as for-profit establishments.[59] In August state police executed raids in Albuquerque and Santa Fe, confiscating seventy-four video machines in the process, including those belonging to the Santa Fe Fraternal Order of Police.

In actions that had ramifications for Indian gaming in New Mexico and nationally, Federal District Court Judge John

Conway dismissed the lawsuits brought by Sandia Pueblo and the Mescaleros in late 1992. In both cases the court found that in allowing tribes to bring suit against the states for failing to negotiate in good faith, Congress had acted without authority in abrogating state Eleventh Amendment sovereign immunity. The court's holding acted to fundamentally undermine the method established by the IGRA for settling tribal-state Class III controversies. The tribes appealed the decision to the Tenth Circuit Court of Appeals, and their cases were latter joined with similar lawsuits brought by the Kickapoo Tribe of Kansas and the Ponca Tribe of Oklahoma.

In 1993 the New Mexico Indian Gaming Association (NMIGA) was created by the state's gaming tribes. The mission of NMIGA, as adopted by the association in November 1993, is

> to protect and preserve the general welfare of tribes striving for self-sufficiency through gaming enterprises in Indian Country. To fulfill its mission, NMIGA works to develop sound policies and practices, provide technical assistance and advice on gaming-related issues. In addition, NMIGA seeks to maintain and protect Indian sovereign governmental authority in Indian Country.[60]

The tribes had been cooperating on gaming issues without a formal organization since the mid-1980s, relying on what Frank Chaves has referred to as an "ad-hoc committee on Indian gaming."[61] Their efforts included providing congressional testimony during consideration of the IGRA and hiring an attorney to file an amicus curiae brief in the *Cabazon* case.

By 1993 ten New Mexico tribes had gaming operations of one kind or another: the Jicarilla Apache and Mescalero Apache tribes and the Pueblos of Acoma, Sandia, Pojoaque, San Juan, Taos, Isleta, Santa Ana, and Tesuque. The gaming facilities employed a total of 597 individuals and paid more than $4.8 million in wages and salaries. A study prepared for NMIGA by the Center for Applied Research of Denver estimated the total income attributed directly and indirectly to

Indian gaming at more than $65.5 million, with the state collecting $1.3 million annually in tax revenue.[62]

Governor King's apparent refusal to negotiate in good faith soured his relations with the tribes. They were further strained by his vetoes in 1993 of economic development legislation supported by New Mexico tribes. These included a bill to create an intergovernmental tax credit on oil and gas production from Indian lands (S.B. 126); a bill to create a task force to study dual taxation of businesses located on Indian land (H.B. 982); a bill permitting wholesale liquor dealers to sell alcohol to tribes with liquor ordinances conforming to state law and approved by the secretary of the interior (H.B. 685); and line items providing money to Isleta Pueblo to study the creation of an intergovernmental network to deal with Rio Grande–related environmental issues and to the Office of Indian Affairs for a full-time arts and crafts investigator.

King signed H.B. 181, restricting the use of reimbursed funds for Indian tribes with cross-deputized police officers who cite non-Indians to appear in tribal court, which the tribes opposed. He vetoed similar legislation, H.B. 708, supported by the tribes that did not contain this restriction. In a position paper summarizing these actions, NMIGA noted, "There is general sentiment within Indian country that Governor King, Western Governors' lead Governor for Tribal State Relations, is not responsive to Indian policy issues and needs."[63] King also vetoed H.B. 41, legislation that took authority to negotiate tribal-state gaming compacts away from the governor and placed it in the Office of Indian Affairs. As Frank Chaves noted in a letter to the author, "By this legislation, it is clear the NM Legislature believed the Governor of the State had authority to negotiate compacts."[64]

TRIBAL–DEMOCRATIC PARTY RELATIONS

Governor King's legislative record and refusal to sign gaming compacts jeopardized the relationship that had been established between New Mexico's tribes and the state Democratic party. This was occurring at a time when Indian voters were playing a larger role in the state's electoral politics. According to Fred Harris and LaDonna Harris, "Voter registration drives have greatly increased the numbers of New Mexico Indians who vote in local, state, and national elections."[65] The increase in the number of Indians who are registered to vote has in turn benefited the Democratic party, for New Mexico's Indians tend to vote overwhelmingly for Democratic candidates. As Paul L. Hain and F. Chris Garcia have noted, along with Hispanics, New Mexico's "Indian citizens are exceptionally concentrated within the Democratic Party."[66] New Mexico Democratic party chairman Ray Powell estimates that half of President Bill Clinton's margin of victory in New Mexico in 1994 can be attributed to Indian votes.[67] Twenty years earlier, according to a study by Leonard Ritt, the Indian vote was "crucial" to the election of Democratic gubernatorial candidate Jerry Apodaca.[68]

Powell had been working to build the relationship between the party and tribes since at least the 1992 presidential election. Albuquerque attorney Kevin Gover had worked with the party's executive director to draw up a plan to gain Indian support. According to Powell, this plan set an example for other states with a significant Indian vote.[69] Gover, a Pawnee and an Oklahoma native, became heavily involved in organizing national Indian support for Bill Clinton's presidential campaign against George Bush.[70]

Indian voters were the New Mexico Democratic party's "most loyal constituency."[71] In turn, the party had worked for the election of Indian officeholders and "encouraged" the six Democratic Indian members of the state legislature, five of whom are Navajo and one of whom is from Jemez Pueblo. (See table 3 for the Indian members of the legislature in 1995.)

The 1992 party platform contained a strong plank on tribal sovereignty:

> [We are committed] to establishing a strong and respectful government-to-government relationship between the State of New Mexico and the twenty-three Native American tribal governments within the state, and to honor the

TABLE 3
Indian Members of the 42d New Mexico Legislature, 1st Session

SENATE		
John Pinto	Democrat	Gallup
Leonard Tsosie	Democrat	Crownpoint
HOUSE		
Wallace Charley	Democrat	Shiprock
Lynda M. Lovejoy	Democrat	Crownpoint
James Roger Madalena	Democrat	Jemez Pueblo
Leo Watchman II	Democrat	Navajo

treaties between the United States and Indian tribes throughout the United States. The state and federal governments should work in partnership with tribal governments to improve Native American health, education, housing, and general welfare. The federal government should develop and implement policies to stimulate sustainable economic development and encourage tribes to develop revenue-raising programs. We believe that lasting progress on these and other issues will occur by following the guidance of Native American tribal governments, which are in the best position to determine which policies and programs will improve the quality of life in tribal communities.

As the 1994 gubernatorial primary approached, Indian gaming became one issue that distinguished King from his two Democratic opponents, Lt. Gov. Casey Luna and former federal Bureau of Land Management director Jim Baca. While King stood by his opposition to expanded gaming, Luna and Baca both promised to sign compacts with the tribes if they were elected. Republican candidates Gary Johnson, David Cargo, and John Dendahl all said they too would sign gaming compacts if successful in their bids to be elected governor.

Lieutenant Governor Luna's support for Indian gaming resulted in his endorsement by some tribal leaders as well as considerable financial help from gaming tribes. Mescalero Apache tribal president Chino and Pojoaque Pueblo governor Jacob Viarrial publicly supported Luna. Direct tribal financial contributions to Luna's campaign totaled $46,000, and tribal gaming enterprises contributed $15,290 (see table 4).

After gaining 60 percent of the delegates at the state Democratic party convention, King faced a tough primary challenge from Luna and Baca. King won the June primary election with 39 percent of the vote; Luna received 36 percent and Baca 25 percent. Gary Johnson, owner of a construction company, won the Republican primary with 35 percent of the vote to former state representative Dick Cheney's 33 percent.

After the primary Governor King resumed discussions concerning gaming compacts. In July he and tribal representatives met with a mediator sent by Secretary of the Interior

TABLE 4

Tribal Contributions to Casey Luna for Governor

Pojoaque Gaming, Inc.	$ 5,000
Pojoaque Gaming, Inc.	5,000
Pojoaque Gaming, Inc.	290
Pueblo of Pojoaque	10,000
Pueblo of Pojoaque	15,000
Pueblo of Sandia	5,000
Sandia Indian Bingo	4,000
Pueblo of Santa Ana	10,000
Pueblo of Acoma	5,000
Jicarilla Apache Tribe	1,000
Isleta Gaming Palace	1,000
Total	$ 61,290

Source: New Mexico Secretary of State, File #2: "Casey Luna 1994 Candidate Reporting."

Bruce Babbitt at the request of Congressman Bill Richardson. As negotiations were reopening, at least two pueblos took steps to enlarge their gaming operations. Santa Ana Pueblo signed an agreement with the Lady Luck Gaming Corporation of Nevada to build and develop a $25 million casino and hotel.[72] That same month Tesuque Pueblo's Camel Rock Gaming Center managers began making plans to offer card games and San Juan Pueblo's Ohkay Casino began offering poker tables to customers.[73] These games, if banked by the house, were Class III and not permitted under New Mexico law. However, U.S. Attorney John Kelly acknowledged that nonbanked card games would be Class II.

Kelly himself played a role in reducing at least some of the tension in the increasingly volatile gaming issue. On July 1 Kelly signed a "standstill" agreement with Acoma, Isleta, Pojoaque, Sandia, San Juan, Santa Ana, and Tesuque pueblos and the Mescalero Apaches regarding the number of permissible video gaming machines. Each Indian gaming tribe would be limited to 275 video machines, which required Sandia and Tesuque to remove some of their machines. The tribes also agreed to provide the U.S. Attorney's Office and the FBI with information about their gaming operations. Kelly said, "What we're trying to do here is just maintain the status quo and do it responsibly."[74]

In early August, as the fall gubernatorial race began to take shape, Governor King appeared to soften his opposition to expanded Indian gaming. At a press conference he acknowledged the "possibility" that he would sign the compacts before the election. "I kind of like to get elected," King said, "so I wouldn't say it didn't have anything to do with it [his softened stance]."[75]

King's public position on the issue was further muddied by a late August meeting in Santa Fe with Navajo president Peterson Zah to discuss gaming. When Zah said that Navajos were interested in casino-style gambling, King said, "That's further than I'd like to go."[76] King also announced that he had received a draft compact from the gaming pueblos and the

Mescalero Apacje Tribe. He said, "[I]t "carries Indian gaming way beyond what I would expect to go."[77]

In mid-September King finally made his position on the compacts clear: he would not sign them before the November election. He said what the tribes wanted was impossible under New Mexico law. "I took an oath to uphold the constitution and laws of the state of New Mexico," King said, "and I have no authority as an executive officer to allow any group of citizens to do anything illegal."[78]

Although Indian leaders were not surprised, neither were they forgiving. Pojoaque Pueblo governor Jacob Viarrial said, "I think Gov. King has proven he's very anti-Indian. . . . Gov. King is hurting us and we're very, very unhappy and very hurt. It would be a sad day for Indian people if King were to get elected." Tesuque Governor Paul Swazo also spoke of the political repercussions: "This is the death blow for his life."[79]

It had appeared from the primary results that Governor King might have a rough race ahead of him, particularly in a year that was shaping up nationwide as being anti-incumbent at the polls. King's reelection was further threatened by continuing divisions within the Democratic party unrelated to Indian gaming and by the presence of a well-known third party candidate, Roberto Mondragon.

Throughout the fall campaign Lieutenant Governor Luna resisted pressure to endorse his former running mate. These included a personal plea by President Clinton when he came to New Mexico in October to campaign for King and Jeff Bingaman, incumbent Democratic U.S. senator. In a private meeting with Clinton arranged by Bill Richardson, Luna reiterated his continuing opposition to King's reelection.[80] Later in October Luna bought Mondragon $250 worth of airtime on a Las Vegas, New Mexico, radio station.

Mondragon, a former Democratic lieutenant governor, was running for governor as the candidate of New Mexico's Green party. The popular Mondragon posed a particular threat to King in the heavily Hispanic northern counties, such as Rio Arriba. But Mondragon's campaign was hampered by lack of funds, and only a frantic fund-raising effort by the Green party late in the campaign prevented him from withdrawing from the race.

Mondragon's continued presence in the race was looked on favorably by the tribes, which, in fact, strategically but quietly supported his campaign.[81] Among the contributors to Mondragon's last-minute plea for financial support were the Santa Ana Discount Smoke Shop ($10,000) and Sandia Indian Bingo ($1,000).[82]

An added twist to both the governor's race and the Indian gaming controversy was presented by two gaming referenda: one before the voters of New Mexico, the other to be decided by residents of the Navajo Nation. In 1993, after several years of debating the expansion of legalized gambling in the state, the New Mexico legislature passed House Joint Resolution 11, a proposed constitutional amendment that the voters would have to approve. The result was the appearance on the November 1994 ballot of Constitutional Amendment 8 (Issue 8) asking the voters to decide whether the New Mexico constitution should be amended to permit a state lottery and video gambling machines. If the referendum passed, the legislature would have to enact regulations governing the lottery and the newly legal games.

The gubernatorial candidates differed in their stance on Issue 8. Reflecting his opposition to expanded gaming, Governor King opposed it, although he said that he would ask the legislature to create a lottery. Gary Johnson took a position similar to King's. Declaring that he was in favor of a state lottery but opposed to video gaming, Johnson came out against Issue 8. Mondragon's views on the referendum were not as clear. Although he joined King and Johnson in favor of a lottery, he indicated that he favored continued video games for fraternal and nonprofit organizations.[83] NMIGA took no position on Issue 8.

Navajo voters faced a similar ballot issue when Peterson Zah vetoed a Navajo Council resolution legalizing gambling in the Navajo Nation in August. In his veto message Zah said, "The

Navajo people must be given the opportunity to vote on the question of whether they favor the establishment of gaming operations on Navajo land."[84] Two Navajo Nation chapters, LeChee and Cameron, had earlier voted resolutions opposing gaming.

Soon after King's final declaration against expansion of Indian gaming, Republican candidate Johnson and Green party candidate Mondragon affirmed their commitment to negotiating compacts. Johnson said that the real gambling issue "is sovereignty." He also said that he would like to see the state "have a portion" of tribal gaming revenues. Mondragon agreed with the latter point as well.[85]

In early September the Tenth Circuit Court of Appeals handed down a decision in the Sandia and Mescalero suits against the state. The court combined the two New Mexico suits with one by the Ponca Tribe against Gov. David Walters and the state of Oklahoma and another by the Kickapoo Tribe against the state of Kansas.[86] Overturning the district court's decision, the appeals court held that the Tenth and Eleventh amendments did not bar the tribes from bringing suit against the state under the IGRA. The court found that Congress may abrogate a state's Eleventh Amendment sovereign immunity under the Indian Commerce Clause of the Constitution (Article I, Section 8). According to the court, this was the intent of Congress in passing the IGRA.

The court also found that the IGRA's "good faith" negotiation requirement did not violate the Tenth Amendment because it did not require the states to actually do anything else. A finding by a federal district court that a state had not negotiated in good faith merely shifted the action to the secretary of the interior.

Although the court's Tenth and Eleventh Amendment decisions were a victory for the tribes, it also ruled that suits against Governor King and Oklahoma governor David Walters were barred by the Supreme Court's ruling in *Ex parte Young*. This case established the conditions under which a state official may be sued for enjoining federal law violations. By having the major issues involving the IGRA and tribal-state negotiations on Class III gaming decided in their favor, New Mexico tribes believed they were in a much stronger position to push for their desired gaming ends. Soon after the Tenth Circuit's decision, the Jicarilla Apache Tribe and San Juan, Pojoaque, Isleta, Acoma, and Tesuque pueblos filed suits in federal district court alleging the state had not negotiated in good faith.

In late September Pojoaque Pueblo became the first tribe formally to endorse Johnson over King. Viarrial announced that the tribe would donate at least $20,000 to Johnson's campaign.[87] Isleta Pueblo soon followed with its own endorsement of Johnson. Santa Ana, Acoma, and Tesuque pueblos and the Mescalero Apache Tribe would eventually also endorse Johnson.

By the end of the campaign, seven tribes had formally endorsed or contributed to Johnson's campaign, as had the Ten Southern Pueblos Governors Council.[88] Tribes and their gaming operations contributed a total of $189,000 to Johnson's campaign, more than 10 percent of Johnson's general election total of $1.17 million.[89] This included a contribution of $20,000 made the day before the election by the Mescalero Apache Tribe. King and Mondragon had both announced their opposition to the proposed facility.[90] Table 5 shows contributions to Johnson by tribes and tribal enterprises.[91]

TABLE 5
Tribal Contributions to Gary Johnson's Campaign

Isleta Bingo	$50,000
Sandia Pueblo	50,000
Santa Ana Pueblo	25,000
Santa Ana Golf	20,000
Southern Sandoval Investment, Ltd. (owned by Santa Ana Pueblo)	20,000
Mescalero Apache Tribe	20,000
Acoma Pueblo	4,000

SOURCE: *Albuquerque Journal,* December 25, 1994.

During the campaign King sought to make an issue of the financial support Johnson was receiving from the tribes and called on him to return the contributions. King said that the tribes' campaign contributions appeared to him "like a hell of an obligation."[92] King also asked Johnson to be specific about the kinds of gaming he would ãgree to. In addition, Johnson was criticized for his tribal contributions from opponents of Issue 8.

Both King and Johnson campaigned in Indian Country. King toured the Navajo Nation, accompanied by Democratic state senator John Pinto, one of two Navajos in the New Mexico Senate. Late in the campaign Johnson attended a rally at Santa Ana Pueblo and visited Window Rock, Arizona, capital of the Navajo Nation. While at Window Rock, Johnson met with Zah and spoke about tribal-state conflict and tribal economic development.

In a December 1994 column in the *Albuquerque Journal,* Frank Chaves and Greg Histia explained the tribes' involvement in the fall campaign. Accusing former Governor King of "doubletalk and empty promises," Chaves and Histia praised Johnson for having promised to respect tribal sovereignty "as a basis for carrying out the government-to-government relationship that exists between the state and tribes." The tribes' support of Johnson was not, they wrote, based solely on his promise to sign Class III compacts: "First and foremost, Johnson agreed to talk with us, listen to our concerns on many issues, and respond to us openly and honestly."[93]

Chaves and Histia argued that making campaign contributions enabled the tribes to act to protect the "investment in the future" that gambling represents and to help Johnson, in the hope that he would be able to continue his dialogue with them. "We did not create this campaign contribution system," they wrote, "yet we have long been victimized by the manner in which others have often used the system to deprive us of property and use of our resources."[94]

The November election resulted in a changed climate for gambling in New Mexico, both Indian and non-Indian. Gary Johnson defeated Governor King by a surprising margin of 49 to 40 percent, with Green party candidate Mondragon receiving a respectable 11 percent.[95] Issue 8 passed with 54 percent of the vote, apparently changing at least part of the debate over the scope of gaming permitted in New Mexico.[96] However, at the same time New Mexico voters were expanding legalized gaming in the state, voters of the Navajo Nation rejected a referendum legalizing gaming in that jurisdiction by a vote of 27,022 to 21,988.[97] Navajo voters also defeated their incumbent chief executive, Peterson Zah. Zah, a strong supporter of President Clinton, lost by 4,543 votes out of more than 55,000 cast.

In his 1998 autobiography, *Cowboy in the Roundhouse,* Bruce King continues to state his view that gambling is bad for the state and contributions from gambling interests bad for governance. While he writes that he "suffered from the influence of gambling money," King goes on to say,

> I didn't lose as much of the Indian vote as some thought— the Navajo Nation stayed with me, and they make up more than half the New Mexico Indian population. Rather than lost Indian votes, I was hurt more by the financial impact of the campaign contributions from supporters of Indian gaming. I also took hits for supposedly not letting Indians exercise their rights, though I always believed I was just following the law.[98]

In mid-December Governor-elect Johnson chose attorney Fred Ragsdale, a member of the California Chemehuevi Tribe, to begin negotiations with the tribes. Johnson said that negotiating compacts with the tribes "is more than just keeping a campaign promise. . . . [I]t is the right thing to do."[99] Johnson said that the compacts should include provisions dealing with types of gaming, revenue sharing, regulatory mechanisms, safety codes, and employee background checks.

The overall New Mexico gaming picture became more confused in early January 1995 when the state supreme court found Issue 8 to be unconstitutional. Supporting the position of both antigaming activists and New Mexico Attorney General Tom

Udall, the court held that linking the lottery and other types of gambling in one referendum violated Article XIX, section 1, of the New Mexico constitution. By combining the two forms of gambling in one issue, the legislature had engaged in "log-rolling," a practice "whereby the legislature joins two or more independent measures to ensure that voters who support any one of the measures will be coerced into voting for the entire package in order to secure passage of the individual measure they favor."[100] Not only were the lottery and video games sufficiently different to require separate issues, the court found that the ballot language describing Issue 8 "contributed to the logrolling" and "exacerbated the problems inherent in the vice of logrolling."[101]

The Ragsdale negotiations and the continuing political and legal fallout from Issue 8 presented the legislature and non-Indian gaming interests with an opportunity to enter the debates over the future of gambling in New Mexico, on and off Indian land. Some state lawmakers demanded that the legislature have a role in reviewing, if not in approving, any compact concluded between the governor and the tribes. Although the legislature would have had to address the implementation of Issue 8 had the court upheld its constitutionality, the effect of the ruling was to increase the pressure on legislators to settle once and for all the status of gaming in New Mexico.

In the weeks leading up to the January 16 start of the sixty-day legislative session, the Legislative Council's Subcommittee on Gaming held a series of public hearings on a wide variety of gambling-related matters.[102] The hearings were designed to help provide legislators with guidance as they began to consider gaming legislation. Witnesses included some of the leading experts on gambling in the nation, including William N. Thompson of the University of Nevada at Las Vegas and I. Nelson Rose of Whittier College. Other witnesses included gaming officials from states with various kinds of legalized gambling, horse racing and other gambling interests, law enforcement officials, and representatives of New Mexico's Indian gaming tribes, including NMIGA's co-chair, Frank Chaves.

New Mexico's non-Indian gaming interests began to lobby the legislature and the public to demand that tribes not be given an unfair advantage. Two broad groups were concerned with protecting, if not expanding, their present status: for-profit enterprises such as racetracks and gambling paraphernalia providers and nonprofit charitable organizations.

The intensity of interest in what the legislature was going to do to resolve New Mexico's gaming status is apparent in the number of gambling lobbyists registered with the secretary of state. Individuals and firms representing horse racing, video devices, gambling equipment suppliers, and gambling consultants registered as lobbyists. (See table 6 for non-Indian gaming

TABLE 6

Non-Indian Gambling Interests with Registered Lobbyists
for the 1995 New Mexico Legislative Session

Automated Wagering International*
Citation Bingo
Hubbard Enterprises*
International Gameco, Inc.*
Lady Luck Gaming Corp.*
New Mexico Horsemen's Association
Nuevo Sol Turf Club, Inc.
Ruidoso Downs, Inc.
Santa Fe Racing, Inc.
Scientific Games*
SODAK*
Sunland Park Race Track
Vending, Amusement & Music Operations, Assoc.
Vending, Amusement and Music Operations
Video Lottery Technologies*
Webcraft Games, Inc.*

* Firms located outside New Mexico.

SOURCE: New Mexico Secretary of State, "Registered Lobbyists and the Organizations they Represent: 1995," March 8, 1995.

organizations with registered lobbyists during the 1995 legislative session.)

Most firms had registered lobbyists from the state in which they were located as well as from New Mexico. Ruidoso Downs, one of the three permanent horse racing tracks in the state, had lobbyists who also represented, among others, Phillip Morris, the New Mexico Hotel and Motel Association, SODAK, AT&T, and the New Mexico Beverage Alcohol Wholesalers. Representatives for International Gameco, Inc., also represented, among others, General Motors, the New Mexico Press Association, the Santa Fe Railroad Co., the New Mexico Petroleum Marketers Association, and Ruidoso Downs. Ray Shollenbarger of Santa Fe represented Ruidoso Downs, Santa Fe Racing Co., and Webcraft Games, Inc. None of the lobbyists for non-Indian gaming represented an Indian tribe.

Shollenbarger, who had served as former Governor Carruthers's gaming negotiator, also had strong political and personal ties to Governor Johnson. A lawyer and former alcohol and gaming director, Shollenbarger and his wife, Kay, had contributed close to $8,000 to Johnson's campaign. Kay Shollenbarger had been an employee of the Johnson campaign and after the election worked in Johnson's office assisting in filling state government jobs. Shollenbarger had served in Johnson's postelection transition team. After a lawsuit was filed in April challenging Johnson's authority to sign gaming compacts with the tribes, Jonathan Sutin, an attorney in Shollenbarger's law firm, Sutin, Thayer & Browne, was retained to represent the governor before the state supreme court.[103] SODAK is the exclusive distributor of International Game Technology (IGT) video gambling machines to Indian tribes. Manuel Lujan, former secretary of the interior and New Mexico Republican congressman, joined the company's board of directors in 1993.

Indian interests also registered lobbyists (see table 7). Those registered as lobbyists for New Mexico tribes or other Indian organizations often represented other groups. These tended not to be of the same economic clout as the interests represented by non-Indian gaming lobbyists. Odis Echols of Albuquerque was an exception. He represented six pueblos, NMIGA, the New Mexico Dietetic Association, the New Mexico Nurses Association, the Northwest Bank of New Mexico, and the City of Bernalillo. Significantly, Echols also represented Nuevo Sol Turf Club and Scientific Games, two non-Indian organizations with a stake in the outcome of gaming legislation. Echols, a former state senator, is widely acknowledged to be one of the state's premier insiders. An Associated Press study of reports filed with the secretary of state's office found that Echols spent more money during the 1995 legislative session— $33,468—than any other lobbyist.[104] This was nearly half of what all registered gaming lobbyists reported spending.[105]

Other tribal lobbyists with significant non-Indian clients were Vincent J. Montoya, also of Albuquerque, who represented the

TABLE 7

Indian Tribes and Organizations with Registered Lobbyists, 1995 New Mexico Legislative Session

Acoma Pueblo
Eight Northern Indian Pueblos Council
Isleta Pueblo
Jicarilla Apache Tribe
Laguna Pueblo
Navajo Nation, Office of the President
New Mexico Indian Gaming Association
New Mexico Office of Indian Affairs
Pojoaque Pueblo
Sandia Pueblo
San Ildefonso Pueblo
San Juan Pueblo
Santa Ana Pueblo

SOURCE: New Mexico Secretary of State, "Registered Lobbyists and the Organizations they Represent: 1995," March 8, 1995.

Jicarilla Apache Tribe and the Belen Consolidated Schools, the
City of Belen, El Paso Electric Co., Los Lunas Board of Education, Lovelace Health Systems, Inc., the Wine Institute, and the
Village of Bosque Farms. Susan Williams, one of Kevin Gover's
law partners, represented Pojoaque Pueblo.

The opponents of gambling were also represented but at a
very low level of visibility and institutional clout. The New
Mexico Coalition Against Gambling had three registered lobby-
ists, including Guy C. Clark, the head of the organization.
Coalition lobbyist Nima D. Ward also represented the Human
Needs Coordinating Council and the Rocky Mountain Synod
Evangelical Lutheran Church in America.

Additional indicators of interest group activity in the legislature are the individuals and organizations testifying before the
Senate Select Committee on Gaming. According to committee
records, ten hearings were held during which representatives
for a wide variety of groups appeared. By far the largest number
were those associated with non-Indian for-profit gaming. Tribal
representatives were also quite visible. As was the case throughout the debate on gaming, the least numerous representatives
before the committee were those opposed to expanded gambling
generally. (See table 8 for the organizations that testified before
the committee.)

Non-Indian gambling interests also attempted to influence
public opinion outside the legislature, particularly as they
claimed to be affected by Indian gaming. On Sunday, January
29, 1995, the New Mexico Racetrack & Horsemen's Association
took out nearly identical full-page advertisements in the sports
sections of both the *Albuquerque Journal* and the (Santa Fe) *New
Mexican*. Under a bold five-line headline, "When It Comes to
Economic Development, Gaming and Horse Racing Are Your
Winning Combination," the ad read, "Ask your legislator to
support the Gaming Control Act." This was followed by the
assertion, "New Mexico's Indian Pueblos have petitioned our
government to give them a virtual monopoly on gaming." The
result of this, according to the ad, would be the possible "extinc-
tion" of New Mexico's horse racing industry.

TABLE 8
Non-Indian Interests Testifying Before
New Mexico Senate Select Committee on Gaming

NONGAMING INTERESTS	GAMING INTERESTS
Lutheran Office of Governing Ministries in New Mexico	New Mexico Horsemen's Association, jockeys, owners, trainers, breeders, agents
New Mexico Coalition Against Gambling	
Alamagorda International Order of Eagles	Sundland Park
Scholastic, Inc., of Albuquerque	Ruidoso Downs
Representatives of veterans and fraternal clubs	Santa Fe Downs
	San Juan Downs
Albuquerque Boys and Girls Clubs	IGT
	Nevada Gaming Control Board
Santa Fe Eagle Club	Hubbard Industries
"citizen"	Racing Resources Group, Inc.
"6th grader"	Ruidoso businessmen
	Video Lottery Technology
	International Game Co.
	New Mexico Hospitality Retailers Assn.
	Giant Southwest Convenient Stores
	Coin Operators of New Mexico
	Automated Wagering International

Governmental	*Indian*
New Mexico State Racing Comm.	Pueblo of Pojoaque
Mayor of Eagle Nest, NM	Pueblo of Santa Ana
Sandoval County Commission	National Indian Gaming Assn.
State Agency on Aging	
Municipal League	
State Senator Shannon Robinson	

SOURCE: New Mexico Senate Select Committee on Gaming, 1995.

Touting the economic impact of the industry, the ad declared that the horse racing industry was "merely" suggesting "that the economic-development opportunities of gaming be shared by the Indian communities so that everyone benefits." The ad in the *New Mexican* did not have the association's disclaimer. The bottom of the ad read, "Friends of New Mexico's Horse Racing Industry." The *Albuquerque Journal* ad contained both the association disclaimer and the Friends notation. The ads were part of a $30,000 campaign by Santa Fe Racing, Inc., operator of racetracks in Santa Fe and Albuquerque.

On February 7 Governor Johnson announced that negotiations had produced an agreement acceptable to him and the tribes, but the signing of the compacts was delayed so that the fraternal and charitable organizations could conduct their casino nights. On February 13, in a ceremony in the governor's office attended by eleven gaming tribes—Taos, San Juan, Santa Clara, Pojoaque, Tesuque, San Felipe, Santa Ana, Sandia, Isleta, and Acoma pueblos and the Jicarilla and Mescalero Apache tribes— Johnson signed the compact.[106]

Calling the signing of the compact "an historic event in our state," Johnson continued, "This compact is essentially a government to government agreement—and it helps define the relationship between Indian sovereign nations and the state of New Mexico. It describes and defines what is already occurring in New Mexico today."[107]

Having acted as interest groups with a political agenda in the previous year's gubernatorial campaign, the tribes were now received in the governor's office as sovereigns entering into a government-to-government relationship with the state of New Mexico.

Johnson said that the final signed version of the compacts and side agreements contained changes designed to address concerns that had been raised following the initial announcement. He pointed out that without a compact achieved through negotiations between the state and tribes, the federal government "would force a compact on the state." The result would be no state role in Indian gaming and no share in the revenues such games would generate, both guaranteed by the negotiated compact.

The uniform compact, signed by each tribe individually, provided for (1) authorization for "any and all Class III Gaming"; (2) mechanisms for state review of tribal gaming records; (3) tribal regulations and audit procedures; (4) licensing requirements and background checks for casino employees; (5) standards for gaming equipment, supplies, and suppliers; (6) casino patron liability; and (7) criminal prosecution under federal law.[108]

A separate side agreement provided for revenue sharing with the state "to compensate the State and Local Government(s) for maintaining market exclusivity of tribal gaming." The tribes agreed to share "Three Percent (3%) of the First Four Million Dollars ($4,000,000) of net win at each Gaming Facility derived from Class III games of chance" and "Five Percent (5%) of the net win over the first Four Million Dollars." Sixty percent of the total revenue to be shared would be paid to the state of New Mexico and 40 percent to a "Local Government" to be determined by each tribe. The side agreement would be terminated "if the State permits any expansion of non-tribal Class III Gaming in the State." A state lottery, gaming operated by "fraternal, veterans or other non-profit membership organization," and electronic gaming devices operated by horse racing tracks on racing days were excluded from this requirement.[109]

The signing of the compacts did not resolve all of the questions concerning non-Indian gaming, nor were all legislators agreeable to the compacts themselves. The legislature continued to debate the future of legalized gambling in New Mexico. Intense, visible pressure from non-Indian gaming interests continued on both the legislature and the governor. Indian gaming interests also made their presence felt, and Governor Johnson stood by his commitment to the tribes. Representatives of the state's horse racing industry argued that without the draw of video gambling at their tracks their livelihood was threatened. They claimed that competition from other forms of legalized gambling was threatening their very existence. Ruidoso

Downs faced competition from the Mescalero Apache casino; Sunland Park, located in extreme southern New Mexico, competed for gambling dollars with the Texas Lottery and the Texas Tigua Tribe's bingo and card games. They therefore lobbied intensively for a change in the law that would allow them to offer their patrons such additional entertainment.

The Senate created the Select Committee on Gaming to handle the legislature's expected heavy gaming-related workload. The committee was chaired by Democratic senator John Arthur Smith of Deming. Other members were Democrats Joseph Fidel of Grants, Pete Campos of Las Vegas, and Fernando Macias of Mesilla and Republicans Emmit Jennings of Roswell, Leonard Lee Rawson of Las Cruces, and Don Kidd of Carlsbad. Neither of the chamber's two Indian members was appointed to the committee. The regular relevant standing committees handled gaming bills in the House.

One of the most heated gambling questions was whether to eliminate all types of non-pari-mutuel gaming, including the casino nights operated by fraternal and charitable organizations. Some legislators, most notably Max Coll (D-Santa Fe) and Richard Knowles (R-Roswell), argued that by eliminating all electronic gaming, pull tabs, and casino nights the state would be in a better position to oppose the expansion of Indian gaming. Understandably, the nonprofit organizations that benefited from such legal forms of gambling opposed these efforts, although they acknowledged that competition from Indian gaming was hurting them financially. In an op-ed article in the *Albuquerque Journal*, Richard B. Archuleta of the Charitable Gaming Committee contended that "charity gaming dropped from 350-400 patrons per session to less than 200, while Indian halls regularly have far in excess of 1,000 customers.[110]

Although the legislature at times seemed preoccupied with the gaming question, the answer appeared to be elusive. As the secretary of the Senate Select Committee on Gaming told me, the issue seemed "to have a life of its own," and the more legislators tried to control it, the more out of control it became.[111]

At least thirty-nine gaming-related bills were introduced into
the legislature. The legislature's general uncertainty on the
issue is clearly seen in the contradictory bills that passed one or
both houses during the session:

- H.B. 29: passed both houses, vetoed by the governor.
  Would have outlawed slot machines and casino nights
  operated by fraternal and charitable groups.
- S.B. 510: passed in the Senate, failed in the House.
  Would have permitted off-track betting on horse races.
- H.B. 1090: passed in the House, failed in the Senate.
  Would have permitted electronic gaming machines at
  horse racing tracks.
- S.B. 1052: passed in the Senate, failed in the House.
  Would have created a state lottery and permitted elec-
  tronic gaming machines at horse racing tracks, large
  hotels, fraternal and veterans' clubs, and some bars and
  restaurants.
- S.B. 1151: passed in the Senate, failed in the House.
  Would have permitted veterans' and fraternal clubs to
  have no more than twenty-five electronic gambling
  machines.
- S.B. 853: Passed both houses and was signed into law
  by Governor Johnson. Created a state lottery.

The conflicts and indecision over what to do about gaming
were vividly demonstrated in the Senate two days before the
close of the session. In the course of one evening and after-
noon, senators voted four times on whether to forbid gambling
interests from making campaign contributions. The first effort
succeeded 20 to 8 as an amendment by Sen. Roman M. Maes of
Santa Fe. It passed even though Sen. Joseph J. Carraro, a restaurant owner, pointed out that he might be prevented from
donating to his own campaign if he installed gambling devices
at his establishment. Carraro later successfully amended the
amended version of the bill and removed the Maes amendment
on a tie-breaking vote by Lt. Gov. J. Walter Bradley.

Senator Maes tried again with an amendment to H.B. 1090, this time with what he termed the "Carraro fix." For the first time in the debate on this issue concern was raised about its impact on Indian tribes. Sen. Duncan Scott worried that a ban on contributions by gaming interests would "disenfranchise American Indian tribes." Without the ability to make campaign contributions, he argued, tribes would be "completely removed from the political process." Maes replied that "they have a right to vote" and that money is not the only way for Indians to participate in politics. The amendment failed 19 to 23. One last effort was made late in the day when Sen. Don Kidd offered a similar amendment to the same bill. This time it passed 26 to 16. H.B. 1090 passed 32 to 10.[112]

Johnson's position during the remainder of the session was firm. The only additional legalized gaming he would support was a state lottery and slot machines at racetracks and the veterans' and fraternal groups. Both of these options were permitted by the compacts he had signed with the tribes. This was a blow to the horse racing industry. Its position had evolved from advocating slot machines at the tracks to calling for full-blown casinos. The work of Kevin Gover, Odis Echols, and Rex Hackler and James Rivera, two political consultants brought in by Gover, was largely responsible for defeating the efforts of the tracks to open their own casinos.[113]

Hovering over the legislators as they grappled with the issue was the impending approval of the Indian gaming compacts and the presence of Indian and non-Indian lobbyists. The horse racing lobbyists were especially active in attempting to pass legislation allowing track casinos. R. D. Hubbard, owner of Ruidoso Downs, was very visible at the Capitol and attended a meeting of the horse racing industry with Governor Johnson. Hubbard threatened to close his track if the legislature did not vote to approve track casinos. A group calling itself Citizens for a Level Playing Field met with Johnson to argue for track casinos. Among the least visible, if not the least passionate, gaming lobbyist was Guy Clark of the Coalition Against Gambling. The only people who came to his antigambling rally at the Capitol were members of the press.

As the legislature rushed to complete its work and as gaming appeared more complex each day, Sen. Leonard Tsosie (D-Crownpoint), one of two Navajos in the Senate, submitted a substitute version of S.B. 1132, The Level Playing Field Act. The bill would require that non-Indian gaming profits be paid to the state and would give tribes approval of any new off-reservation gaming in the state. It was clearly designed to draw attention to the charges being leveled against Indian gaming by turning them around on its critics. On behalf of NMIGA, Chaves issued the following statement:

> With unbelievable gall, wealthy track owners demand "a level playing field. If they were allowed to expand their racing operations to include casino gambling, where would their profits go? The same place their horse racing profits go: their own pockets."[114]

Continuing to express his displeasure at the compact, House Speaker Raymond G. Sanchez introduced House Joint Resolution 11, "A Joint Resolution Expressing Disapproval of the Manner in Which the Governor of the State of New Mexico Executed the Compact that Provides for the Conduct of Casino Gaming with the Indian Tribes." The resolution reasserted Sanchez's view that the governor had rushed approval of the compact without adequate legislative review. It expressed disapproval of both the substance of the compact and the authority of the governor to enter into such agreements. It asked first that the compact be withdrawn and second that the secretary of the interior disapprove of the compact "until the completion of a process that assures the proper accommodation of the interests of all the citizens of New Mexico." The House passed the resolution on March 15 by a vote of 34 to 30, two days before eleven of the thirteen compacts were given formal approval by the Interior Department.[115]

The Interior Department's approval of the compacts did not end Sanchez's efforts. While congratulating the tribes on the approval of the compacts, Sanchez continued to insist that the "health and welfare of all New Mexicans" be protected. He asked the tribes to raise the age requirement from eighteen to twenty-one; not cash Social Security or payroll checks at casinos; provide support for programs for problem gamblers; and not expand the existing scope of Indian gaming in New Mexico.[116] Tribal representatives agreed to meet and discuss these issues, but Chaves said that they were "market driven" and "not negotiable."[117]

The legislative sound and fury produced by the gambling issue resulted in only one significant change in the status of legalized gambling in New Mexico: at long last the state would have a lottery. The tribes and Governor Johnson were clearly the major winners on this issue. The governor kept his commitment to the tribes, and the tribes maintained their preeminent position in gaming in the state. Legislators and non-Indian gaming interests were unable to develop a coherent gaming policy that met either of their goals.

FLEXIBLE TRIBAL STRATEGIES AND THE SCOPE OF CONFLICT

As we have seen, New Mexico tribes used three strategies—litigation, lobbying, and electoral pressure—in a Schattschneider-like search for the sphere of conflict most likely to result in the desired policy.[118] The tribes' strategies were consistent with the state's political culture. Jose Garcia and Clive S. Thomas have noted that "interest groups in New Mexico operate in four sectors in attempting to influence public policy in their favor: elections and campaigns; the legislature; the executive branch; and the judiciary."[119]

Four factors make such multifaceted strategies both possible and necessary in New Mexico: (1) the state's political, social, and institutional arrangements; (2) the status of tribes as sovereigns with extensive political, cultural, economic, and social interests; (3) tribal/state conflict established by the Indian Gaming Regulatory Act; and (4) the resources generated by Indian gaming.

Allen J. Cigler and Burdett A. Loomis have noted that "most groups and interests seek to narrow the scope of conflict."[120] In many respects the IGRA narrows the conflict artificially. Tribes seeking to engage in Class III gaming must negotiate with the state and, failing fruitful negotiations, go to federal court. New Mexico tribes followed the law and engaged in the required narrow conflict. But by entering the electoral process, tribes expanded the conflict to bring about a change in the arena of narrow conflict. Both arenas of conflict, the narrow one of government-to-government negotiations and federal lawsuits and the broader one of electoral politics, are open to tribes because of their flexible political status. And the financial resources generated by the tribes' gaming operation provided the flexibility required to implement their multifaceted strategy.

The nature of gaming as a policy issue and its central role in defining the extent of tribal sovereignty motivated tribes to coalesce and engage in a multifront campaign to protect tribal gaming specifically and tribal sovereignty generally. At times the tribes' tactics were reactive; at other times, proactive. At all times they appeared ready and able to bring to bear the multiple resources available to them in their dual roles as sovereign entities and interest groups.

In fighting to uphold tribal sovereignty, the tribes were at the same time fighting to hold on to an instrument of great potential economic power. Both of these tribal interests, sovereignty and economic development, found opposition among those seeking to limit tribal gaming opportunities. Governor King and two U.S. Attorneys at times sought to limit the exercise of tribal sovereignty by refusing to allow the expansion of Indian gaming. Non-Indian gaming interests fought to maintain what they considered a "level playing field" for tribal gambling operations. Their actions directly and indirectly threatened the economic foundation of Indian gaming, as did the acts of government itself. This is not surprising given the context of interest group activity in the state. A number of observers have classified New Mexico as a state where interest groups are strong.[121] In none of these surveys of the state's interest group activity, however, were Indians or Indian tribes cited as influential interest groups.

Whereas many elected and appointed officials placed obstacles in the path of the tribes' efforts to achieve their goals, it was the *cooperation* of two officials—Gary Johnson and John Kelly—that ultimately allowed the tribes to succeed. The change from King to Johnson in the governor's office is the most significant development, from both the political and the policy perspectives. Governor King's philosophical opposition to gaming and his states' rights interpretation of the scope of Indian gaming and Indian sovereignty were replaced by Johnson's need to fulfill a campaign pledge.

U.S. Attorney Kelly proved to be less of an adversary than previous occupants of that office. Although he refused to allow uncontrolled expansion of Indian gaming, the standstill agreement he reached with the tribes on the number of allowable video slot machines permitted them to continue their gaming operations uninterrupted. Arguably, it also strengthened their hand in negotiations with whoever sat in the governor's office, as the continued existence of the machines implied an endorsement of the tribes' interpretation of the scope of gaming.

Kelly also publicly supported the negotiations between the tribes and Johnson.[122] Indian leaders found Kelly to be easier to work with than previous U.S. Attorneys. With a background in Indian law, Kelly did not have to learn the intricacies of this complicated field, and discussions between him and the tribes proceeded more smoothly.[123] It is important to note that Kelly is the former law partner of one of the leading tribal attorneys, Richard Hughes.[124] Kelly's actions through the first half of 1995 appear to support James Eisenstein's observation that personal experience is often important in how a U.S. Attorney exercises his or her discretion.[125]

The strength of the collective tribal effort to protect and expand Indian gaming is in large measure due to the ability of the tribes to present a united front. The Pueblos have a centuries-long history of cooperation and have three significant organizations that bring them together to discuss and make policy as well as operate programs: the All Indian Pueblo Council, the Southern Governors Council, and the Eight Northern Pueblos Council. The nineteen pueblo governors represent their people on the All Indian Pueblo Council. "According to tribal legends and oral history," writes Sando, "the All Indian Pueblo Council has existed for many centuries, and 1598 is used by the people as its date of origin because that is the recorded meeting date with the Spaniards under Governor Juan de Oñate."[126]

As the *New Mexico Business Journal* observed, New Mexico's Indian "communities are diverse and have long histories of interrelationships with one another, both positive and confrontational."[127]

Thus, while there are cultural, political, and other differences that cause New Mexico's twenty-two Indian tribes to act independently, on the issue of gaming the relevance of state government was clear and the interests of the pueblos and the two Apache tribes converged. This allowed the tribes to present a stronger united front in pressing their demands. In this sense the combined intertribal effort meets Alan Rosenthal's definition of a coalition: "a loose collection of organizations that cooperates to accomplish common objectives."[128] There was no disagreement among the gaming tribes on the broad questions of tribal sovereignty and scope of gaming. The Navajo Nation, which opposed gaming on their reservation, was not a significant actor in the gaming issue.

NMIGA might also be considered a kind of public interest group working in an "interest group sector," defined by Cigler as "a set of organized groups that share broadly similar policy concerns."[129] Cigler observes that public officials join public interest organizations "not only to advance policy positions, but also to promote core political-system values: responsiveness, representativeness, accountability, equity, efficiency, and effectiveness."[130] NMIGA seeks each of these within the context of Indian gaming and Indian sovereignty, the tribes' most significant "political-system value."

INSIDE LOBBYING: THE EXECUTIVE BRANCH

As Alan Reed and Denise Fort note, executive power is "fragmented" in New Mexico.[131] Executive responsibilities are distributed constitutionally and by statute across a number of elected and appointed bodies. The tribes' lobbying efforts with New Mexico's governors primarily consisted of campaign contributions (or withholding them) and negotiations designed to lead to a Class III gaming compact. The IGRA requires tribes to attempt to negotiate with state officials on Class III gaming issues. The New Mexico tribes began this process almost immediately after the IGRA took effect.

The negotiating process required by the IGRA is clearly of an intergovernmental relations nature, one unique in American federalism. Although it is designed as a mechanism to resolve tribal-state differences, it may in fact exacerbate them. As in New Mexico, these difference may involve policy differences as well as fundamental differences over the nature of Indian sovereignty itself. The question of the scope of gaming permitted under the IGRA is also fundamentally a question of the scope of state and tribal sovereignty.

In a December 1993 letter to me, Governor King outlined his position regarding Indian gaming and tribal-state relations. While reiterating his past support of tribal sovereignty, King wrote, "I do not believe distinctions between state and tribal governments need to be clear-cut. There is room for overlapping responsibilities and cooperative undertakings." He cited cross-deputizations of law enforcement as an example.

But gaming was clearly a different matter to the governor. "On the question of gaming," he wrote,

> I have insisted that tribal governments should be permitted to offer any form of gaming *otherwise legal in the state* and should be able to offer it under their own rules and jurisdiction. . . . However, I do not believe that I as governor am obligated or even entitled to grant a particular

group of citizens the right to engage in activities otherwise illegal in my state.[132]

This was still King's position after leaving office. In March 1995,
soon after his successor had signed compacts with New Mexico
tribes, he repeated his opposition to compacts that permitted
games not specifically permitted under New Mexico law. He
added that Johnson was "giving everything to the Indians."[133]

King's interpretation of the IGRA is quite different from that
of the tribes, and his view of tribal sovereignty recalls a states'
rights position going all the way back to President Jackson:
tribes are *within* the borders of a state, and Indians should be
subject to the same laws as all other "citizens" of the states
wherein they reside. This irreconcilable difference in interpretation of the scope of both tribal/state sovereignty and the
IGRA doomed negotiations between the tribes and King. King
could not be lobbied out of his position.

King had adopted what Wolf describes as "a two-phase
strategy to stymie Indian gaming operation."[134] The first part of
the strategy is to "delay or refuse to negotiate compacts with the
Indians." Then, when tribes follow the IGRA and sue in federal
court, "states assert that the constitutional defense of sovereign
immunity, under the Eleventh Amendment, bars such suits."[135]

Newly elected Governor Johnson did neither. He told the
Senate Committee on Indian Affairs in June 1995, "Adopting
compacts with the Indian tribes is not based on some philosophical idea of whether gambling is right or wrong. Rather, it
is the result of federal law." Taking a position strikingly different
from King's, Johnson said that "all Indian gaming in New
Mexico is consistent with New Mexico state law and public
policy."[136]

Whether or not Johnson had a better grasp than King of
Indian sovereignty generally or the scope of Indian gaming
specifically, his willingness to carry through on his campaign
commitment meant that the tribes had a sympathetic ear. The
responsiveness of the governor's office was strengthened by
the appointment of Fred Ragsdale as the governor's gaming

negotiator. As was the case with U.S. Attorney Kelly, Ragsdale knew the area of law he was negotiating. As Chaves noted, with Ragsdale they "negotiated regulatory issues as opposed to law."[137] Negotiations between Ragsdale and tribal attorneys apparently were conducted without significant impediments to achieving the mutually desired end: a Class III gaming compact.

Johnson told the Senate committee that in negotiating the compacts "the most important goal was to use the negotiation and compacting process as a model for future state and tribal affairs." He pointed to a recent "tribal summit" that his administration held on a variety of issues as resulting from "the ground work" laid by the gaming negotiations.[138]

INSIDE LOBBYING: THE COURTS

While it is well established that interest groups have increasingly turned to the judicial process to achieve their policy ends,[139] the IGRA establishes a unique set of circumstances that may lead tribes to federal court. By providing that tribes may bring suit in federal district court against states that do not negotiate Class III compacts in good faith, the IGRA provides a forum in which to resolve tribal/state conflict. It also leads to a major role for attorneys in the gaming policy area.

As we have seen, Sandia Pueblo and the Mescalero Apache Tribe were the first New Mexico tribes to sue under the IGRA. While these tribes and those who filed subsequent similar lawsuits were direct parties in a tribal/state conflict, New Mexico tribes have also come to the aid of non–New Mexico tribes involved in similar disputes. This legal support is not confined to the issue of gaming.

When there are significant questions of tribal sovereignty in litigation before the U.S. Supreme Court, attorneys for New Mexico tribes have often supported the tribe's position by filing amicus briefs. Because the boundaries of tribal sovereignty and Indian policy have so often been established by Court decisions, that venue has historically been the one that tribes have turned to to assert or defend their rights.

The 1980s provided several major opportunities for the Court to further define the limits of tribal sovereignty. At the same time, interest groups generally[140] and tribes specifically were attempting to influence judicial policy making. A number of scholars have noted the increased use of amicus curiae briefs by interest groups before the Supreme Court, but none of them looked at the role of amicus briefs in Indian law cases.[141]

A number of New Mexico tribes filed amicus curiae briefs with the Supreme Court supporting the position of the Cabazon Band of Mission Indians in its significant and historic 1986 litigation against California's efforts to regulate their bingo operations. Sandia, Acoma, Tesuque, and San Juan pueblos joined in an amicus brief filed by the Albuquerque attorney L. Lamar Parrish. Alan R. Taradash of Albuquerque submitted a brief on behalf of the Jicarilla Apache Tribe and Isleta and Santa Ana pueblos. All of the briefs supported Cabazon's assertion that California lacked jurisdiction to interfere with the band's bingo games.

New Mexico lawyers active on behalf of Indian tribes in the state are also engaged in supporting the efforts of other tribes seeking to protect sovereign interests. As we have seen, the Albuquerque law firm of West, Gover, Stetson & Williams (later Gover, Stetson & Williams) has been a major player in Indian issues and state politics. Similarly, the firm filed amicus briefs on behalf of a number of tribes supporting other tribes with cases before the Supreme Court in the 1980s and 1990s. In 1983 the firm filed an amicus curiae brief on behalf of the Cheyenne River Sioux Tribe of South Dakota, the Standing Rock Sioux Tribe of North and South Dakota, and the Association of American Indian Affairs in *Solem v. Bartlett*. This case involved the question of whether Congress had diminished the Cheyenne River Sioux Reservation in South Dakota, thus giving the state jurisdiction to try an Indian accused of a crime committed on the disputed land. The Court held that the reservation had not been diminished and that South Dakota did not have jurisdiction.

In 1988 Gover, Stetson & Williams filed amicus briefs in two significant Supreme Court cases, *Cotton Petroleum Corporation v. New Mexico* and *Berndale v. Confederated Tribes and Bands of the Yakima Indian Nation*. The first was filed on behalf of the Crow Tribe of Montana, the Shoshone Tribe of the Wind River Reservation, the Arapaho Tribe of the Wind River Reservation, the Yavapai-Apache Tribe, the American Indian Resources Institute, the National Congress of American Indians, the Apache Tribe of the Mescalero Reservation Housing Authority, and the Pueblo of Laguna Housing Authority. The second brief was filed on behalf of the Swinomish Tribal Community.

The following year the firm filed an amicus brief in one of the most significant recent cases affecting tribal criminal jurisdiction. In *Duro v. Reina* the firm filed on behalf of fourteen tribes, bands, and reservations, none of which was from New Mexico, and the Association of American Indian Affairs. The issue in this case was whether a tribe could exercise criminal jurisdiction over nontribal Indians. The Court held that a tribe had criminal jurisdiction only over its own members. The brief filed by Gover et al. had argued that the tribe involved in the dispute, the Salt River–Maricopa Indian Community of Arizona, did have jurisdiction over the nontribal member charged with discharging a firearm on the reservation.

Four facts should be noted about this activity by Gover et al. First, in all four of these cases Gover et al. had argued on behalf of tribal sovereignty against efforts by the states to curtail it. In all but one case the party supported by the firm lost before the Supreme Court. This is notable given the recent literature attempting to discern the effectiveness of amicus briefs.[142] Second, nearly all of the tribes represented by the firm were located outside New Mexico. Third, only one of the cases, *Cotton Petroleum*, involved an issue of direct concern to tribes located in New Mexico. Fourth, in two of the cases the firm represented one of the oldest non-Indian, pro-Indian rights interest groups in the country, the Association of American Indian Affairs of New York City.

New Mexico tribes were directly affected by *Cotton Petroleum,* one of the most significant cases of the decade concerning the rights of states to impose severance taxes on businesses operating on Indian lands and already subject to tribal taxes. In addition to the brief filed by Gover, Stetson & Williams, amicus briefs were filed by attorneys for the Jicarilla Apache Tribe of New Mexico and by the Navajo Nation's Department of Justice. Both supported Cotton Petroleum in its efforts to avoid paying the New Mexico state tax. The case was of special concern to the Jicarilla as it was the tax on Cotton Petroleum's Jicarilla Apache Reservation wells that was at issue. The Court subsequently held that New Mexico could impose its tax on Cotton Petroleum absent a congressional statute preempting the state from doing so.

INSIDE LOBBYING: THE LEGISLATIVE BRANCH

The extent of the formal participation of the New Mexico legislature was in its power to change the parameters of the state's gaming policy, which was in large measure driven by the tribes. A series of legislative sessions, culminating in the 1995 session, wrestled with the conflicting pro- and antigaming interests attempting to influence the legislature's decisions. With the support of Governor Johnson, the tribes have emerged from these legislative battles with their gaming rights untouched.

Tribal leaders and representatives were not on the sidelines of the legislative process, however. As noted above, tribal representatives appeared before legislative committees and most tribes had registered lobbyists with authority to represent their interests before the legislature. The introduction of the Level Playing Field Bill by Senator Tsosie with the support of NMIGA was a not-so-subtle reminder to the public and lawmakers of what was taking place among the competing gaming interests in the final days of the legislative session. Finally, and perhaps most significantly, the deep inside work of Odis Echols and Kevin Gover in the final days of the legislative session was an example of lobbying at its most basic and sophisticated.

The legislature is also a forum for partisan politics and ongoing issues of checks and balances among the three branches of New Mexico's government. This was apparent in the demands made by some legislators that Johnson submit the Indian gaming compacts to the legislature before signing them and Democratic House Speaker Sanchez's efforts to influence the issue. Sanchez made public his criticisms of the compacts and his private meetings with Indian leaders. By the latter action, the tribes recognized Sanchez's pragmatic need that to provide himself with political cover.[143]

It is also important to note that after the end of the legislative session two legislators joined with the executive director of the New Mexico Coalition Against Gambling to file suit challenging the governor's power to sign the compacts. State Representatives George Buffett and Max Coll asked the New Mexico Supreme Court to invalidate the compacts on the grounds that Johnson lacked statutory authority to enter into the gaming agreements with tribes without legislative consent.[144]

At the congressional level, New Mexico Indian tribes were active in efforts to shape the nation's Indian gaming policy. Tribal and NMIGA representatives testified at congressional hearings on Indian gaming. Examples of this include testimony before the Senate Select Committee on Indian Affairs by Pueblo of Santa Ana tribal administrator Roy Montoya and Acoma governor Mule L. Garcia, Frank Chaves, Sandia governor Esquipula Chaves, and Donald L. Walker, president of Sandia Indian Management Co., in 1985; Herman Agoyo, chairman of the All Indian Pueblo Council, in 1987; and Wendell Chino, president of the Mescalero Apache Tribe, in 1992. Similar appearances were made before the House Interior and Insular Affairs Committee.

New Mexico tribes were also represented on the joint National Congress of American Indian/National Indian Gaming Association Task Force and Negotiating Team. These two bodies were created to help the Senate Select Committee on Indian Affairs resolve tribal/state differences over gaming. The Negotiating Committee met with representatives of state governments.

Isleta Pueblo governor Alvino Lucero and Pojoaque governor Jacob Viarrial served on the task force. Chaves served on the task force and the negotiating committee. Attorneys Susan Williams and Henry Buffalo served on the task force, negotiating team, and the work group established to hammer out the details of a possible compromise with a similar group representing the states.[145]

OUTSIDE LOBBYING: PUBLIC RELATIONS

While the major substantive work to protect and expand Indian gaming was done before government bodies, the tribes did not ignore the public at large. As Rosenthal notes, "One way to generate support is to place an emphasis on communications."[146] The gaming tribes communicated their position to the public individually and collectively through the New Mexico Indian Gaming Association.

The work of NMIGA was crucial to both inside and outside lobbying. Chaves was frequently interviewed by the media, and he and Histia wrote several op-ed articles for the *Albuquerque Journal*.

Although it engaged in outside lobbying, NMIGA was not a traditional grassroots interest group.[147] Its base comprised the tribes that had gaming operations, principally the Pueblos of the Rio Grande. It was not a mass membership organization, and the interests of its constituency were narrow and outside the frame of reference of most public officials and the public at large.

In September 1994 NMIGA came to the public defense of Kelly, with whom the tribes had earlier reached a standstill agreement on the number of allowable video gambling devices. Kelly had been attacked by the director of the New Mexico Coalition Against Gambling for having a conflict of interest in a business dispute with Sandia Pueblo. The association charged that Kelly had "become the stand-in target" for those opposed to Indian gaming.[148]

The tribes individually attempted to convince the New Mexico public of the benefits of Indian gaming. Isleta Pueblo,

for example, ran thirty-second television commercials presenting Indian gaming in a positive light, and Tesuque Pueblo
governor Paul Swazo wrote a column for the *New Mexican*
presenting the tribes' economic argument for gaming.[149] The
Isleta ads came at a time during the gubernatorial race when
the antigambling Association for the Protection of Community
was attacking Indian gaming in general and Johnson's support
for compact negotiations in particular.

Arguably one of the best public relations outlets available to
the tribes was their casino advertisements. Slick promotional
advertisements appeared in various media outlets. The Isleta
Gaming Palace was often seen in commercial spots on Albuquerque television stations.

The tribes also attempted to use their casino patrons to lobby
lawmakers. For example, the Isleta Gaming Palace made pre-
addressed postcards available to their patrons urging members
of the New Mexico legislature and New Mexico's congressional
delegation to support Indian gaming. Patrons could sign these
cards and leave them in a box for mailing by casino employees.
The cards read:

> I urge you to support Indian Gaming in New Mexico. I
> do! Indian Gaming provides well-run, legitimate enter-
> tainment for thousands of New Mexicans and visitors
> every day.
>
> Indian Gaming is a governmental enterprise sup-
> porting the tribes and surrounding area by creating jobs,
> new tax revenue and new business revenues within the
> state of New Mexico.
>
> I request that you support our Native American friends
> and oppose any effort that limits or reduces Indian
> Gaming. *I will be supporting Indian Gaming With My Vote!*

Outside Lobbying: Political Campaigns

Having failed in their efforts to sway Governor King and
negotiate Class III compacts on a sovereign-to-sovereign basis,

the tribes sought to remove the obstacle, namely, the governor, and turned to the political arena. In the American political system neither units of government nor associations of government officials endorse political candidates.[150] There are legal and practical reasons for this. First, it would be illegal to use government funds for partisan purposes, and many states prohibit partisan activities by public employees. Second, what might be called "professional courtesy" ensures that an organization comprising elected officials will not seek the removal of others similarly situated. Third, partisanship could destroy the unity needed for achieving the common goals of elected or appointed officials holding comparable offices. Fourth, government officials have other ways of getting their agenda before public decision makers.

These constraints are generally absent among Indian tribes. So long as federal and state funds are not used, tribes are free to dispose of their resources as they see fit. While tribes run the risk that contributions will back a losing campaign, they enjoy the benefits when they back a winner, as the tribes in New Mexico did in 1994. Given the relatively small numbers of registered Indian voters in New Mexico, campaign contributions and endorsements guaranteed that their voice would be heard. New Mexico's tribes saw that their interests would be served by a governor other than Bruce King.

Partisanship mattered a great deal less than the candidates' willingness to support the tribes on an issue critical to their sovereign and economic interests. Hence, while first endorsing Democrat Casey Luna in the gubernatorial primary, the tribes supported the Republican nominee when King won renomination.

Cherokee Nation Bingo Outlet, Catoosa, Oklahoma.

Comanche Nation Games, Lawton, Oklahoma.

The new Isleta Pueblo Police substation, built in part with the tribe's gaming revenue.

The Isleta Gaming Palace hot air balloon.

Indian gaming supporters and employees at a pro-Indian gaming rally, Isleta Pueblo Gaming Palace, January 15, 1996.

Indian gaming supporters interviewed by news media along Interstate 25 during pro-gaming rally at Isleta.

Pro-Indian gaming supporters at Isleta Gaming Palace rally, January 15, 1996. Note the sign protesting U.S. Attorney John Kelly.

Pro-Indian gaming rally, Isleta Pueblo Gaming Palace, January 15, 1996.

Pro-Indian gaming supporter with a political message, Isleta Pueblo
rally, January 15, 1996. Note the voter registration tent.

Front of Casino Sandia with trailer used to coordinate the pro-gaming activities of the tribes.

Billboard advertisement for Casino Sandia just off Interstate 25, north of Albuquerque.

National Indian Gaming Association director Tim Wapato speaking at a pro-gaming rally outside the New Mexico state capitol in Santa Fe during the February 1996 legislative session.

Employee of an Indian gaming facility at pro-gaming rally, state capitol, Santa Fe, February 2, 1996.

Pro-gaming signs, state capitol, Santa Fe, February 2, 1996.

Bumper stickers printed by Isleta Gaming Palace. A number of gaming tribes printed similar pro-gaming materials.

Santa Ana Pueblo Star Casino, Bernalillo, New Mexico.

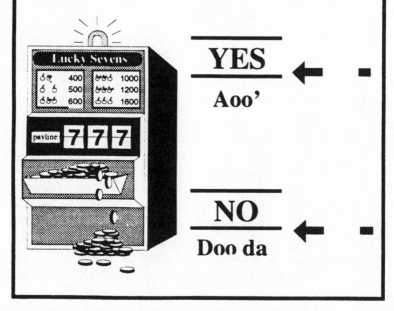

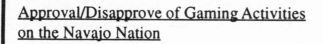

Detail from a sample ballot for the 1997 gaming referendum on the Navajo Nation.

"We'll Remember in November"

The future of Indian gaming appeared to be secure after the compacts had been signed and the legislature had adjourned without changing the gaming status quo in New Mexico. Tribal gaming operations expanded rapidly, and full-scale casino gambling became a reality along the Rio Grande. The months between March and July 1995, however, were like the brief bloom of a high desert flower. The harsh realities of New Mexico politics soon threatened the new vitality of tribal economic life and tested the ability of the tribes to stave off the political and legal challenges to the gaming compacts. Defeating the threats to what tribal leaders believed was their legal right to offer Class III gambling under the compacts required a campaign that would bring to bear all of the resources and political acumen gained in their previous battles and made possible by gaming revenues.

The impact of decisions by non-Indian political institutions and the deficiencies of the Indian Gaming Regulatory Act became apparent in New Mexico in the latter half of 1995. Two decisions by the New Mexico Supreme Court cast doubt on the status of the compacts and created a political and legal crisis for tribal, federal, and state officials. The court's decisions demonstrated again the vulnerability of tribes to political questions that on their face have little, if anything, to do with Indian policy. Their practical effect was to threaten not only the economic revival under way in Indian Country in New Mexico but also the fundamental ability of the tribes to conduct their own affairs free from the vagaries of non-Indian politics. Accordingly, the tribes proceeded to demonstrate their continued willingness to enter the political arena to protect their interests.

Gaming became even more important to the tribes in the months following the signing of the compacts. While continuation of gaming operations remained a fundamental question of sovereignty for the tribes, their economic importance dramatically increased. Tribal gaming operations were expanded and became full-blown casinos. Card tables were added and the banks of video slots enlarged. Tesuque Pueblo moved out of its bingo hall and temporary casino into the newly constructed Camel Rock Gaming Center. In November, two weeks before the court's first decision, San Felipe Pueblo opened the doors of its Casino Hollywood, with twenty thousand square feet of gaming space, just off Interstate 25 halfway between Albuquerque and Santa Fe.[1] Taos Pueblo added additional video slots to its small casino, the northernmost in the state.[2]

The success of the gaming operations is first apparent in the amount of money taken in by tribal casinos. The ten Class III gaming operations made a net profit of $46 million in 1995.[3] NMIGA co-chair Frank Chaves told the Senate Select Committee on Gaming that casinos "directly" employed 2,924 people and were responsible for creating an additional 8,436 jobs. According to Chaves, citing a study done for the association, Indian gaming was responsible for $7.6 million dollars in New Mexico gross receipts taxes and $4.3 million in state income taxes.[4]

Robbie Robertson of the Center for Applied Research told a joint hearing of several House committees that during 1995 New Mexicans spent $172 million on Indian gaming in the state, out of a total of $231 million taken in by the casinos for the same period. The tribes spent $184 million on their gaming operations, including $48 million in wages and salaries. Of the

$136 million spent by tribal casinos on goods and services, $124 million were spent within the state. Although Robertson acknowledged that businesses that compete for leisure dollars lost $154 million to tribal casinos, he said that a "counter-vailing" $216 million were spent by tourists who came to New Mexico to gamble.[5]

Beyond the aggregate dollar amounts is what casino revenues enabled the tribes to do that they could not have done other-wise. Restricted by the IGRA in how they can use gaming revenue, New Mexico tribes used their profits on a wide variety of services for tribal members. For example, Isleta Pueblo's youth programs are completely funded by Isleta Gaming Palace revenue; Santa Ana Pueblo expanded its police force and funds scholarship programs; Sandia Pueblo operates a wellness center for tribal members of all ages; and Acoma Pueblo is modern-izing its outdated water system.[6]

At least two tribes used gaming revenues to invest in cultural needs. Pojoaque Pueblo had lost significant aspects of its spiri-tual and cultural heritage, including its sacred societies and kiva. Gaming revenues enabled the pueblo to build a new kiva, the spiritual ceremonial center of all Pueblo people.[7] In another example of what might seem an ironic use of the fruits of an activity often considered immoral, the Taos Pueblo Tribal Council voted to expand its small casino specifically for the purpose of using the revenues to purchase a piece of property to act as a buffer to protect the pueblo's sacred Blue Lake.[8] The loss of gaming revenue would in all probability lead to the pueblo losing the land and its subsequent development for tourism by non-Indians.

THE NEW MEXICO SUPREME COURT RULES: ACT 1

Only four months after the compacts were signed the future of Indian gaming in New Mexico was once again a controversial issue. In July the state supreme court handed down its decision in *New Mexico ex rel. Clark v. Johnson*,[9] the lawsuit filed by gaming opponents after the compacts were signed. In a decision that had as much importance for the office of the governor as for Indian gaming, the court unanimously held that Governor Johnson had exceeded his constitutional authority in negotiating and signing the gaming compacts had violated the principle of separation of powers by performing a legislative function.[10] Without legislative authorization, the court said, Johnson had not only signed compacts he was not authorized to sign but also had in effect legalized certain types of for-profit gaming not permitted under New Mexico law.

> We have no doubt that the compact and agreement authorizes more forms of gaming than New Mexico law permits under any set of circumstances. . . . The legislature of this State has unequivocally expressed a public policy against unrestricted gaming, and the Governor has taken a course contrary to that expressed policy. . . . Further, even if our laws allowed under some circumstances what the compact terms "casino-style" gaming, we conclude that the Governor of New Mexico negotiated and executed a tribal-state compact that exceeded his authority as chief executive.[11]

The court rejected Johnson's contention that the state's Joint Powers Agreement Act[12] and Mutual Aid Act[13] gave him the requisite authority to negotiate the gaming compacts. Furthermore, the court held that Johnson's argument that the IGRA was controlling was "inconsistent with core principles of federalism." It noted that Congress could have legalized all forms of gaming on Indian lands but, in passing the IGRA, had chosen not to do so. Moreover, the court said it did not "agree that Congress, in enacting the IGRA, sought to invest state governors with powers in excess of those that the governors possess under state law." Finally, the court prohibited "all actions to enforce, implement, or enable any and all of the compacts and revenue-sharing agreements."[14]

Two weeks later the court issued an amended order and stay of execution, giving additional force to its earlier holding. It declared "that the compacts executed by the Governor are without legal effect and that no gaming compacts exist between the Tribes and Pueblos and the State of new Mexico. Thus New Mexico has not entered into any gaming compact that either the Governor or any other state officer may implement."[15]

While the legality of gaming was not a direct issue before the state supreme court in *Clark,* the justices nevertheless made it clear that they narrowly interpreted New Mexico's gambling statutes. They clearly viewed the state gaming law as prohibitory and criminal rather than permissive and regulatory. They drew a sharp line between what was permitted under the Permissive Lottery Law[16] and forms of "for-profit gambling." Justice Pamela B. Minzer wrote that "New Mexico has expressed a strong public policy against for-profit gambling by criminalizing all such gambling with the exception of licensed pari-mutuel horse racing."[17] For those who could see into the future, these words would send a clear signal that the court was not finished with the issue of gambling in the state.

The broader political implications of the decision were as significant as the narrower issue of gaming. In a system of government generally acknowledged as having an already weak chief executive,[18] the further limitations imposed on the governor were significant. As one observer noted, New Mexico's governors would now be limited to their appointive and line item veto powers.[19] *Clark* also began to raise concerns among some that the court's decision was politically motivated. A unanimous decision by a Democratic court on a question involving a Republican governor who had defeated the incumbent Democrat with the assistance of Indian tribes seemed not to be coincidental. This feeling would intensify with a decision handed down by the court later in the year.

The reaction to the decision and the amended order by Indian and non-Indian officials was swift. Tribal leaders argued that the compacts were valid because they had been approved by the secretary of the interior in conformity with the IGRA. They therefore would continue to operate their casinos consistent with the compacts.[20] Chaves said, "I can tell you that our position is that the compacts have been approved in accordance with federal law and the Indian Gaming Regulatory Act."[21] And Governor Johnson also continued to hold the position that the compacts were valid.[22] New Mexico's attorney general, Tom Udall, however, said that he believed the compacts were invalid.[23]

To further complicate matters for the state, in accordance with the compacts' revenue-sharing agreement, Sandia Pueblo sent a check for $290,839 to the New Mexico Treasurer's Office.[24] By the second week of August the tribes had forwarded nearly $900,000 to the state. Treasurer Michael Montoya accepted the money but was criticized for doing so by Udall.[25] Montoya soon thereafter decided to return the money to the tribes, although he did not do so until May 1996.[26]

U.S. Attorney John Kelly's response to *Clark* provided further evidence of the wide discretionary authority of his office and the personal nature of that authority.[27] During the same period that the U.S. Attorney for the Northern District of Oklahoma was preparing to act against a tribe in his jurisdiction, Kelly resisted mounting pressure to move against New Mexico's Indian casinos. Increasingly, in the weeks following *Clark*, Kelly was criticized by state legislators, antigaming advocates, and the press for not closing the casinos.

While acknowledging the significance of the state supreme court's ruling, Kelly urged the state's elected officials to quickly resolve the issue in a special session of the legislature. He said that any action by the U.S. Justice Department would be "inappropriate and premature."[28] "We intend, at least for the near term," he said, "to defer to what I hope will be fruitful state/tribal efforts to resolve, locally, the issues raised by the New Mexico Supreme Court."[29] Kelly also held separate meetings with Governor Johnson and the legislative leadership to discuss the growing controversy.

While Kelly advocated a political solution to the Indian gaming crisis, the state's top elected officials took significantly different positions that reflected their own responsibilities. Although Johnson first stood adamantly behind the compacts as negotiated, he soon indicated a willingness to renegotiate the details, a prospect immediately rejected by Frank Chaves.[30] In early August Johnson wavered even more, suggesting that Laguna and Santo Domingo pueblos and the legislature negotiate the compacts requested by the two tribes. These compacts, Johnson said, could then replace the ones he had negotiated with the fourteen other tribes.[31]

House Speaker Raymond Sanchez's role was potentially the most crucial if a political resolution was to be achieved. The Albuquerque Democrat had held meetings with the tribes during the legislative session on the compacts. After the state supreme court decided *Clark,* he announced his willingness to talk with Johnson about resolving the issue.

The tribes continued to press their position that the compacts were valid as negotiated. In "An Open Letter to Governor Gary Johnson from 11 People Affected by Indian Gaming," published in the *Albuquerque Journal* on August 13, 1995, tribal leaders thanked the governor for his past support and urged him to hold the line.

> [We express our] gratitude, not so much for keeping your word, for in a simpler world a man keeping his word would not be exceptional, it would be expected. Rather, our gratitude is for your courage and for all your efforts to bring the state and tribal governments together in mutual respect for the benefit of all people. You are one of the few who understand the contributions made to this state by Indian people, Indian culture, and Indian owned natural resources. . . . Take heart, Gary Johnson. Do not lose your honesty in a time of dishonesty. Do not fall victim to cynical and opportunistic politics. Remain resolute in your belief that great nations, like great men, should keep their word.

THE NEW MEXICO SUPREME COURT
RULES: ACT 2

With the January 1996 legislative session nearing and a political solution apparently no closer, the state supreme court handed down another decision on November 29 that not only raised the stakes for those already involved in the controversy but also expanded the scope of conflict to include a whole new set of interests. Overturning the 1994 appeals court decision in *Infinity Group, Inc. v. Manzagol,* the court found the "Power Bingo" computer game to be an illegal "gambling device" under New Mexico law.[32] The court surveyed federal and state gaming statutes and concluded that only an express statutory authorization had ever permitted electronic gaming devices.[33] The court noted that New Mexico's legislature had never enacted such a statute.

The unanimous decision written by Justice Richard E. Ransom reaffirmed the court's view that New Mexico has a "strong public policy against gambling" and declared that, "with limited exceptions, gambling is a crime in New Mexico."[34] Asserting that only the legislature can legalize forms of gambling, the court concluded, "It is for the people acting through their duly elected representative, and not for this Court, to effect any change in the public policy against gambling."[35]

The impact of *Citation Bingo* was even more profound than that of *Clark.* Not only was Indian gaming in question; the compacts had specifically tied tribal gaming to those forms legal in the state. The court's finding that "Las Vegas Night gambling" was not legal under the Bingo and Raffle Act also meant that all of the fraternal, veterans', and charitable organizations that operated video gaming devices were now in violation of state law. On December 4 the state Regulation and Licensing Department notified nonprofit organizations that electronic gaming machines were illegal. Within two days of this notification state agents began conducting raids to assure compliance with the law.[36]

KELLY SHOWS HIS HAND AND
THEN DEALS

In the six weeks following the state supreme court's latest decision, Kelly escalated the threat to the tribes and then stepped back from direct confrontation with them. He first responded by pointing out that the ruling in *Citation Bingo* overturned the 1994 *Infinity* decision that had been interpreted as the "judicial authorization for putting slots and other electronic gambling devices in Indian casinos." He went on to say, "This is the kind of decision that prosecutors and policy-makers alike will applaud, because it takes the guesswork out of interpreting state law."[37] Kelly also said that he was going to consult with the Justice Department on how to proceed. In a December 8 meeting requested by the tribes, Kelly asked tribal leaders to voluntarily close the casinos. For their part, the tribes made it clear that they would keep the casinos open and operating.[38]

Less than a week after his meeting with tribal leaders, Kelly finally acted to end Class III Indian gaming in New Mexico. On December 14 he faxed letters to each of the leaders of the ten casino tribes informing them that they must cease operations by January 15 or he would initiate forfeiture proceedings in federal court that would result in the government taking possession of the tribes' gaming equipment. He repeated his assurance, made at the meeting with the leaders the previous week, that he did not intend to physically seize the machines by "calling law enforcement to the reservations." He said that he was basing his actions on the *Citation Bingo* case, "whose reaffirmation of the scope and purpose of the state's gambling laws has far-reaching implications for the future of Indian gaming in New Mexico."[39] And in a press release the same day he anounced, "The leaders of the New Mexico tribes are among this state's most law-abiding citizens. I doubt very seriously that the tribes will do anything other than comply with this request."[40]

Kelly was also clearly looking at the political climate in the state. The legislature was to go back into session on January 16, at which time it would take up the matter of Indian gaming.

Because there was no consensus on the gaming issue, "either within the Legislature or as between the Legislature and the Governor," he rejected the suggestion that the casinos remain open during the duration of the session. The tribes were given until December 22 to respond to his ultimatum.[41]

According to one tribal attorney, the response of tribal leaders was "harsh and not the least conciliatory."[42] In a December 22 letter, Acoma Pueblo governor Ron Shutiva informed Kelly that the tribe's casino would remain open, asserting that the state supreme court's ruling "does not affect Acoma Pueblo's rights under the Compact" it had signed with Johnson. "Problems with the Gaming Compacts arise from the State side," wrote Shutiva. "The Governor's authority and state approval process are not among things that Acoma Pueblo controls."[43] Isleta Pueblo governor Alvino Lucero responded,

> Our Pueblo has acted conscientiously and honestly at all times. . . . Congress could not have intended for tribes to enter into compacts for gaming which was permitted by the state, for tribes relying on those compacts to establish and expand gaming operations, or moreover to obligate themselves to expend future monies truly investing for the future of their people, only to have the compacting state change its mind and try to back out of the compact. It could not have been the intent of Congress to permit states through either treachery or legal trickery to reach this result.[44]

By January 3 all but two of the tribes had replied in writing to Kelly's letter; none had agreed to close their casino. That same day the nine gaming pueblos—Santa Ana, San Juan, Tesuque, Acoma, Sandia, Isleta, Pojoaque, San Felipe, and Taos—filed a motion in federal court for an injunction against Kelly, Secretary of the Interior Bruce Babbitt, and Attorney General Janet Reno to prevent them from interfering with their gaming operations. By including both Babbitt and Reno in the action, tribal attorneys hoped to demonstrate the apparent interagency conflict: a representative of the Justice Department was pursuing the tribes for an activity officially approved by the Department of the Interior.

As the legislature began its January session and as the tribes escalated their campaign for compact ratification, Kelly and tribal leaders signaled their willingness to step back from an increasingly bitter direct confrontation. Anti-Kelly sentiment had been growing among Indians since his December 14 letter, and tensions were generally growing across New Mexico Indian Country. The threats by Viarrial and Lucero to close the highways that ran through their pueblos got a great deal of attention, not only in the state but also nationwide, and caused state law enforcement personnel to begin planning for that eventuality.[45] Governor Viarrial told CNN, "We're prepared to die or go to prison in order to save that valuable way of making a living for our people."[46]

As a result of talks between Kelly and tribal representatives, a stipulation was presented to Federal District Court Judge Martha Vasquez. Each side agreed to halt further proceedings against the other and seek an expedited court decision on the legality of the tribes' casinos. Kelly agreed not to proceed with forfeiture actions against the casinos, and the tribes agreed to comply with the ultimate decision of the court and to close the casinos if the court found "that the tribal casinos are operating in violation of federal law." The tribes also agreed to "refrain from taking any and all action to close public highways and thoroughfares crossing Indian land in New Mexico, or otherwise interfering with the public's right to travel . . . [and] renounce the use of force or violence in the pursuit of their goal of keeping the casinos open and agree to take no action that would otherwise violate applicable state or federal law."[47]

After receiving editorial and public praise for his December ultimatum to the tribes, Kelly was severely criticized for entering into the stipulation. A January 21, 1996, editorial in the *Albuquerque Journal* charged that he had given in to threats of violence.[48] Guy Clark and state representatives Max Coll and George Buffett, the plaintiffs in *Clark*, asked the federal court to allow them to intervene in the case.

Kelly responded to the criticism in a column in the *Albuquerque Journal* on January 23. He reasserted his opinion that the tribal casinos were illegal and argued that his ultimate goal of closing the casinos would still be accomplished but without having to send U.S. marshals to seize the gaming machines. "The real story this week," he wrote, "is about 'conflict defused.'"[49]

THE TRIBES RAISE THE ANTE

In the aftermath of their success in achieving signed compacts, the tribes' unified political activity had subsided. However, following the second state supreme court decision, Kelly's intervention, and the approach of the legislative session, the tribes began a well-funded and highly coordinated campaign to protect their interests. Directed at both public officials and the general public, the tribes' campaign involved both inside and outside strategies. Rex Hackler, the Bernalillo campaign consultant recruited by Kevin Gover in the waning days of the 1995 legislative session, was brought in to coordinate the effort. Odis Echols, whom Hackler described to me as the "lord god king of all lobbyists," was again the ultimate insider. Walking the halls of the Roundhouse and buttonholing legislators and other lobbyists, Echols attempted to protect and advance the interests of the fourteen sovereigns for which he was working.

As the 1996 thirty-day legislative session opened, the tribes began executing what Echols and Hackler termed a "three-tier" lobbying effort.[50] The first tier consisted of Echols and his assistants working the legislative process inside the Roundhouse. The second tier consisted of the public relations campaign and the casino employees who contacted their legislators. The final tier was composed of tribal leaders and attorneys. A budget of more than half a million dollars supported the combined effort. Echols called this "the largest single lobbying effort" in the thirty legislative sessions he had worked, as a senator and as a lobbyist.[51] The strategic goal included providing an environment in which it would be easier for legislators to support the tribes and vote to ratify the compacts.[52]

Coordinated by Hackler out of a suite in the Hotel Santa Fe, which is owned by Picuris Pueblo, the tribes conducted what in many respects resembled any political campaign. Hackler's desk was a large table in what was normally a bedroom but that had been converted into the "war room." The telephone was rarely silent. Over the doorway leading into this room hung a red, white, and blue hand-lettered sign proclaiming "Warriors Only." On top of a television set usually tuned to CNN was a box labeled "Lobbying Forms." Hanging on the wall behind the television were five full-page ads that had recently appeared in the state's major newspapers. Leaning next to the dresser were large color photographs exhibited at a state senate hearing to illustrate the importance of Indian gaming to New Mexico tribes. Assisting Hackler were tribal members and casino workers on loan to the campaign. As one person would leave for the Roundhouse, another would come in for her marching orders. This was the command center for a new dimension in American politics: the sophisticated, highly coordinated, well-financed campaign by New Mexico Indian tribes to win the hearts, minds, and votes of the state's electorate and legislators. Their message was simple and direct: ratify the compacts.

This message was most visible in the media, in public rallies, and in the work done at the casinos themselves. The tribes used their usual casino advertising budgets to buy airtime to push support for Indian gaming.[53] The thrust of the messages was threefold: no more broken treaties; Indian gaming is working for New Mexico; don't let the feds decide this question for New Mexicans. Both television and radio ads urged those who heard them to contact the legislature. Clearly, the ads offered the public a variety of reasons to support the tribes. An argument that simultaneously appealed to morality, economic self-interest, and a mistrust of the federal government presumably would reach many, if not most, New Mexicans.

The first rally, held the day before the opening of the legislative session, took place on a brilliant January New Mexico

morning at Isleta Pueblo along Interstate 25, fifteen minutes
south of downtown Albuquerque. Supporters of Indian gaming
begin to gather early at the Isleta Gaming Palace. As some
headed toward the highway with their support Indian gaming
signs, others began to line up in front of the refreshment tent,
to join others seeking to register to vote in a tent erected for
that purpose, or simply grabbed a good seat in front of the large
canopy-covered stage to await the day's events. As the crowd
grew, the casino parking lot filled to capacity and people began
to park their cars along the interstate. By the time the rally was
under way, parked cars lined I-25 in front of the pueblo's
gaming facility for nearly a mile in both directions. Albuquerque and Bernalillo County police, the Highway Patrol, and
Isleta Pueblo police parked in the median with emergency
lights flashing, attempting to keep through-traffic flowing and
pedestrians safe in their journey across the highway and up the
hill to the rally.

As rally attendees passed the moored bright yellow Isleta
Gaming Palace hot air balloon, they could hear the eclectic
selection of recorded music coming from the speakers near the
stage: a little country, some classic rock, and a smattering of
Dakota Sioux folk singer Floyd Westerman. An interview with
a former governor of Isleta Pueblo was conducted amid the
merging sounds of Westerman's "Custer Died for Your Sins"
and the drums and chants of singers from Laguna Pueblo
preparing for their performances later in the day. Five thousand New Mexicans gathered at the part revival meeting, part
old-time political rally.

Casino employees were bussed to Isleta. Most wore T-shirts
and buttons printed by their employers urging support for
Indian gaming. Hand-painted signs with slogans about gaming,
voting, and sending messages to elected officials were carried
by gaming supporters of all ages and ethnicities. Three recur-
ring themes were "Save our jobs," "We will remember in
November," and "No more broken treaties."

Among the speakers were many elected pueblo officials,
some of whom renewed talk of road blockades and raised the

possibility of closing the pueblos to outsiders. Several women casino employees recounted their experiences of moving off the welfare rolls into productive, secure employment. To demonstrate the national significance of what was occurring in New Mexico, Ron Allen, National Congress of American Indians executive director, and Rick Hill, National Indian Gaming Association chair, appeared and assured the tribes of their organizations' support and the support of tribes nationwide.

A second rally was held two weeks later at the Roundhouse. Despite a bitter snowstorm late the previous night, more than three hundred people gathered in front of the Capitol, a building designed to resemble the Zia Pueblo sun symbol. Twelve busloads of people from around the state, including four or five from the Navajo Nation, had to cancel because of road conditions.[54] As at the Isleta rally, tribal leaders and casino employees emphasized the importance of ratifying the compacts. National support was again demonstrated by the presence of a representative of the Oneida Nation of Wisconsin and Tim Wapato, executive director of the National Indian Gaming Association. There was a significant change in the tone of this rally, however. The confrontational language of Isleta was muted and speakers representing non-Indian gaming interests took the podium. Among the latter were representatives of the fraternal and veterans' organizations whose fund-raising gaming had been halted by the court's *Citation Bingo* decision. Also speaking, and appearing somewhat uncomfortable, was a spokesman from the New Mexico Horsemen and Breeders Association.

The visible presence of non-Indian gaming organizations represented a strategic change for the tribes. Unlike the 1995 session, this time the tribes figured that their best chance of success lay in a joint effort with others who had been adversely affected by the state supreme court. This resulted in a piece of legislation Hackler termed the "everybody wants something bill."[55] The fraternal, charitable, and veterans' groups, along with the racetracks and resorts, sought to be included in whatever form of legalized gaming emerged from the legislature.

The tribes agreed and participated in the drafting of the omnibus legislation.[56]

The casinos themselves provided a valuable outlet for pro-gaming outreach among New Mexicans. They not only provided manpower for the campaign but also proclaimed their cause to the customers who streamed through casino doors twenty-four hours a day. To motivate this unorganized mass of potential electoral support, the tribes publicized their campaign among the poker tables and slot machines. Cards supporting Indian gaming were distributed, collected, and mailed to legislators by the casinos. Several casinos printed pro-gaming bumper stickers and lapel pins, most of which had some variation on the message "I support Indian gaming and I vote." Several casinos provided business cards with the following message: "The money used to make this purchase at your business today came from employment in the Indian Gaming Industry! Please pass this card to your management. Thank You!"

The public campaign seemed to have an effect. An *Albuquerque Journal* poll published on January 21 reported that by a margin of 60 to 33 percent New Mexicans favored the legislature allowing Indian casino gaming. Support for all kinds of gaming at a variety of venues did not have the same level of support as Indian gaming. By a margin of 47 to 43 percent New Mexicans opposed legalizing video slots at racetracks, and only 22 percent favored video slots in bars and restaurants; however, 53 percent favored legalizing the machines for fraternal and charitable organizations. A strong majority of 56 percent of the respondents also agreed that the legislature should act on gaming during its current session.

While the outside public relations and campaign-style activities were under way, Echols, tribal leaders, and attorneys were active inside the Roundhouse, testifying at hearings, building coalitions, rounding up votes, writing legislation, and working to reach an agreement with the significant legislators. After discussions with Senate President Pro Tem Aragon, the tribes announced they were willing to modify the compacts if the legislature would ratify them. This represented a change in strategy by the tribes and was initiated by them.[57]

Many of the concessions were relatively minor and had been raised in previous discussions with legislators. These included a minimum age of twenty-one, closing four hours a day from Monday to Thursday, and no free food and liquor at the casinos. Other concessions were more substantial, including an increase in the revenue-sharing requirements. The current 3 percent up to $4 million and 5 percent of any amount over that would be changed to 3 percent of the first $4 million, 5 percent of the next $6 million, and 6 percent over revenues of $10 million.[58]

One of the most potentially significant activities by a tribal attorney was the drafting of legislation to rectify the constitutional quandary raised in *Clark*. In an effort to avoid the separation of powers issue used by the court to nullify the compacts negotiated by Johnson, Richard Hughes tackled the procedural question of joint executive-legislative compact approval.[59] Based largely on a similar Kansas statute, Hughes drafted a bill that was the basis for legislation introduced by House Speaker Sanchez (H.B. 703) and Senate President Pro Tem Aragon (S.B. 684).[60] The bills would create a joint House-Senate committee to review compacts negotiated by the governor and recommend to its respective bodies whether approval should be granted. Hughes and Sanchez testified on behalf of H.B. 703 before a combined hearing of several House committees sitting to take gaming-related testimony.[61] Hughes's behind-the-scenes role was not openly noted in the press but was alluded to in a February 11, 1996, *Albuquerque Journal* editorial on the legislation. The editorial observed, "The terms specified in advance in the Sanchez-Aragon bill inure only to the benefit of the Indian side of the negotiations—not a surprising turn of events since the bill reportedly was drafted by a lawyer for one of the gaming tribes."

The fate of this legislation was indicative of the ultimate success of the tribes during the session. Aragon's version passed the Senate, but Sanchez saw his bill killed in the House Judiciary Committee. Similarly, the omnibus gaming bill passed the Senate but was unanimously defeated by voice vote when brought to the floor of the House. The status of gaming in New Mexico was thus the same at the end of the session as it had been since *Clark* and *Citation Bingo*. The only legal gaming in the state was bingo, paper pull tabs, pari-mutuel horse and bicycle racing, and the state lottery, scheduled to begin in April. As far as the state was concerned, the compacts were null and void.

TRIBES, THE STATE, AND PARTISAN POLITICS: CHECKS AND BALANCES OR GRIDLOCK?

The tribes' strategic response to late 1995 and early 1996 threats was in effect an attempt to control the scope of conflict of the gaming controversy. What was remarkable was the ability of the tribes to respond to the shifting fronts of the battle and to continue to adjust to the ever-changing rules of the game. At each step of the process—from the first request for compacts made during Governor Carruthers's administration to the federal lawsuit against Governor King to the gubernatorial campaign to the signing of the compacts to lobbying the legislature—the tribes had mobilized the appropriate resources to participate at the appropriate level. As time went on, the field of battle continued to change. Each time the tribes appeared victorious in one arena of the political or legal system another arena nullified the victory.

The shifting arenas of battle led Frank Chaves in January 1996 to ask the Senate Select Committee on Gaming, "Who is the State?" Two fundamental problems facing the tribes made Chaves's question significant. First, in a separated system of shared powers among independent branches, checks and balances not only prevent the concentration of power. They also mean that a policy question is not finalized until the three branches have at least resolved the process of policy formulation. For groups with a policy interest, such as Indian tribes, this system ensures a high probability that the scope and arenas of conflict will shift. New Mexico tribes were thus caught in a classic institutional conflict over the legitimate constitutional scope of power of the state's three institutions.

The second reason for the salience of Chaves's question results from the Indian Gaming Regulatory Act itself. Section 2710(3)(A) of the act provides as follows:

> Any Indian tribe having jurisdiction over the Indian lands upon which a Class III gaming activity is being conducted, or is to be conducted, shall request the State in which such lands are located to enter into negotiations for the purpose of entering into a Tribal-State compact governing the conduct of gaming activities. Upon receiving such a request, the state shall negotiate with the Indian tribe in good faith to enter into such a compact.

Nowhere does the IGRA define "the state," or, specifically, to which state official the Indian tribe must make its request. This ambiguity is a tacit recognition of federalism and the right of a state government to determine its own constitutional and administrative procedures. For Indian tribes wanting to negotiate Class III compacts with "the state," this ambiguity can stall and even prevent the expansion of gaming options. New Mexico tribes had faced this dilemma when they first wanted to begin such negotiations in 1988 and decided to make the request to the Office of Indian Affairs. Governor Carruthers then removed the Office of Indian Affairs from the process and conducted the negotiations between his staff and the tribes. Then, once the compacts had been negotiated, signed by a subsequent governor, and approved by the Secretary of the Interior, the tribes were told that the gaming allowed as a result of the process was illegal.[62]

Consequently, as they had in the past, the tribes engaged in a simultaneous multifront battle: in the federal court, in the Roundhouse, and among the general public. The tribes were defending their sovereignty and the fruits of that sovereignty—the economic opportunities made possible by the casinos.

Protecting that status again required them to bring to bear all of the options available to them.

Importantly, losing this battle could limit their options in the future. Being prohibited from operating casinos would not only be a diminishment of their self-governing powers; it would also reduce the financial resources that had helped to make the tribes a significant actor in New Mexico politics. Although they would still have the opportunity to make political endorsements and register tribal members to vote, the tribes would lose the ability to mount the kind of campaigns that had given them influence in the gubernatorial race and allowed them to appeal directly to the public during the 1996 legislative session. The greater meaning of a loss is that, as Office of Indian Affairs executive director Regis Pecos told me in an interview, an infringement in one area of sovereignty threatens all other areas of sovereignty. Without gaming resources the tribes' fight to protect and expand all aspects of their sovereignty would be curtailed.

INSIDE LOBBYING: THE EXECUTIVE BRANCH

For the first time in nearly a decade the tribes did not have to worry about convincing the state's chief executive to support them. But Johnson's support was largely verbal and not substantive. Although he publicly continued to support Indian gaming, the governor did little before or during the session to advance the issue in the legislature.[63] He did make a strong appeal in his State of the State Address, but it was at the end of the speech and was not included in the bound version distributed to the public. The reaction to the address indicated the apparent weakness of Johnson's influence in the legislature. The title of the January 17 editorial in the *New Mexican* summed it up: "The Sound of No Hands Clapping." Notwithstanding his public support for Indian gaming, Johnson did not present his own legislation for compact approval until the second week of the session. House Majority Leader Michael Olguin (D-Socorro) blamed the governor for the legislature's failure to ratify the compacts, saying, "I believe he turned his back on the Native

Americans."[64] But whether he could have delivered Republican votes is questionable, because the Senate minority leader opposed any legislative action on gaming. Olguin contended that gaming was an issue that "went way beyond party, and the governor did not coach his Republican legislators as to what would be best for everyone."[65]

INSIDE LOBBYING: THE COURTS

While the political battle was being fought in the legislature and in the court of public opinion, the tribes were fighting in the court of law. Attempting to seize the initiative from Kelly, the tribes countersued in federal court. This led to the January stipulation that set the stage for what could be the ultimate determination of the legality of tribal casino gaming in New Mexico. As tribes could not afford to rely on the political arena alone, they took this step while still working for a legislative solution.

INSIDE LOBBYING: THE LEGISLATIVE BRANCH

Gaming dominated the thirty-day legislative session; the intricacies and conflicting interests seemed at times to overwhelm the legislature. House Majority Leader Olguin wrote in the *Albuquerque Journal* that gaming was "by far the most complicated and controversial issue ever to be thrust upon this Legislature."[66] In the end its social, political, and economic ramifications seem to have paralyzed legislators and prevented any action on the compacts.

The tribes were inside players within the Roundhouse. Not only did tribal leaders, attorneys, and casino employees testify at legislative hearings, individual legislators were lobbied by both elites and nonelites. Casino employees personally contacted their legislators. At the same time, according to Echols's strategy, tribal leaders and attorneys worked behind the scenes to negotiate a solution, round up votes, form coalitions, and draft legislation. They took the offensive and attempted to define the issue on their terms. The tribes worked with whomever could further their interests, but their efforts ultimately fell short. As Hackler said after the session had ended, the tribes "did everything right and still got beat."[67]

There were at least three reasons for the legislature's failure to ratify the compacts. First, partisan politics was a significant dynamic in the battle for Indian gaming and the tribes found their interests being used as a pawn in party positioning. During the administration of Governor King the Democrat-controlled legislature passed legislation giving the governor power to negotiate gaming compacts; King vetoed the bill. Now that there was a Republican who supported Indian gaming and who in turn had been supported by the tribes, the Democratic-controlled leadership balked at approving the compacts that had been negotiated by a Republican. "The shifting political winds" noted Sen. Tsosie, "catches the tribes in a crossfire."[68]

The partisan battles went beyond the narrower issue of Indian gaming. Budgetary differences between the governor and the Democratic majority were deep. The Senate also refused to confirm several of the governor's appointees to state office. And there were fundamental differences over the scope of state government itself. As the *New Mexican* reporter Barry Massey wrote following adjournment, "Whether the issue was the budget, prisons or nominations, the outcome in the Legislature usually hinged on a philosophical or partisan battle between the Democrats who control the House and Senate and the conservative Republican occupying the governorship." House Minority Whip Kip Nicely (R-Albuquerque) told Massey, "Really, the underlying theme of this whole session has been: Who is in charge of this place?"[69]

Second, the Democratic leadership of the legislature was unable to develop a consensus on gaming and was thus unable to deliver a bill to the governor. The "something for everyone" bill hammered out by Aragon and pro-gaming lobbyists passed the Senate but was quickly killed in the House. Sanchez was not able to build a consensus for any gaming legislation, including his bill to create a process for compact approval. His inability to free that legislation from committee was a surprise and demonstrated the risk of supporting any gaming legislation in the House, even in light of the polls showing overwhelming approval for Indian gaming.

While some legislators suggested that the significant divisions on gaming among the public killed its chances,[70] there is a third and even more intriguing possibility for the legislature's failure to act. Gover argues that what was at stake in the battle over Indian gaming was a redistribution of political and economic power in the state, a battle that the entrenched establishment was determined to win.[71] He believes this explains the opposition of such groups as the Santa Fe County Chamber of Commerce, the Albuquerque Business Alliance, and most of the Republican party. Pecos argues that it is the money generated by Indian gaming that led to the "heightened confrontation."[72] In a statement that was daringly candid, antigaming attorney Victor Marshall told the *Los Angeles Times,* "Politically, non-Indians are not going to allow Indians to make hundreds of millions of dollars in profits without getting a piece of the action—either everybody does it or nobody does it."[73] Hackler believes "this whole thing is not about gaming" but about "money and power."[74]

What is curious is that whereas the sources of Indian support were quite apparent, the opposition was much more amorphous. Four names were consistently linked to efforts to kill Indian gaming: Max Coll, George D. Buffett, Guy Clark, and Victor R. Marshall. The first three were the plaintiffs in *Clark,* and Marshall was their attorney. Clark, a dentist from Corrales, was the leader of the New Mexico Coalition Against Gambling, an apparently understaffed and underfunded organization. Representative Coll, a Santa Fe Democrat, was chairman of the House Appropriations and Finance Committee and Representative Buffett was a senior Republican member of the same committee.

Marshall, an Albuquerque attorney, was involved in other efforts to legally end gaming in the state. First, he filed an amicus curiae brief for Clark, Coll, and Buffett in the *Citation Bingo* case. Second, he filed suit against several banking institutions on behalf of a group of people alleging that they had suffered losses at Indian casinos. The suit was filed under a Civil War era

New Mexico antigambling statute.[75] Third, he sent a letter to the Financial Institutions Division, the state banking regulator, asking it to revoke approval of automatic teller machines (ATMs) at Indian casinos, since, he contended, the casinos were illegal.[76] The use of ATMs to withdraw welfare payments at Indian casinos had become a public issue, one that the tribes indicated they were willing to address.

Clark himself continued his public opposition to gaming, which he claimed was based on a moral objection to the activity, as was much of the opposition among the general public.[77] He was a frequent visitor to the Roundhouse, including testifying before legislative committees. Clark also filed a complaint with the Federal Communications Commission over the airing of casino advertisements and pro-compact commercials paid for by the casinos.[78]

Whatever the sources of opposition, tribes had to deal with their political consequences. As Rosenthal has noted, "Any lobbyist who ignores the politics of the state and of the legislature cannot possibly succeed at the job. Politics drives the process."[79] Because of traditional political inclinations as well as the locus of legislative power, tribal leaders focused on members of the Democratic party, particularly Aragon and Sanchez. Both powerful leaders were inclined to support the tribes, but Sanchez was careful not to jeopardize his obvious ambition to run for governor. Personality politics emerged when Aragon and the tribes agreed to certain concessions in the compacts and Sanchez held back, notwithstanding his own extensive negotiations with tribal leaders over the past year.[80]

Protecting their traditional alliance with the Democratic party was made difficult by tribal support for Republican Gary Johnson in his 1994 race. Gover and others, including pueblo governors, worked to maintain the relationships with party leaders. For example, Pojoaque governor Viarrial attended a $10,000-a-plate party fund-raiser in Washington, D.C., and sat at Vice President Al Gore's table. Tribes bought ten of the forty tables at the Democratic party fund-raiser at the opening of the 1996 New Mexico legislative session.

One important factor in the legislative effort to get the compacts ratified was the unity of the six Indian legislators, two senators and four representatives, all Democrats. Tsosie, the point man for Indian gaming in the Senate, noted that having a bloc of legislators united on the issue was an important factor in furthering the tribes' position.[81] Representative James Roger Madalena (D-Jemez Pueblo) was point man in the House.

There is circumstantial evidence that Indian gaming politics had a role in defeating efforts to override some of Governor Johnson's vetoes left over from the 1995 legislative session. Among that evidence is the fact that Senator Tsosie was only one of two Democrats to vote against override of several pieces of legislation.[82] Tsosie worked closely with the tribal leaders and attorneys on legislative strategy.

The role of tribal attorneys in the lobbying process disproves Rosenthal's contention that "legal work and lobbying generally do not overlap."[83] The work of Gover, Hughes, and other lawyers was crucial to the tribes' lobbying strategy. From strategic planning to bill drafting, their work was indispensable.

OUTSIDE LOBBYING: APPEALING TO THE PUBLIC

The tribes' outside campaign in the media paralleled the inside effort. The television, radio, and newspaper ads were designed to define the issue and give New Mexicans, and ultimately legislators, a reason for supporting compact ratification. As noted, the appeals to morality, self-interest, and anti-Washington feelings were expected to persuade a wide segment of the population and apparently did so. The success of the public relations campaign was due to strategic planning, flawless execution, and the availability of resources to carry it out.

Rosenthal writes that "the objective of a grass-roots campaign is to prove to legislators that their constituents are concerned about a particular issue."[84] The tribes' campaign was designed to accomplish that end. As Rosenthal also notes, an outside lobbying effort "cannot be independent of the inside one."[85] The inside and outside efforts of the tribes were tightly linked;

Echols, the tribes' deep inside man, had veto power over the outside publicity campaign.

THE U.S. ATTORNEY

John Kelly continued to demonstrate the crucial role that a U.S. Attorney can play in public policy. Eisenstein has observed that the "aggressiveness and interpersonal skills, and the conception of the position's prerogatives . . . also determine the impact" of the U.S. Attorney.[86] Although he resisted public pressure to move against the Indian casinos after *Clark*, following *Citation Bingo* Kelly could not ignore the changed legal and political environment. He acted only after the questions surrounding the legality of the compacts became extraordinarily muddled. When he issued his ultimatum in December, he apparently was weighing the political considerations. Earlier in the summer he had suggested that a special session of the legislature be called to clear up the legality of the compacts; the timing of the ultimatum's deadline seemed to have been made with similar political considerations. He set the deadline one day before the legislative session was to open, apparently believing that this would somehow induce a political settlement, when in fact it may have provided additional reasons for some legislators to strike a wait-and-see pose.

His willingness to continue to negotiate with the tribes in an attempt to defuse the situation is notable, especially when compared to what took place in Oklahoma in September (see chap. 5). As Kelly noted in his *Albuquerque Journal* article, he did not want to have to send armed U.S. marshals to the reservations to confiscate the allegedly illegal machines. Eisenstein has posited that in exercising discretion, U.S. Attorneys "represent their locality, and the interests and policy preferences of important segments of the local community sometimes conflict sharply with those of the national administration."[87]

But Kelly had a broader problem than his New Mexico critics and their opposition to Indian gaming. For a considerable time after the state supreme court reshaped the realm of legal gaming, Kelly had no clear indication from Washington what the administration's position was. There was in fact evidence of a lack of coherent policy. While the Interior Department had approved the compacts prior to *Clark* and *Citation Bingo*, the Justice Department would not indicate a clear opinion on their continued legality. By mid-December, however, Kelly apparently had received at least a tacit go-ahead from the Justice Department to move against the casinos.[88] A special committee on Indian gaming within the Justice Department is supposed to review any action contemplated by U.S. Attorneys on the issue. The committee deferred to Kelly's decision.[89]

An interesting aspect of Kelly's role is his public visibility. Kelly was not only the subject of alternating newspaper attacks and praise, the tribes themselves contributed to making him a visible player in the gaming controversy. In a humorous but pointed incident, Kelly's office telephone lines were jammed after the tribes ran a number of radio ads asking listeners to contact the U.S. Attorney's office to let him know their views. This occurred after the December meeting between tribes and Kelly and before Kelly sent his ultimatum. Because tribal leaders emerged from the meeting believing that Kelly would take no immediate action, they attempted to cancel the airtime they had bought. For whatever reason, they were not able to stop all of the ads, resulting in the lines being tied up. After that, callers to the U.S. Attorney's office who had a question about Indian gaming were immediately transferred to a recorded message inviting them to offer their views.

Kelly was also one of the significant targets of speakers and signs at the Isleta rally. Speaker after speaker derisively referred to the U.S. Attorney, some comparing him to General Custer. One hand-lettered sign contained Kelly's name inside a circle with a diagonal arrow drawn through it.

INTERTRIBAL UNITY

Intertribal unity continued to be the crucial element in the tribes' efforts. Although there were disagreements among the pueblo governors and Mescalero Apache president Wendell Chino maintained a low public profile, the tribal front appeared to be solid. The threats by Pojoaque governor Viarrial and Isleta governor Lucero to close portions of Route 84-285 and Interstate 25 were not supported by most of the other leaders.[90] Chino, in fact, spoke out directly against such actions.[91] But at crucial moments, such as when the decision was made to enter into the stipulation with Kelly, the pueblo leaders came together behind a unified strategy.[92]

Once again the New Mexico Indian Gaming Association and its co-chairmen were visible in the Roundhouse and in the press. Both Frank Chaves and Ken Paquin testified at legislative hearings, and the association provided data supporting the economic contributions of Indian gaming and the potential harm if the casinos were forced to close. The association was indeed acting increasingly like a nascent political party. Its strategic and tactical efforts were fundamentally no different from those employed by political parties, with the exception of a ballot line. This latter attribute will be replicated, however, if the association or the tribes through the association become more involved in the active support or opposition of candidates for public office. Gover believes that NMIGA is already at least as significant a player in New Mexico politics as state's two major political parties.[93]

The gaming tribes provided the finances necessary to run the campaign, paying for television, radio, and newspaper ads, as well as for other, related expenses.[94] A significant resource available to the campaign was the manpower provided by the casinos. Casino employees were loaned to the "war room" for the duration of the legislative session to provide whatever legwork was needed.

The tribes were not only coordinated in the public relations and lobbying effort. As noted, tribal leaders unified behind the legal strategy that led to the mid-January agreement with U.S. Attorney Kelly.[95] To achieve this unity, the governors who had advocated direct action had to agree to tone down their rhetoric and avoid any activity that could lead to confrontation.

Finally, the public leadership of the Indian effort must be noted. For the most part, tribal leaders presented a united front in public. While Chino criticized the threats to close the highways, he did nothing to interfere with the broad strategic and tactical goals of the other NMIGA tribes. Navajo Nation president Albert Hale spoke to the legislature about the importance of tribal gaming even though his tribe had rejected legalized gaming.[96] Pueblo leaders and NMIGA leaders consistently demonstrated a calm public presence in the face of increasingly difficult political and legal obstacles.

The interethnic effort must also be noted. The non-Indian consultants, such as Hackler and Echols, appeared to have a relationship with the Indian leadership based on trust and confidence. At the level of "campaign workers," Indian and non-Indian casino employees worked together to achieve their common goal. Various participants warmly described the closeness of those who worked long hours in the Hotel Santa Fe war room.

THE FUTURE

The failure of the tribes to convince the legislature to act on Indian gaming in no way alters or diminishes their political status. In fact, in the latter months of 1995 and in early 1996, the tribes demonstrated their flexibility within the political system. New Mexico tribes again demonstrated that their status within that system is fraught with both possibilities and dangers. The possibilities can be seen in their flexibility and in the gaming resources available to them. But the historic fragility of their status and of fleeting tribal resources are also apparent. Because of their ambiguous constitutional and political status, Indian tribes have more ways in which to engage their opponents. As the IGRA has shown, tribes are clearly both within and outside the normal avenues of American politics.

The opportunities for New Mexico tribes to win either a political or a legal victory remain. Although the legislature adjourned without resolving the gaming issues raised by *Clark* and *Citation Bingo,* the tribes' efforts did not end; they only moved to other arenas. With the ultimate legality of the casinos still an unresolved question, the tribes will continue a multi-tiered effort to protect their gaming operations. The matter of the compacts remained in federal court. Whatever decision is eventually reached by Federal Judge Vasquez, the tribes and New Mexico officials faced months of continued uncertainty over the ultimate outcome. For their part, the tribes prepared to once again take their case to the voters. The 1996 legislative elections would provide an opportunity to exert electoral influence through strategic endorsements and financial contributions. Tribal strategists spoke of becoming involved in districts held by legislators—Democrats as well as Republicans—who had actively opposed them during the session.

CHAPTER FIVE

A Clash of Sovereigns,
A Clash of History

The conditions that resulted in gaming compacts between New Mexico tribes and the state are absent in Oklahoma. Public policy, institutional attitudes toward Indians, and the degree of cohesion among tribes are all significantly different in Oklahoma. Similarly, the strategies followed by Oklahoma tribes in pursuit of their gaming rights differed in kind and in intensity from those of New Mexico tribes. The differences in strategic approaches were directly related to (1) Oklahoma's gaming policy and how it is interpreted and implemented, (2) the differing political culture as reflected in non-Indian officials and institutions and their policies and relationships with Indian tribes, and (3) cultural and historical differences among the thirty-nine federally recognized Indian tribes in Oklahoma (see table 9). Because these three factors are critical to understanding the environment in which Oklahoma Indian gaming is set, it is necessary to explore them in some detail.

OKLAHOMA'S INDIAN TRIBES

No other state in the nation has a history as inextricably linked to American Indians as does Oklahoma, Choctaw for "land of

TABLE 9
Indian Tribes in Oklahoma

Absentee Shawnee Tribe	Alabama Quassarte
Apache Tribe	Caddo Tribe
Cherokee Nation	Cheyenne-Arapaho Tribe
Chickasaw Nation	Choctaw Nation
Citizen Band Potawatomi	Comanche Tribe
Delaware Tribe of East Ok.	Delaware Tribe of West Ok.
Eastern Shawnee Tribe	Fort Sill Apache Tribe
Iowa Tribe of Oklahoma	Kaw Tribe of Oklahoma
Kialegee Tribal Town	Kickapoo Tribe
Kiowa Tribe	Miami Tribe
Modoc Tribe	Muscogee (Creek) Nation
Osage Nation	Otoe-Missouria Tribe
Ottawa Tribe	Pawnee Tribe
Peoria Tribe	Ponca Tribe
Quapaw Tribe	Sac and Fox Nation
Seminole Nation	Seneca-Cayuga Tribes
Thlopthlocco Tribal Town	Tonkawa Tribe
Wichita Tribe and Affiliated Tribes	Wyandot Tribe
United Keetoowah Band of Cherokees	

the red people." Nor does any other state have as pervasive an Indian presence.

The 1990 U.S. Census counted 252,420 Indians in Oklahoma, more than in any other state. The Cherokee Nation of Oklahoma is the second-largest tribe in the country. The cultural and political impact of this Indian presence within Oklahoma has been great. "In fact," write David R. Morgan, Robert E. England, and George M. Humphreys in *Oklahoma Politics and Policies,* "relatively speaking, the history of Oklahoma is to a large extent a story of Native Americans, their cultures, and their interactions first with Europeans and later with the United States government."[1] These "interactions" have often been one-sided as Indian ownership of the land and natural resources flowed into non-Indian hands. The existence of Oklahoma as

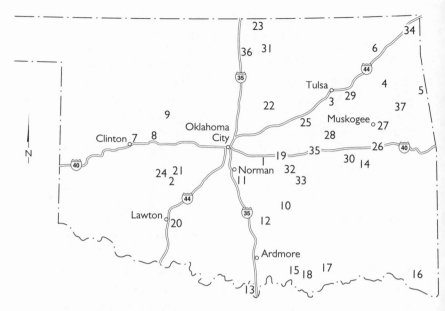

Map 2. Oklahoma Indian Bingo Facilities, October 22, 1998 (Based on infor mation from the National Indian Gaming Commission.)

1. *Absentee-Shawnee Tribe of Oklahoma*
   Thunderbird Entertainment Center
   Norman, Okla.
2. *Apache Tribe of Oklahoma*
   Na-I-Sha Games
   Anadarko, Okla.
3. *Cherokee Nation of Oklahoma*
   Cherokee Nation Bingo Outpost—
   Catoosa
   Tahlequah, Okla.
4. *Cherokee Nation of Oklahoma*
   Cherokee Nation Bingo Outpost—
   Roland
   Tahlequah, Okla.
5. *Cherokee Nation of Oklahoma*
   Cherokee Nation Bingo Outpost—
   Siloam Springs
   Tahlequah, Okla.
6. *Loyal Shawnee Tribe of Oklahoma*
   Loyal Shawnee Bingo
   Vinita, Okla.

7. *Cheyenne and Arapaho Tribes of Oklahoma*
   Clinton High Stakes Bingo
   Concho, Okla.
8. *Cheyenne and Arapaho Tribes of Oklahoma*
   Lucky Star Bingo
   Concho, Okla.
9. *Cheyenne and Arapaho Tribes of Oklahoma*
   Watonga Bingo
   Concho, Okla.
10. *Chickasaw Nation of Oklahoma*
    Ada Gaming Center
    Ada, Okla.
11. *Chickasaw Nation of Oklahoma*
    Goldsby Gaming Center
    Norman, Okla.
12. *Chickasaw Nation of Oklahoma*
    Sulphur Gaming Center/Chickasaw
    Motor Inn
    Sulphur, Okla.
13. *Chickasaw Nation of Oklahoma*
    Touso Ishto Gaming Center
    Thackerville, Okla.

14. *Choctaw Nation of Oklahoma*
Chcotaw Indian Bingo—Arrowhead
Canadian, Okla.

15. *Choctaw Nation of Oklahoma*
Choctaw Indian Bingo—Durant
Durant, Okla.

16. *Choctaw Nation of Oklahoma*
Choctaw Indian Bingo—Idabel
Durant, Okla.

17. *Choctaw Nation of Oklahoma*
Choctaw Indian Bingo—Pocola
Durant, Oklahoma

18. *Choctaw Nation of Oklahoma*
Choctaw Travel Plazas & Smoke Shops
Durant, Okla.

19. *Citizen Band Potawatomi Indians of Oklahoma*
Firelake Entertainment Center
Shawnee, Okla.

20. *Comanche Indian Tribe*
Comahcne Nation Games
Lawton, Okla.

21. *Delaware Tribe of Western Oklahoma*
Gold River Bingo
Anadarko, Okla.

22. *Iowa Tribe of Oklahoma*
Cimarron Bingo Casino
Perkins, Okla.

23. *Kaw Nation of Oklahoma*
Kaw Bingo Enterprise
Kaw City, Okla.

24. *Kiowa Tribe of Oklahoma*
Kiowa Bingo
Carnegio, Okla.

25. *Muscogee (Creek) Nation*
Bristow Indian Community Bingo
Bristow, Okla.

26. *Muscogee (Creek) Nation*
Checotah Indian Community Bingo
Checotah, Okla.

27. *Muscogee (Creek) Nation*
Creek Nation Muskogee Bingo
Muskogee, Okla.

28. *Muscogee (Creek) Nation*
Creek Nation Okmulgee Bingo
Okmulgee, Okla.

29. *Muscogee (Creek) Nation*
Creek Nation Tulsa Bingo
Tulsa, Okla.

30. *Muscogee (Creek) Nation*
Eufaula Indian Community Bingo
Eufaula, Okla.

31. *Ponca Tribe of Oklahoma*
Ponca Tribal Bingo
Ponca City, Okla.

32. *Seminole Nation of Oklahoma*
Seminole Nation Bingo
Seminole, Okla.

33. *Seminole Nation of Oklahoma*
Wewoka Trading Post
Wewoka, Okla.

34. *Seneca-Cayuga Tribe of Oklahoma*
Seneca-Cayuga Gaming Operation
Miami, Okla.

35. *Thlopthlocco Tribal Town*
Thlopthlocco Tribal Bingo
Okemah, Okla.

36. *Tonkawa Tribe of Oklahoma*
Tonkawa Tribal Bingo
Tonkawa, Okla.

37. *United Keetoowah Band of Cherokee Indians*
United Keetoowah Bingo
Tahlequah, Okla.

---

a state resulted not from a mutually agreed on decision by the Indian sovereigns of Indian Territory and the federal government but from unilateral acts on the part of the U.S. government. The circumstances surrounding Oklahoma's birth may in large measure have helped to shape the state's political culture.

According to Daniel Elazar, Oklahoma is "on the border between traditionalistic and individual political culture areas," because it lies "at the intersection between the South and the West," and "the fault line between those two spheres runs right through the heart of the state."[2] Elsewhere Elazar has placed Oklahoma in what he terms "the greater South," that area south of the Ohio and Potomac rivers, west of Lake Michigan, and east of the Mississippi, "plus Missouri, Arkansas, Louisiana, Oklahoma, and Texas."[3]

The geocultural picture of the state is further confused by the classification system of Ronald J. Hrebenar and Clive S. Thomas. In their fifty-state study of interest group politics in the United States, they place Oklahoma in the Midwest. For their purposes, Oklahoma is excluded from the South because it is "not primarily 'southern'" in "social, economic, or political terms."[4]

The cultural center of the state is no less difficult to locate. Morgan, England, and Humphreys write of the "clash between traditional and modern values": "Oklahoma remains a paradox— a state struggling with its sense of identity, a place where the old and new vie for the attention and allegiance of its people. In some ways still backward and traditional; in other ways, quite modern and up-to-date." In discussing the social and economic implications of the state's political culture, they write, "Historical ties to the land and spatial living arrangements carry with them long-lasting social and economic consequences."[5] This is no doubt true of all people but arguably more so for the state's Indian population. The "land and spatial living arrangements" of the Oklahoma Indians are the result of historic political and policy decisions that continue profoundly to affect the state's political culture.

How Indians and non-Indians view the history that produced these contemporary "arrangements" is often dramatically different. Clear evidence of this occurred during the observance of the centenary of the various land runs opening Indian Territory to white settlement. For non-Indian Oklahomans, this was a time to celebrate the proud heritage of brave and noble settlers staking claim to the frontier. For many Indians in the state, those century-old events were a reminder of *their* brave and proud ancestors forcibly removed to the state, promised the land forever, and finally subjected to laws designed to take that land and eviscerate their tribal identity. As Rennard Strickland has noted, "History is an act of remembrance."[6]

Diametrically opposed interpretations of the state's history have existed from the beginning. Angie Debo writes that Oklahoma "had been the slowest of all the states to admit that the liquidation of tribes and of tribal lands to which it owed its existence had not brought all the separated individuals into happy assimilation with the dominant society."[7] Arrell Morgan Gibson has termed Indian Territory "a tribal colonization zone," because before the removal of tribes to Indian Territory, only a handful of the federally recognized tribes in Oklahoma had made use of the future state.[8] The remainder arrived in Oklahoma as a result of forced or voluntary compliance with the national policy of settling all Indians in the trans-Mississippi west in what became known as "Indian Territory."

The most famous removals to Indian Territory are those of the Five Civilized Tribes of the southeastern United States—the Cherokee, Chickasaw, Choctaw, Seminole, and Creek nations. Each experienced a tragic and nation-defining "trail of tears" along which thousands of tribal members fell and died. After arriving in their new homelands, these tribes began to reestablish the cultural and political structures that they had so successfully organized in the East. According to Debo, the Five Civilized Tribes "had a natural genius for politics. Trained through countless generations in the proud democracy of primitive councils, they found their borrowed Anglo-American institutions in perfect harmony with their native development. . . . Few communities have ever equalled these small Indian republics in political skill."[9] These "republics" survived relatively intact until just before statehood.

A handful of members of the Five Civilized Tribes had migrated to Indian Territory more than a decade before the Removal Act of 1830. They had entered a land occupied by, among other transplanted tribes, the Osage, Seneca, Quapaw, and Shawnee. In the years following the Civil War, as the U.S. Army fought the Plains and southwestern tribes in the Indian Wars, more tribes were forced to settle in unfamiliar Indian Territory. The Southern Cheyenne, Kiowa, Apache, Kickapoo, Nez Perce, and Comanche were among the tribes forced to sign treaties ceding their aboriginal lands in trade for a reservation in Indian Territory.

The result of this colonization process was a territory with the most varied Indian population in the nation. Each tribe or group of tribes had its own unique cultural and political characteristics. Kirke Kickingbird notes that "the status and stature of the Five Civilized Tribes in Oklahoma came from their level of political organization [whereas the] wild tribes of the Western Plains derived their influence from force of arms."[10] Even as the western tribes became less warlike and fell more under the sway of government agents, the Five Civilized Tribes, even after the Civil War, continued to assert an independence and political sophistication that they lacked. This difference became a significant factor in how each group of tribes succumbed to the increasing demands for statehood by white land seekers.

When Congress passed the Dawes General Allotment Act in 1887, it exempted the Five Civilized Tribes and the Osage, Miami, Peoria, and Sac and Fox tribes. The lands of each were later allotted by separate congressional action.[11] All other tribes in Indian Territory were allotted under the Dawes Act. The breakup of tribal holdings began the process that led to the opening up of Indian Territory to legal non-Indian settlement and eventually to statehood. A series of laws paved the way for this to take place.

- The Organic Act, passed in 1890, established two separate territories, Oklahoma Territory and Indian Territory, the latter comprising the Five Civilized Tribes, the Cherokee Outlet, the Cherokee Strip, and the tribes of the Quapaw Agency (26 Stat. 81).

- The Curtis Act, passed in 1898, made the civil laws of the Five Civilized Tribes unenforceable in federal courts and abolished tribal courts. A commission was established with the purpose of preparing the rolls of members for each of the Five Civilized Tribes necessary for the allotment of tribal landholdings (30 Stat. 495).
- The Five Tribes Act, passed in 1906, severely restricted the self-governing powers of the affected tribes by, among other provisions, giving the president authority to appoint the tribes' chief executive and requiring presidential approval of all tribal laws (34 Stat. 137).
- The Enabling Act, passed in 1906, provided for the admission of the combined Oklahoma and Indian territories into the Union as one state (34 Stat. 267).

Other laws dealt specifically with the status of the Osage Tribe and its oil and gas holdings and the allotment and restriction of land held by the Five Civilized Tribes. The latter was facilitated by the work of the Dawes Commission and the tribal membership rolls it drew up.

President Theodore Roosevelt proclaimed Oklahoma a state on November 16, 1907, after a constitution had been ratified. The Enabling Act had reserved to the United States the right to make laws affecting the new state's Indians, including "their lands, property, or other rights by treaties, agreements, law, or otherwise, which it would have been competent to make if this law had never been passed."[12] Article 1 of the Oklahoma Constitution disclaims any right or title to Indian lands within the state.

After statehood Oklahoma tribes continued to lose their land, a process speeded up by the discovery of oil throughout the former Indian Territory during the first three decades of the century. The grab for land and the Indians' natural resources produced a group of men, most of them white, known as "grafters." As Debo documents with such passion and detail in *And Still the Waters Run,* these men systematically manipulated the law and individual Indians to procure for themselves great wealth and power, often with the complicity of federal employees. The tragic loss of material wealth paled only to the murder and disappearance of scores of Indians living on desirable land.[13]

The unique history and status of Oklahoma tribes continued to have an impact on policy during the 1930s and the New Deal. Because of the intense lobbying of some assimilationist Indians and the power of the Oklahoma congressional delegation, Oklahoma tribes were exempted from the Indian Reorganization Act (IRA).[14] The chairman of the Senate Committee on Indian Affairs was Oklahoma Democrat Elmer Thomas, a man generally opposed to New Deal programs; the House Indian Affairs Committee was chaired by Oklahoma Democrat Will Rogers. After getting Oklahoma tribes exempted from the IRA, these two men introduced legislation that became the Oklahoma Indian Welfare Act (OIWA), passed in 1936. With some significant exceptions, this law generally applied the IRA to Oklahoma tribes. Two of the most important of these were the total exemption of the Osage Tribe from this law and the provision leaving probate matters involving members of the Five Civilized Tribes and the Osage Tribe to state courts. Carter Blue Clark has observed that "exemption of the Osages from the act confirmed that the OIWA was uniquely concerned with oil and gas lands."[15]

The OIWA gave tribes the right to organize and adopt a constitution and bylaws, a provision that would later prove to be pivotal for the revival of Oklahoma tribal governments. Muriel H. Wright has noted that "Oklahoma Indians were conservative in taking advantage of" the OIWA.[16] Only eighteen tribes organized under the act between 1937 and 1942. Clark argues that mixed-bloods benefited most from the OIWA, which shifted tribal government away from traditional forms to constitutional democracies. "To many Indians," writes Clark, "the Anglo-American system, election districts, secret ballots, and tribal presidents were alien."[17]

Oklahoma tribes were subject to the same ebb and flow of federal policy in the decades after the Indian New Deal as were other tribes in the United States. Several Oklahoma tribes were directly affected by the Termination Era of the 1950s. The Wyandot, Peoria, Ottawa, and Modoc tribes were terminated by acts of congress; a 1959 law concerning the Choctaw Nation was interpreted by the BIA to be a termination act; and, according to Debo, only action by the state's congressional delegation prevented the termination of the Osage Tribe.[18] As federal Indian policy shifted during the 1960s, Oklahoma tribes began the long process of emergence that would culminate in revitalized tribal governments in the 1980s. Significantly, the self-determination policy had its origins in Oklahoma when several tribes began contracting for services in the Lawton area.[19] Oklahoma tribes also participated in War on Poverty programs such as the Office of Economic Opportunity.[20]

Just as Indians across the nation became more motivated politically, so did those in Oklahoma. One of the leading young "militant" Indian leaders of the National Indian Youth Council was Oklahoma Pawnee Clyde Warrior. Oklahomans for Indian Opportunity was founded in 1965 under the leadership of LaDonna Harris (Comanche), wife of U.S. senator Fred Harris. LaDonna Harris went on to found Americans for Indian Opportunity and served on the National Council on Indian Opportunity created by President Lyndon Johnson.

Although tribal governments began to perform more administrative duties in the 1960s, the environment for broad and unified Indian political action remained mired in the cultural, political, and legal mind-set that had existed since before statehood. Tribes in Oklahoma have for decades had the *form* of organization. However, the success of their efforts were, and continue to be, generally minimal on a statewide level because of the general inability to coalesce behind specific issues. Organizations such as the United Indian Nations of Oklahoma and the Inter-Tribal Council of the Five Civilized Tribes meet to discuss issues and respond to proposed policy changes. However, unity and coordinated action have generally not been sustained on any given issue because tribal diversity is often more jealously guarded than intertribal unity.

The differences among Oklahoma tribes are significant. They result from the historic circumstances of each tribe's Oklahoma experience and from the wide variety of Indian cultures found in the state. While written in a slightly different context, the attorney F. Browning Pipestem's observation that "there is no 'Oklahoma Indians' tribe" is fundamental to understanding the state's complex Indian political environment.[21]

Observers of contemporary Oklahoma Indian affairs often divide the state's tribes geographically into east and west groupings roughly divided by Interstate 35.[22] "East" refers to the Five Civilized Tribes and tribes that generally have their roots east of the Mississippi River and north of the Ohio River. "West" refers to Plains tribes and tribes with roots in the southwestern United States. There are thus significant cultural differences among the tribes that make unity difficult. Lujan (Kiowa-Taos) points out that the differences even include ways of communicating.[23]

There are also cultural resentments, with the western tribes often viewing the eastern tribes as both more affluent and more politically adept.[24] Chickasaw governor Bill Anoatubby asserts that there are "philosophical differences" among the tribes. He contends that the Five Civilized Tribes differ "in the way we approach business," including "business as government."[25] There are historic distrusts that linger among some tribes, the Osage and Cherokee and the Osage and Kiowa, for example.[26] Former Oklahoma Indian Gaming Association president Robert R. Stephens (Chickasaw) observes that the western tribes "don't trust the eastern tribes" and have been "plum put out with some of the dealings" of the Five Civilized Tribes.[27]

Jess Green (Chickasaw/Choctaw), an attorney for a number of tribes throughout Oklahoma, argues that there are really *five* major divisions among the state's tribes: (1) the Five Civilized Tribes; (2) the tribes in extreme northeastern Oklahoma (Miami, Eastern Shawnee, Quapaw, etc.); (3) the northern tribes near the Oklahoma-Kansas border (Osage, Tonkawa, etc.); (4) the central tribes east of Oklahoma City (Sac and Fox, Citizen Band Potawatomi, etc.); and (5) the western tribes (Kiowa, Apache, Delaware, etc.). Green contends that each grouping has characteristics that are similar among the tribes within it and different from the other groupings.[28]

As a result of federal policy there are also contemporary tribes and tribal groupings that do not reflect traditional arrangements. The Muscogee people, now the Muscogee Creek Nation, were a loose confederacy of autonomous towns.[29] The Cheyenne and Arapaho, historically two distinct but allied tribes, were combined during the reservation era to form the Cheyenne-Arapaho Tribe, which shares a common land base.[30] Both of these two groups are thus artificial creations that do not reflect traditional indigenous social and political structures.

This balkanization of Oklahoma tribes has usually meant that unified political action rarely occurs. According to Strickland, Oklahoma tribes "have vastly different approaches to governance."[31] Similarly, Oklahoma state senator Kelly Haney (Seminole) points out that the tribes even have "different ideas of sovereignty."[32] Unlike tribes in New Mexico, Oklahoma tribes, with some exceptions, do not have "age-old dealings" with one another.[33] According to Kickingbird (Kiowa), there are too many differences among Oklahoma tribes "real or perceived" for there to be real unity.[34]

A significant recent intertribal division occurred when four of the Five Civilized Tribes signed compacts with Gov. David Walters resolving a dispute over state cigarette taxes. In 1992 the U.S. Supreme Court ruled in *Oklahoma Tax Commission v. Citizen Band Potawatomi Tribe* that the state of Oklahoma could not tax cigarettes sold at tribal smoke shops to Indians. The Court also held, however, that the cigarette tax was applicable to sales by tribes to non-Indians. The Court complicated matters for the Oklahoma Tax Commission by protecting the tribe from lawsuits to collect the tax based on tribal sovereign immunity.

Recognizing that the Tax Commission would continue to press for payment of the taxes due on sale to non-Indians, the Cherokee, Chickasaw, Choctaw, and Seminole tribes and the state began negotiating an agreement to stave off further litigation. The result was a 1992 tribal-state compact providing payments "in lieu of taxes" by the four tribes to the state. It provided that the tribes would pay the state 25 percent of the estimated tax on these sales. Cherokee principal chief Wilma Mankiller said, "[T]he agreement is] not a threat to our sovereign status. It is because of our sovereignty that we can take this kind of action." And Chickasaw governor Bill Anoatubby said, "This government-to-government compact is the most reasonable method of settling our disputes. It is a true exercise of tribal sovereignty."[35]

Many other Oklahoma tribes strongly disagreed with the compact and its implications for tribal sovereignty. Intertribal meetings were held to protest the compact and to oppose the legislation that would make the compact possible, S.B. 759. Sac and Fox principal chief Elmer Manatowa attacked S.B. 759 because it "pre-empts treaty rights, violates sovereign rights, and is unconstitutional."[36] Representatives from twenty-two tribes passed a resolution attacking S.B. 759 as a "violation of the sovereign rights of tribal governments and an infringement to the sovereign status and integrity of Indian Nations, Tribes and/or Bands whose jurisdiction overlaps that of the State of Oklahoma."[37]

Tribal unity and opposition to S.B. 759 did not result in the bill's defeat, nor did opposition to compacts end these tribal-state agreements. Threatened with continued battles with the Oklahoma Tax Commission, including the possibility of confiscated cigarettes, several tribes came to the realization that the compacts were "not a bad deal" for the tribes.[38] By June 1995 a total of fifteen tribes had signed in lieu of tobacco tax payment compacts with the state, including the Sac and Fox Tribe and the Muscogee Creek Nation, two of the strongest opponents of the original compact.[39]

The battle over the tobacco tax demonstrated two important points about the political influence of Oklahoma tribes. First, the Five Civilized Tribes often are able to act individually or in concert in dealing with state government while most other tribes are not able to do so. This no doubt results from their long history of political sophistication and their willingness to accommodate when necessary. Second, even when a large number of tribes takes a position on an issue and attempts to influence state government, success is not likely; it is even more unlikely if the Five Civilized Tribes do not participate.

While tribes generally have had little influence in Oklahoma politics, individual tribal members have frequently become political powers in the state. A governor, Johnston Murray (Chickasaw); a Speaker of the Oklahoma House, William Durant (Choctaw); at least two members of the state supreme court, N. B. Johnson (Cherokee) and Earl Welch (Chickasaw); and four members of the U.S. House of Representatives, W. W. Hastings (Cherokee), Charles D. Carter (Cherokee), Charles D. Carter (Chickasaw), and William G. Stigler (Choctaw), were enrolled tribal members by birth. One of Oklahoma's first U.S. senators was Robert L. Owen, "a Virginian of Cherokee descent who had been admitted to tribal membership."[40]

Since statehood, numerous members of the Five Civilized Tribes have served in the state legislature. In addition to Speaker Durant, at least two other principal chiefs of the Choctaw Nation were elected to the legislature: E. M. Frye (Senate) and Harry J. W. Belvin (House and Senate).

The irony of politically powerful Oklahoma Indians is twofold. In order for an Indian to achieve political power in Oklahoma, he or she must do so as an Oklahoman who happens to be Indian, emphasizing the first loyalty over the second. Once having achieved power in the secular politics of the state, the successful tribal member then does little to advance the agenda of tribes independent of an agenda for all Oklahomans. It is probably not coincidental that in recent years those Indians who have achieved statewide electoral success have tended to be mixed bloods not closely identified with tribal politics. Although one can argue that this represents a profound success for the policies of assimilation, it clearly does little to further the separate political status of tribes.

The minimal effect of the successes of individual tribal members on tribal-state relations is obvious in the ongoing serious conflicts between state and tribal governments on a number of issues. The tribal-state conflict in Oklahoma is unlike any other in states with sizable Indian populations and land bases. In South Dakota and Arizona, for example, the state government attempts to assert its authority in Indian Country even while acknowledging that Indian Country and tribal governments exists within its borders. For much of this century Oklahoma officials have denied that Indian Country existed in the state; that Indians living in their former homelands are beyond the reach of Oklahoma law; and that tribal governments have little more than minimal administrative authority. As Gover noted in his 1976 report for the American Indian Policy Review Commission, "Because of the Allotment Acts, which caused the reduction of Indian lands, the State of Oklahoma contends that it has exclusive jurisdiction in the State with the United States having proprietary jurisdiction on trust lands."[41]

The belief that somehow Indian land and tribal authority meant something different in Oklahoma was a result of the confusing and contradictory policies of the federal government during the transformation of Indian Territory into the state of Oklahoma. The subsequent decades-long confusion about the status of tribes in the state was often shared by tribal leaders. The status of tribal lands was the source of most of the confusion. As Kickingbird has written, "Misinformed but conventional wisdom tells us that Oklahoma has no reservations except the Osage Reservation."[42] This belief is what Pipestem and G. William Rice have termed "the mythology of the Oklahoma Indians."[43]

As Kickingbird has noted, even influential Indian leaders publicly professed their uncertainty about the legal status of Indian land in Oklahoma. In testimony before a task force of the American Indian Policy Review Commission in 1976, Cherokee Nation principal chief Ross Swimmer said, "In the past seventy years we have acquired land, forty thousand acres, we own it, control it, held in trust for us by the United States but we're still not reservation, never have been and hopefully never will be." On the applicability of state taxes on Indian-operated businesses, Swimmer testified, "I don't know what the status is of the Cherokees."[44]

Absent a theory or evidence to the contrary, the state of Oklahoma, with the acquiescence of the federal government, acted under the presumption that its criminal and civil laws were enforceable on Indians residing, working, or operating a business on Indian-owned land. In a 1953 letter to Secretary of the Interior Orem Lewis, Oklahoma governor Johnston Murray, an enrolled member of the Chickasaw Nation, asserted the generally accepted view of tribal-state jurisdiction and its impact on P.L. 83-280.

> When Oklahoma became a State, all tribal governments within its boundaries became merged in the State and the tribal codes under which the tribes were governed prior to statehood were abandoned and all Indian tribes, with respect to criminal offense and civil causes, came under State jurisdiction.[45]

As Kickingbird has noted, "This hopeful though unfounded belief of Governor Murray became Oklahoma's final comment on Indian jurisdiction for many years."[46]

In his 1976 report Gover wrote, "The fact is that no one really knows the extent of the powers of the tribes in Oklahoma. The Federal government and the state government carry out policy toward the tribes without an understanding of the status of tribes, and this has resulted in a situation where the tribes do not have the resources they need, or even all of the resources available to other tribes." Among the consequences of this state of affairs was that "the tribes of Oklahoma do not exercise most of the powers of sovereigns."[47] "After 1950 and until 1977," Kickingbird wrote, "Oklahoma exercised all aspects of civil and criminal jurisdiction over Indian lands."[48]

The 1970s saw the rebirth and flowering of Indian self-governance in Oklahoma. In 1970 Congress restored the ability of the Five Civilized Tribes to select their own chief executives.[49] Occurring in the context of the Johnson-Nixon policy of self-determination, Oklahoma tribal self-governance more directly resulted from lawyers and judges rereading treaties and statute books and coming to the awareness that most assumptions about tribal sovereignty in Oklahoma were wrong. The consequence of the challenges to the conventional legal wisdom was a recognition that Indian tribes in Oklahoma had the right of self-government over their members and their lands. This right of self-governance included executive, legislative, and judicial authority.

As with most advances in tribal sovereignty in Oklahoma, the rebirth of tribal government began in court. Three decisions involving tribes from the two former territories alerted Oklahomans, Indian and non-Indian, that a new era in tribal-state relations was beginning. Taken together, these three cases provided a framework for the renewed exercise of tribal jurisdiction throughout Oklahoma. The first two addressed the self-governing powers of the Creek Nation; the third concerned the reach of Oklahoma criminal law in Indian Country.

In *Harjo v. Kleppe,* the U.S. District Court for the District of Columbia had to determine to what extent the government of the Muscogee Creek Nation had been terminated at the turn of the century. Allen Harjo, elected representative of Fish Pond Tribal Town and unsuccessful candidate for principal chief, challenged the Interior Department's recognition of the principal chief as the legitimate government representative of the Creek Nation. In a lengthy decision that considered both the particular history of Creek self-governance and democratic theory, the court held that the Nation's government had never been completely terminated by the federal government. The court traced the often-conflicting legislative, judicial, and executive acts altering the traditional form of Creek government, including the promises made to the Muscogee by the U.S. government.

> While the credibility of these promises has been gravely undermined by various federal actions, culminating in the abolition of the tribe's territorial sovereignty, the essence

of those promises, that the tribe has the right to determine its own destiny, remains binding upon the United States, and federal policy in fact now recognizes self-determination as the guiding principle of Indian relations. Plaintiffs' claim is, at bottom, simply an assertion of their right to democratic self-government, a concept not wholly alien to American political thought.[50]

The court established a procedure by which members of the Creek Nation could change their government consistent with what had existed under the Creek Constitution of 1867. The district court's opinion was upheld two years later by the U.S. Court of Appeals for the District of Columbia in *Harjo v. Andrus*. In 1979 the Creek Nation ratified a new constitution "which reopened membership rolls and substantially reshaped the tribe's government."[51]

In addition to providing for legislative and executive branches, the 1979 Muscogee Creek Constitution also provided for a judiciary. The Nation's 1982 judicial code established a court system with criminal and civil jurisdiction over tribal members. However, the BIA refused to fund the Nation's courts in 1983, contending that the Curtis Act had abolished the tribe's court system. The U.S. District Court for the District of Columbia upheld the BIA's decision in *Muscogee (Creek Nation) v. Hodel* (1987), finding that "Congress did explicitly abolish the power of the Muscogee (Creek) tribe to maintain a court system and never acted to restore that power."

A year later the appeals court reversed the district court. Overturning the BIA's decision and reading the law much differently than the lower court, the appeals court held that the Oklahoma Indian Welfare Act had repealed the Curtis Act. Therefore, the court held, "the Muscogee (Creek) Nation has the power to establish Tribal Courts with civil and criminal jurisdiction, subject, of course, to the limitations imposed by statutes generally applicable to all tribes."[52]

The question the tribes in the western part of the state addressed was the limit on state criminal jurisdiction in Indian

Country. In 1975 a Kiowa named Littlechief was accused of killing his father on a trust allotment in Caddo County. In a "startling decision"[53] that had far-reaching ramifications for tribal self-government, the U.S. District Court for the Western District of Oklahoma held that the crime was committed in Indian Country as defined by 18 U.S.C. 1151c and thus outside Oklahoma criminal jurisdiction.[54]

In 1978, in Oklahoma v. Littlechief, the Oklahoma Court of Criminal Appeals conceded the federal nature of the case against Littlechief and agreed with the federal court that Oklahoma lacked jurisdiction to try Littlechief. This implicitly overturned the 1936 decision *Ex parte Nowabbi* by the same court upholding the conviction of one Choctaw for the murder of another on restricted land. Oklahoma attorney general Larry Derryberry subsequently issued an opinion affirming the lack of state jurisdiction in Indian Country located in the state: "It is clear, then that the State of Oklahoma is without jurisdiction to prosecute crimes committed upon Indian trust allotment lands defined as 'Indian Country' when such crimes are committed by an Indian against another Indian."[55]

In retrospect, Governor Murray's 1953 opinion about the need for Oklahoma to assume P.L. 280 jurisdiction meant that Oklahoma had no congressionally authorized basis for exercising jurisdiction in Indian Country. Furthermore, the conventional wisdom about the existence of Indian Country in Oklahoma and the nature of the Curtis Act was shown to have rested more on myth than fact.

One of the most dramatic effects of the changes in legal understanding of tribal status was the "rebirth" of tribal courts, "the most important Indian event since statehood."[56] In 1979, following an opinion by the BIA solicitor, the Court of Indian Offenses for the Anadarko Area was established.[57] In 1991 similar courts were authorized for the Muskogee Area. By 1993 every tribe in the state had either its own separate tribal court deciding issues arising under tribal ordinance or a Code of Federal Regulations (CFR) court applying CFR rules (see table 10).

TABLE 10
Oklahoma Indian Tribal and CFR Courts

TRIBAL COURTS	CFR COURTS
Absentee-Shawnee Tribe	Apache Tribe
Cherokee Nation	Caddo Tribe
Cheyenne-Arapaho	Comanche Tribe
Chickasaw Nation	Chickasaw Nation
Choctaw Nation	Choctaw Nation
Citizen Band Potawatomi	Delaware Tribe of Western
Muscogee Creek Nation	Oklahoma
Iowa Tribe	Eastern Shawnee Tribe
Kaw Nation	Fort Sill Apache Tribe
Kickapoo Tribe	Kiowa Tribe
Otoe-Missouria Tribe	Miami Tribe
Sac & Fox Nation	Modoc Tribe
Seminole Nation	Osage Nation
	Ottawa Tribe
	Pawnee Tribe
	Peoria Tribe
	Ponca Tribe
	Quapaw Tribe
	Seneca-Cayuga Tribe
	Tonkawa Tribe
	United Keetoowah Band of
	Cherokee
	Wichita Tribe
	Wyandot Tribe

SOURCE: Arvo Q. Mikkanen, comp., "1993 Directory of Tribal Courts in Oklahoma," Oklahoma Indian Bar Association.

Two events have demonstrated how far tribal justice has come in less than twenty years: volume 1 of *Oklahoma Tribal Court Reports* was published in 1994 containing the opinions of Oklahoma Indian courts;[58] and in 1992 the Oklahoma legislature passed a law affirming the state supreme court's power to issue standards for the extension of full faith and credit to tribal court decisions.59 By June 1995 full faith and credit status had been granted to the Creek Nation, the Cherokee Nation, and Seminole tribal courts, as well as the Kiowa, Comanche, Apache, Wichita, Caddo, Delaware, Ft. Sill Apache, Ponca, and Tonkawa CFR courts.[60]

While *Littlechief* made the exercise of tribal jurisdiction possible, it also raised practical law and order problems for all law enforcement officials. As David McCullough has noted, "State law enforcement officials faced the dilemma—brought about in part by the 'checker-board' tribal jurisdiction within the state—of not knowing whether (1) the crime was committed in Indian Country and (2) the perpetrator and/or victim were Indian or non-Indian."[61] Law enforcement officers could not be sure where one jurisdiction began and another ended. In his opinion noting the absence of state jurisdiction in Indian Country, Attorney General Derryberry also opined that there was nothing to prevent tribal and state law enforcement officers from being cross-deputized.[62] Thus the issuance of deputy special officers (DSO) commissions to local and BIA law enforcement officers continued for the next several years.

In 1984 Oklahoma attorney general Michael Turpin issued an opinion that contradicted the earlier one by Derryberry: he wrote that DSOs violated the state constitution.[63] Following this opinion, the Sac and Fox Tribe and the Pottawatomie County sheriff entered into an "intergovernmental cooperative agreement" providing for the cross-deputization of tribal and county law enforcement officers.[64] Six years later, in *Ross v. Neff* (1990), the Tenth Circuit Court of Appeals held that the arrest of a Cherokee man by the Adair County sheriff for an offense committed on trust land was invalid.

Ross added to the jurisdictional confusion of law enforcement personnel who were faced with answering calls on what might be Indian land. As Oklahoma assistant attorney general A. Diane Hammons has noted, prior to *Ross*, Oklahoma law enforcement officers "typically responded to those calls and have worried about jurisdiction, if they worried about it at all, after the fact."[65] After *Ross*, the Oklahoma Highway Patrol refused to allow its officers to enter Indian Country, even at the request of federal officials, unless it had a specific and detailed agreement with federal agencies. To reduce potential liability, the Highway Patrol insisted that these agreements make clear that when called in by federal agencies the state officers would be acting as federal, not state, officers. County sheriff's departments soon adopted this policy for their officers.

In response to the confusion in law enforcement, the Oklahoma legislature passed the State-Tribal Relations Act in 1991.[66] This legislation was significant in three respects. First, after years of balking, the legislature acknowledged the federally recognized tribes in Oklahoma. Further, the law commits the state to working "in a spirit of cooperation with all federally-recognized Indian tribes in furtherance of federal policy for the benefit of both the State of Oklahoma and tribal governments."[67] Six years earlier the legislature had failed to pass H.B. 1199, a bill introduced by Rep. Kelly Haney providing for the state and tribes to cooperate on a government-to-government basis.[68] Second, the State-Tribal Relations Act createe a ten-member Joint Committee on State-Tribal Relations, which has the responsibility "for overseeing and approving agreements between tribal governments and the State of Oklahoma."[69] Third, the act provides a mechanism for the state and local jurisdictions to enter into "cooperative agreements" with federally recognized tribes. All agreements have to be approved by the Joint Committee and, when necessary, by the secretary of the Interior.[70]

This truly remarkable piece of legislation laid the groundwork and created a process for changed relations between the state of Oklahoma and tribes. The cooperative agreements section was first used to resolve the major problem it was designed to address: law enforcement in Indian Country. The Sac and Fox and Iowa tribes were the first to have cross-deputization agreements with local law enforcement agencies approved, the former with the Pottawatomie and Lincoln County sheriff's departments, the latter with the Lincoln County

Sheriff's Department. By June 1995 the Cherokee and Choctaw nations and the Delaware Tribe of Western Oklahoma had also signed cross-deputization agreements. In addition to those signed by individual tribes, the BIA signed similar agreements with many jurisdictions throughout the state where individual tribes have no police forces of their own.

As the status of Oklahoma tribes was clarified and as federal policy increasingly enabled tribal governments to expand their political and economic reach, several tribes began to assume the duties previously performed by the BIA. In 1990 Congress amended the Indian Self-Determination and Education Act to create a demonstration project providing a number of tribes throughout the country with the opportunity essentially to eliminate the role of the BIA in many service areas. The Cherokee Nation of Oklahoma and the Absentee Shawnee Tribe were among the original participants in the Self-Governance Demonstration Project (P.L. 100-472). Congress subsequently made the project permanent, expanded the number of participating tribes, and extended it to the Indian Health Service. By fiscal year 1996, eight Oklahoma tribes will be participating in the self-governance project: the Cherokee Nation, the Chickasaw Nation, the Creek Nation, the Choctaw Nation, the Absentee Shawnee Tribe, the Wyandot Tribe, and the Kaw Tribe.[71] Their participation is evidence of the growing ability of Oklahoma tribal governments to operate more fully as sovereign entities.

Oklahoma tribes also developed new economic opportunities on their land. They began to operate smoke shops and gas stations, run bingo games, and issue their own automobile tags. All of these economic enterprises produced revenue for the tribes and at the same time threatened to reduce state revenues because the tribes refused to add state taxes to the goods and services offered. Claiming that state taxes were not enforceable in Indian Country, for example, tribal smoke shops sold cigarettes at reduced cost at what in many cases were structures no larger than a mobile home.

In 1976 Gover had written, "The unclear status of the Oklahoma tribes effectively stifles attempts at forming tribal enterprises with a reasonable rate of return. The major issue is taxation. The State of Oklahoma and municipalities have been taxing tribal enterprises."[72] While tribal status was nebulous and tribal economic endeavors limited, the issue of the applicability of state taxes on Indian land simmered rather than boiled. As Creek principal chief Claude A. Cox stated in federal court in 1985, "They [state authorities] never exercised any jurisdiction when we were selling beads and pottery."[73] This changed as the tribes began to feed the fires with more potential sources of tribal-state tax conflict. As Gover had observed, "It cannot be expected that the State of Oklahoma would protect Indian interests because to do so would deprive the state of sources of revenue."[74]

In the latter part of the 1980s and into the 1990s, as the tribes exercised these more sophisticated aspects of self-governance, they began to run afoul of the Oklahoma Tax Commission. The commission came to embody the greatest source of tribal-state conflict, particularly after cross-deputization began to ease some of the criminal jurisdiction concerns. The conflict was heated because it touched on a fundamental question of sovereignty for both the tribes and the state: where and over whom does each sovereign have jurisdiction to levy taxes to raise the revenue necessary to fulfill its obligations? The commission stated its position in a paper presented at the 1989 Sovereignty Symposium in Oklahoma City: "The Tax Commission's position on this issue begins with the perspective that state law provides no exemptions for tribally owned businesses from state tax law requirements and no federal law exists which pre-empts such an application."[75]

In five major cases reaching the federal courts, including one involving tribal bingo, the commission argued that tribal members and operations were subject to all state taxes because, according to the commission, tribes had no land base separate and immune from the reach of state law. The theory and practice of the commission toward tribal sovereignty and the extent of state jurisdiction are clearly seen in the positions it took in the four cases reaching the U.S. Supreme Court between 1988 and 1995. In each case the commission in effect denied the sovereign status of Oklahoma tribes and the plenary power of Congress in Indian affairs while asserting state jurisdiction over Indian-owned land in Oklahoma.

In 1985, in *Oklahoma Tax Commission v. Graham,* the commission sought to enjoin the Chickasaw Nation from engaging in any further business at its motor inn located in Sulphur, Oklahoma, until it complied with state tax laws. The Nation sought to remove the case to federal court. In its 1988 brief to the Court arguing against removal, the commission for the first time presented its view to that court that there are no reservations in Oklahoma. It made the creative but ahistorical argument that "the reservation system and tribal sovereignty within that system has been disestablished in Oklahoma." Furthermore, the commission argued that there is a "factual distinction" between an "'assimilated' state" and "a 'reservation' state." As to the status of the Five Civilized Tribes, the commission contended that "in the years just prior to Statehood at the turn of the century, these reservations were disestablished."[76]

In *Oklahoma Tax Commission v. Citizen Band Potawatomi Tribe of Oklahoma,* the commission argued that the tribe was required to impose the state's cigarette tax on all sales of that item made in tribal smoke shops. To support the reach of Oklahoma law on such transactions, the commission's brief filed with the Supreme Court contended that "there are no reservations in Oklahoma. . . . [T]he Tribes in Oklahoma have not been set apart from the State on a federal reservation and do not maintain a separate and independent existence apart from the general community." The commission expressed its concern that tribal activities were beginning to have an impact on the affairs of non-Indians: "The State urges that the Tribe should not be allowed to infringe on the States rights to govern its internal affairs."[77]

Two years later the commission was again attempting to impose a state tax on tribal land. This time the commission argued that (1) state income taxes should apply to tribal employees and (2) the motor vehicle excise and license and registration fees should be paid by Sac and Fox members who owned cars and drove on state roads.[78] Echoing its contention in *Potawatomi,* the commission in *Oklahoma Tax Commission v. Sac and Fox Nation* asserted that Sac and Fox land was not a reservation, having been terminated in 1891. Further, "the extent of Indian Country in Oklahoma consists of plots of trust land of various sizes scattered among land which is otherwise within state jurisdiction." Referring to the allotment process, the commission reasoned that "the Indian tribes in Oklahoma were assimilated into the general society by this process and lost the exclusive autonomy enjoyed by tribes which inhabit federal reservations."[79]

In 1995, in *Oklahoma Tax Commission v. Chickasaw Nation,* the commission was once again attempting to tax tribal transactions, this time by imposing Oklahoma's motor fuel tax on gasoline sold at tribal gas stations. The commission also sought to force tribal members employed by the tribe but not living on tribal land to pay state income taxes. Giving up its argument that there is no Indian Country in Oklahoma, the commission merely argued that for some purposes states may impose its taxes on Indian tribal activities. It further argued that treaties made with the Chickasaw Nation in the 1830s did not free individual Cherokees from the reach of all state taxes.[80]

The commission's dealings with the Chickasaw Nation demonstrate the lengths to which it would go to impose its interpretation of the law on Indian land. Chickasaw Nation governor Bill Anoatubby became the target of the commission when it placed a lien on his personal property for taxes it claimed were due on the sale of cigarettes at tribal smoke shops.[81] The commission also fought the Nation's attempts to purchase tax-exempt tags for tribal vehicles, claiming there was no provision in state law for the tribe to receive such tags. The Nation succeeded in getting the legislature to change the law, which now classifies a tribe as an "American Indian Tribal Association" and exempts it from state taxes.[82]

Before the Supreme Court's decision in *Chickasaw Nation* denying the state's right to tax tribal gas stations, Governor

Anoatubby had attempted to negotiate an agreement with the Tax Commission similar to the Tobacco Compacts.[83] The commission rejected these overtures, prompting one observer to say that the effort was doomed because Anoatubby was "negotiating with a stump."

The result of these four cases was a rejection by the Supreme Court of the commission's interpretation of the status of Indian land in Oklahoma. The Court essentially held that Indian Country is Indian Country for purposes of 18 U.S.C. 1151. The commission's attempts to distinguish "reservation" from "allotted land" were rejected. In what can be read as a direct rebuke of the commission's argument concerning the alleged "disestablishment" of the Sac and Fox Reservation, Justice O'Connor wrote, "Nonetheless, in *Oklahoma Tax Comm'n v. Citizen Band Potawatomi Indian Tribe of Okla.*, we rejected precisely the same argument—and from precisely the same litigant.[84]

GAMING IN OKLAHOMA

Morgan, England, and Humphreys have referred to Indian gaming as "the most salient federalism-related issue in Oklahoma today."[85] Although one can make the case that the ongoing controversies over the legality of state taxation in Oklahoma Indian Country have produced more conflict, it is true that Indian gaming has further tested the limits of both state and tribal sovereignty. It has taken considerable litigation to sort out the status of Indian gaming, which remains at a relatively low level in the state.

On its face Oklahoma's gaming policy appears prohibitive. While former state gaming negotiator Linda Epperley notes that "Oklahoma's Constitution does not expressly prohibit or permit gaming," a 1993 Oklahoma Attorney General Opinion asserted that "the criminal statutes of Oklahoma prohibit almost every form of gambling" and that "Oklahoma's gaming laws . . . are pervasively prohibitory."[86] As summarized by Epperly,

Oklahoma basically defines gambling as a combination of three items: (a) a participant who pays something of value, also known as "consideration," "bet" or "wager"; (2) an outcome determined, at least in part on chance; and (3) winnings which constitute "something of value."[87]

"Something of value" is defined as "money, coin, currency, check, chip, token, credit, property, tangible or intangible."[88]

Oklahoma law prohibits "poker, roulette, craps or any banking or percentage, or any gambling game played with dice, cards or any device, for money, checks, credit, or any representatives of value."[89] Law enforcement officers are required to enforce the state's gambling laws and are subject to removal from office if they fail to do so.[90]

Notwithstanding Attorney General Loving's assertion, several forms of gaming are permitted under Oklahoma law. For purposes of the IGRA, bingo and pull tabs are legal Class II games in Oklahoma. Also legal are several types of Class III gaming: pari-mutuel horse racing, including simulcast and off-track wagering, and raffle-type lotteries.[91]

As is the case under New Mexico law, Oklahoma statutes' provisions for charitable gaming seem to widen the scope of gaming available to tribes. For many years charitable organizations and groups supporting charitable activities have conducted so-called Las Vegas or Casino" nights throughout Oklahoma. Whether or not charitable organizations may conduct these activities was addressed in early 1995 by Attorney General Drew Edmondson. In an opinion issued in response to an inquiry from Canadian County District Attorney Cathy Stocker, Edmondson declared such events illegal under Oklahoma law.[92] Shortly thereafter the Shawnee Elks Lodge was raided and five persons were arrested and several gambling devices seized.[93]

Since 1993 two proposals to expand non-Indian gaming in Oklahoma have brought the *potential* of Indian gaming to public notice. The first was Governor David Walters's proposal for a state-operated lottery similar to those in thirty-six other

states, including Texas and Kansas. Walters, under mounting
public and law enforcement scrutiny for alleged campaign
irregularities, led efforts to pass State Question 658 creating a
lottery in Oklahoma. Opponents argued that if the lottery
proposal passed, Indian-operated casinos would soon be
common in the state.[94]

Forrest A. Claunch, chair of Oklahomans Against the Lottery,
wrote in a column for the *Daily Oklahoman* that "a vote for State
Question 658 next Tuesday is almost certainly a vote for casino
gambling on Indian lands—and tribal lotteries as well, if the
tribes want them."[95] Don Nickles, a member of the Senate
Committee on Indian Affairs, echoed this opinion.[96] For reasons
possibly having more to do with the state's political culture and
the backing of Governor Walters than the potential spread of
Indian gaming,[97] the referendum was soundly defeated 417,586
to 280,152.[98]

A June 1995 proposal by Remington Park Racetrack owner
Edward J. DeBartolo, Jr., again raised the specter of widespread Class III Indian gaming. DeBartolo, a leading opponent of State Question 658, proposed a statewide referendum
legalizing casino gambling in four locations in the state:
Remington Park in Oklahoma City, Blue Ribbon Downs in
Salisaw, downtown Tulsa, and Love County. According to the
Daily Oklahoman, Jeff True, executive director of the Oklahoma Quarter Horse Association, "said Remington officials
told the horsemen they hoped to obtain some exclusive rights
for a period of time, effectively blocking Indian tribes from
opening a casino immediately."[99]

Evidence that DeBartolo and casino supporters considered
the potential of Indian gaming a serious part of their campaign
appeared in an advertisement in the *Daily Oklahoman* on June
27, 1955, the day after the planned referendum effort was
announced. DeBartolo, Blue Ribbon Downs manager Dwayne
Burrows, and John H. Williams, former chairman and CEO of
the Williams Company took out a full-page ad in the form of a
letter "To the Citizens of Oklahoma" in support of the casino
proposal. It began, "Recent federal court rulings relating to

Indian tribes all but assure that casino gaming will come to Oklahoma no matter what."

INDIAN GAMING IN OKLAHOMA

Tribal-run high stakes bingo began earlier in Oklahoma than it did in New Mexico and encountered considerably more active resistance from state authorities.[100] The early controversies over Oklahoma Indian gaming were inextricably linked to the rebirthing pains of tribal sovereignty in the state. What tribes could offer in the way of gaming in Oklahoma was also affected by current national trends. In the early 1980s, before Congress addressed the issue, the limits of Indian gaming were usually established in state and federal courts after a tribe began operating games of chance beyond those permitted by state law, usually high stakes bingo. This is what occurred in Oklahoma.

In 1986 Ronald D. Fixico (Creek), then chair of the United Indian Nations in Oklahoma Gaming and Taxation Committee, told the Senate Select Committee on Indian Affairs that the state's tribes' gaming operations "function in an atmosphere whereas the State is antagonistic toward our efforts to become self-sufficient."[101] A year later he described for the committee the tribes' "adverse relationship with our State."[102] Fixico's observations were based on the continuing attempts by state and county officials to curtail tribal gaming enterprises. The conflicts centered around the scope of gaming offered by the tribes and the state's attempts to exercise jurisdiction over them, including the imposition of state taxes.

The first serious legal confrontation over Indian gaming in Oklahoma occurred in March 1983 when Ottawa County Sheriff Floyd Ingram attempted to close the Quapaw and Seneca-Cayuga tribal bingo games.[103] Sheriff Ingram alleged that the games violated state law because they were held on Sunday, were operated without a permit, and offered prizes beyond the legal $100 single game and $500 aggregate limits. Subsequently, the Ottawa district attorney sought an injunction to prevent the tribes from operating the games. The Oklahoma Tax Commission also asserted its authority to collect sales taxes from the bingo games. After initially granting an injunction, Ottawa County District Judge Jon Douthitt dismissed the county attorney's suit, holding that the state had no jurisdiction over the games because they were being conducted in Indian Country.

In July 1985 the Oklahoma Supreme Court reversed Judge Douthitt's decision. The court, while acknowledging that the bingo games were being offered in Indian Country, nevertheless ruled that the state might have jurisdiction "if, and to the extent that, the activity is shown to affect non-Indians and Indians who are non-members of the self-governing unit."[104] The court rejected the tribe's argument that it was protected by sovereign immunity. The case was remanded to the county district court for further determination of the facts consistent with the state supreme court's opinion.

After the supreme court's decision, the tribe asked for and received an injunction from the federal District Court for the Northern District of Oklahoma. The order by Judge Thomas R. Brett barred Judge Douthitt from further proceedings and prevented the state from further attempts to interfere with the tribe's bingo games. While the state appealed Judge Brett's order, all sides agreed that the games would continue.[105] The Tenth Circuit Court of Appeals finally handed down a decision in May 1989. Finding that the case "concerns activities that are necessarily primarily of federal interest" and that "the Tribes have a claim to sovereign immunity which shields them from suit in state court," the court affirmed Judge Brett's order. The court noted the *Cabazon* decision and the Indian Gaming Regulatory Act in determining federal policy and the state's interest in regulating Indian gaming: "The state courts thus lack jurisdiction to hear the State's case against the Tribes. The federal nature of the law and of the issues to be decided, combined with this lack of state jurisdiction, reduce the State's interest in this litigation to the vanishing point."[106]

Two years before the *Seneca-Cayuga* decision, the Tenth Circuit had decided an equally important Oklahoma Indian gaming case, this one directly involving the Tax Commission. One week after the Oklahoma Supreme Court's decision in *Seneca-Cayuga*, Tulsa County District Attorney David Moss had filed suit in county court against the Creek Nation's Tulsa bingo hall. The Tax Commission continued to press the claim it had first made in April that the tribe owed $800,000 in state sales taxes. The Creek Nation immediately sought an injunction against the state in federal district court. Judge James O. Ellison issued a temporary restraining order permitting the bingo hall to remain in operation.

The Creek Nation bingo hall sits on an Arkansas River sand bar near downtown Tulsa. The property was part of a hundred-acre parcel, known as the "Mackey site," owned in fee simple by the Creek Nation. The Nation owned the $2 million, 27,000-square-foot facility and contracted with U.S.A., Inc., a South Dakota company, to manage the bingo operations. The hall offered players some bingo jackpots of $25,000. The tribe used proceeds from the hall "to support tribal operations and tribal health and social services programs."[107]

In a December 1985 hearing on the issuance of a permanent injunction, Judge Ellison heard testimony about the status of the Mackey site, Creek legal history, and the state's claim of jurisdiction over the tribe's bingo games. The state argued that the Mackey site was not Indian Country and that there was a significant risk of organized crime infiltration of the tribal bingo games. Witnesses for the Creek Nation testified about the history of Creek land in Oklahoma, presenting evidence of tribal ownership of the Mackey site. Rennard Strickland testified that the tribe's interest in the land could be traced back to the Treaty of 1832.

Judge Ellison ruled in favor of the Creek Nation on December 20, 1987. He held that the Mackey site was Indian Country and that the state lacked jurisdiction to apply either its gaming laws or its taxes to the Creek Nation bingo. The state appealed to the Tenth Circuit again, claiming that the site was not a reservation and therefore not Indian Country. The state further argued that even if the Mackey site was Indian Country, the state nevertheless had full criminal jurisdiction and taxing authority over the property. Finally, it once again raised the specter of organized crime corrupting the Creek bingo games.

In September 1987 the appeals court upheld Judge Ellison's decision, finding "that under both historical and contemporary definitions, the Mackey site has retained its status as Indian country and land reserved under the jurisdiction of the federal government and the tribe." Relying on treaties, federal statutes, and the Oklahoma Enabling Act, the court held that no explicit act of Congress ever terminated existing Creek tribal lands or gave the state jurisdiction over them.

> In summary, the Mackey site is part of the original treaty lands still held by the Creek Nation, with title dating back to treaties concluded in the 1830s and patents issued in the 1850s. These lands historically were considered Indian country and still retain their reservation status within the meaning of 18 U.S.C. @ 1151(a).[108]

In balancing federal, tribal, and state interests, the court looked for guidance to the U.S. Supreme Court's recently decided *Cabazon* decision. It found all of the contentions made by the state of Oklahoma to be similar to those California made in *Cabazon* and rejected by the Court. Finally, the appeals court upheld the district court's holding that Oklahoma's sales tax was invalid in its application to the Creek Nation bingo games. The Court denied a writ of certiorari in June 1987.

After *Seneca-Cayuga* and *Indian Country, U.S.A.*, high-stakes tribal bingo was apparently free from state regulation and taxation. Tribal bingo games proliferated throughout Oklahoma during the 1980s. It is difficult to precisely pinpoint the number of bingo operations as many were opened but subsequently closed because of management problems or intertribal conflicts. Anecdotal accounts place the number of bingo halls in Oklahoma in the mid-1980s at 20 to 22.[109] Citing the *Tulsa Tribune,* Stefanie A. Lorbiecki placed the number at 24 in a 1985 *Tulsa Law Review* article.[110] In 1986 Ronald Fixico told the

Senate Select Committee on Indian Affairs that there were "18 gaming operations" in Oklahoma; that same year a nationwide survey conducted by BIA Area Offices counted 24 tribal operated games (18 in the Anadarko Area Office jurisdiction and 6 in the Muskogee Area Office jurisdiction).[111] According to the BIA survey, all of the Oklahoma gaming operations offered bingo, and fifteen offered both bingo and pull tabs. One tribe, the Tonkawa, also offered video card games. In November 1990 the *Tulsa World* estimated that there were thirty-four tribal bingo operations in the state.[112]

While the Creek, Cherokee, and Chickasaw bingo operations were among the most successful and appeared to run fairly smoothly, other tribes were not so fortunate. In its early years, for example, the Absentee Shawnee Tribe's Thunderbird Entertainment Center outside of Norman was engulfed in considerable controversy. A dispute over the enterprise's management required intervention by the federal courts.[113] Among the internal conflicts arising over bingo was one involving the Caddo, Wichita, and Delaware tribes. The three tribes established a corporation, W.C.D. Industries, Inc., which opened Fortune Bingo in 1992. The hall closed after a dispute over a management contract with a private firm.[114] In the early 1980s the Ponca Tribe's bingo games were plagued with intratribal disputes and federal audits.[115]

Many Oklahoma tribes turned to gaming as a potentially lucrative revenue source during the 1980s, but the Cherokee Nation was not one of them. The Cherokee Nation Tribal Council voted to establish high-stakes tribal bingo in September 1984, but Principal Chief Ross Swimmer vetoed the tribal council's legislation. According to the *Cherokee Advocate*, Swimmer "said gambling enterprises provide no long range employment, usually prove unprofitable and are constantly being tested in court."[116] The council did not again vote to approve bingo until April 1989, when it voted 7 to 6 in favor of a gaming ordinance.[117] Eight months later the council unanimously voted to invest $3 million in bingo facilities in Roland and Tulsa.[118] The Cherokee Nation Bingo Outpost opened in Roland on November 15, 1990.[119]

INDIAN GAMING IN OKLAHOMA:
MORE THAN BINGO?

Left undecided after *Seneca-Cayuga* and *Indian Country, U.S.A.*,
was what other forms of gaming Oklahoma tribes would be free
to conduct without arousing the ire of state and federal law
enforcement. A 1991 Tenth Circuit Court of Appeals decision
made it clear that the IGRA was the relevant federal statute
governing Indian gaming. The court lifted an October 1987
Northern District Court of Oklahoma injunction against the
United Keetoowah Band of Cherokee Indians prohibiting the
tribe from selling pull tabs. The injunction had been sought by
the state of Oklahoma after the Tulsa County district attorney
seized gambling paraphernalia from the tribe's Horseshoe Bend
Bingo Hall the previous October. The court rejected the state's
argument that the federal Assimilative Crimes Act (18 USC
#13) gave it jurisdiction over gaming in Indian Country.[120] In
lifting the injunction the circuit court observed, "It appears that
a new day has dawned with respect to the regulation of Indian
bingo." Furthermore, "a fair reading of the IGRA leads inex-
orably to the conclusion that this Act now bars federal courts
from enjoining Indian bingo by application trough the ACA."[121]

Passage of the IGRA signaled that at least some additional
forms of gaming ought to be permitted in the state. Tribes
began to approach the state with requests for compacts and
Governor Henry Bellmon named Ross Swimmer, former assistant secretary of the interior for Indian affairs, his negotiator
for Class III games.

Negotiations began between Swimmer and the Comanche
Tribe in late 1989 on a Class III compact that would allow the
tribe to conduct pari-mutuel horse racing in Lawton. A compact
was finalized and signed by Governor Bellmon on May 24, 1990.
Approval was granted by the Joint Committee on State-Tribal
Relations and signed by committee chairman Kelly Haney on
July 12, 1990. However, the compact was never submitted to the
secretary of the for approval, thus concluding Oklahoma's first
experience with legal Class III gaming.[122]

The path of Indian gaming in Oklahoma over the next five years was an obstacle course of stalled negotiations, intertribal conflict, court reverses, and threats by state and federal officials. The fundamental source of conflict between the tribes and the state was the interpretation of what types of gaming Oklahoma public policy permitted to be conducted under Class II or negotiated as Class III games under the IGRA.

Several plans for expanding tribal gaming never materialized. For example, an effort to have the Ponca Tribe become involved in pari-mutuel horse and dog racing failed, apparently "for lack of interest" and financial backing.[123] Similarly, discussions of a possible Sac and Fox tribal bingo in the Bricktown section of Oklahoma City failed to come to fruition.[124] As already noted, the Comanche Tribe's plans for a pari-mutuel track also failed.

Given the ambiguity of the IGRA, it is not surprising that some tribes creatively interpreted the act as permitting them to offer legally questionable games. Epperley wrote, "The newest social pastime in Indian Law circles is a game of 'one-upmanship' played at the expense of the State of Oklahoma. Participants try to 'top' one another in identifying gambling activities which are not actively prosecuted by law enforcement officials."[125] Among the most suspect games were those operated by the Ponca and Tonkawa tribes. In 1991 both tribes closed their gaming establishments after a *Tulsa World* investigation revealed that both tribes had slot machines and that the Ponca facility offered blackjack.[126]

The Absentee Shawnee Tribe's Thunderbird Entertainment Complex, after resolving its management difficulties, became, according to the *Tulsa World*, "one of the favorite places for gamblers" in Oklahoma.[127] One of the reasons for this popularity was a creative interpretation of what constitutes Class II games. The complex offered, in addition to bingo, a form of blackjack called "Bingojack." The game is similar to traditional blackjack except that Ping-Pong balls are used instead of cards. The balls, numbered one through ten, are blown trough a bingo hopper. The balls are lined up in front of the player, who is also playing traditional bingo at the same time. The National Indian Gaming Commission later issued regulations that categorized these types of games as Class III.

Tribal requests for Class III compact negotiations with the state accelerated after David Walters became governor in 1991. Lengthy negotiations between the governor's negotiators and Citizen Band Potawatomi tribal officials resulted in Walters signing a compact with the tribe on July 10, 1992.[128] As Michael W. Ridgeway wrote in an *American Indian Law Review* article, "The process that led to the Potawatomi gaming compact has been an eye opener."[129] During the course of the negotiations, Governor Walters was represented by two different negotiators, Linda Epperley and Robert A. Nance. While serving as the governor's gaming negotiator Epperley was an employee of the State Tourism Commission. She resigned the former position six months after assuming it, thus requiring the process to begin anew when Nance was appointed to the job in February 1992.[130]

In addition to the change in negotiating personnel, two other significant factors slowed negotiations and ultimately doomed the signed compact. After reviewing federal and state law, Nance informed all tribes requesting compacts that only a few games were open for negotiations. When Potawatomi attorney Michael Minnis responded with a list of games the tribes wanted to discuss, Nance replied that only video lottery terminals (VLTs) could be considered.[131]

Nance's position on VLTs led to the second factor that eventually mooted the Potawatomi compact. When informed that VLTs might be brought to the proposed Potawatomi gaming site, the U.S. Attorneys for all three Oklahoma federal districts indicated that such devices might violate the Johnson Act. Nance informed Minnis that the governor did not want to approve games that violated federal law.[132] Further, according to Minnis, Walters had said that "he was personally led to believe that he would be prosecuted if the machines [VLTs] were brought in."[133]

The compact finally agreed to allowed the Potawatomis to offer VLTs if they were ultimately found not to violate federal law. The compact provided that such a determination could be found if either (1) the U.S. Attorney for the Western District of Oklahoma declares the VLTs not in violation of the Johnson Act; or (2) a federal district court declares that the importation of VLTs is not a violation of the Johnson Act; or (3) the Potawatomi import VLTs for the purpose of prosecuting a declaratory judgment. The tribe also agreed "to defend, indemnify and hold harmless Oklahoma from any liability arising to Oklahoma from the importation of the VLTs under this compact."[134]

Following the U.S. Attorneys' refusal to issue the letter regarding the Johnson Act, the tribe sought a declaratory judgement in the Federal District Court for the Western District of Oklahoma. The court held that the importation of VLTs onto tribal land would violate the Johnson Act. In Citizen Band Potawatomi Indian Tribe of Oklahoma v. Green (1993), the tribe appealed to the Tenth Circuit, which upheld the district court ruling. The Potawatomi compact was thus null and void and the tribe was limited to Class II games.

The Potawatomi compact and the resultant court decision were not well received by the state's tribes and the Potawatomis did not receive much support.[125] While criticizing the Potawatomis' judgment in entering into the compact with the VLT provision, the tribes also believed that Walters was not negotiating in good faith as required by the IGRA. According to Gary Pitchlynn, attorney for the Ponca Tribe, four compacts were nearing completion prior to the Green decision. Following the Tenth Circuit's ruling, all video machines in tribal establishments were removed. He was directed by the Ponca and Cheyenne-Arapaho tribes to file suit against Walters and the state of Oklahoma for failing to negotiate in good faith. Although the Cheyenne-Arapaho decided against pursuing the lawsuit, the Ponca Tribe proceeded with its lawsuit in the Federal District Court for the Western District of Oklahoma with the support of some non-Indian gaming interests.

Judge Ralph G. Thompson handed down his ruling on September 8, 1992, holding that the tribe was prohibited by the Tenth and Eleventh amendments from suing both the

governor and the state. Because the IGRA lacks the option for
a state not to act, according to Judge Thompson, Congress
exceeded its authority in requiring good faith negotiations
between a state and a tribe. This section was therefore "precluded by the Tenth Amendment." Judge Thompson went on
to find that Congress had not intended for the IGRA to waive
the states' Eleventh Amendment immunity from suit, nor did
Congress have that power under the Indian Commerce Clause.
Finally, the judge held that the suit against the governor as an
individual was "barred by sovereign immunity."[136]

On appeal, the Tenth Circuit reached a different conclusion
concerning both of the constitutional amendment issues. While
upholding the district court's dismissal of Walters, the appeals
court reversed Judge Thompson on the Tenth and Eleventh
Amendment questions. Finding that the IGRA did not coerce
states into taking any action, the court held that the act did not
violate the Tenth Amendment. On the issue of Eleventh Amendment sovereign immunity, the court found that Congress had
intended to waive sovereign immunity in passing the IGRA,
even if it did not do so in explicit language. Significantly, the
court found that "the Indian Commerce Clause empowers
Congress to abrogate the states' Eleventh Amendment immunity."[137] The decision is on appeal with the U.S. Supreme Court.

In the early 1990s Oklahoma tribes were involved simultaneously in several federal court cases litigating their understanding of what is permissible under the IGRA. While the
Citizen Band Potawatomi and Ponca tribes were pursuing their
claims, the Delaware Tribe of Western Oklahoma joined a
lawsuit led by the Cabazon Band of Mission Indians of California against the National Indian Gaming Commission.[138] The
tribes were fighting the definitions issued by the commission
concerning "electronic, computer or other technological aids"
permitted as Class II games by 25 U.S.C. #2703(7)(A)(i) and
"electronic or electromechanical facsimiles," assigned Class III
status by 25 U.S.C. #2703(7)(B)(ii).

As Federal District Court for the District of Columbia judge
Royce C. Lamberth noted in his opinion, it is "imperative for

the Indians that the definition of aids be as broad as possible."[139]
The tribes, many using electronic video pull tab machines,
argued that the definitions were much too narrow because the
commission's definition of a "facsimile" included the video
machines. As Chickasaw attorney Jess Green has written, "Indian
tribes were uniform in their complaints that NIGC regulations
were more strict than the Act."[140]

Judge Lamberth's June 1993 decision upheld the commission's definitions as consistent with congressional intent under
the IGRA. The U.S. Court of Appeals for the District of
Columbia Circuit upheld his decision in January 1994.[141]

Cabazon II had almost immediate repercussions in Oklahoma.
On February 4, 1994, the three U.S. Attorneys in Oklahoma
sent letters to the tribes informing them that video pull tab
machines "are clearly illegal within the State of Oklahoma" and
offered to meet with tribal representatives. Tribes were given
until February 15 to remove the machines. If the machines
were not removed, the U.S. Attorney's office informed the
tribes, it would "be obliged to take appropriate action without
further notice to you in order to enforce the law."

In February 23, 1994, letters to Oklahoma tribes, all three
U.S. Attorneys offered "guidance on the current position of all
of the United States Attorneys within the State of Oklahoma."
The most significant point of the guidance was the following
paragraph:

> First, machines which are prohibited by *Cabazon II* must
> be disconnected *immediately* and covered, or otherwise
> taken out of the public gaming area of bingo halls or
> stores, and arrangements made for their orderly removal
> from Indian country. We consider all machines which
> display pull tabs on a video screen or display to be in this
> category, regardless of what mechanisms causes the display
> to occur or what else the machine does in addition to
> displaying pull tabs on a video screen.

The Delaware Tribe removed its machines in mid-1994.

Neither *Cabazon II* nor the threats by the Oklahoma U.S. Attorneys ended debate over electronic and video gaming devices. A new dispute between tribes and U.S. Attorneys arose over electronic machines that have video components. Unlike the machines at issue in *Cabazon II,* the devices do not dispense money to the player. John Raley, U.S. Attorney for the Eastern District of Oklahoma and probably the key figure in the ongoing tribal/U.S. Attorney disputes,[142] agreed in March 1994 not to interfere with these machines while a tribe tested their legality.

The Eastern Shawnee Tribe instituted a legal action to determine the legality of its electronic video machines in the Code of Federal Regulations Court, Miami Agency (CFR Court). Soon thereafter and notwithstanding his previous position and the presence of a case in a court of law, Raley contended that the CFR Court had no jurisdiction in the matter. In a January 1995 letter Stephen C. Lewis, U.S. Attorney for the Northern District of Oklahoma, "demanded the tribe cease use of the devices and abandon the proceedings in CFR Court."[143] The tribes complied.

A July 7, 1995, ruling by CFR judge George Tah-Boone held that the machines used by the Eastern Shawnee Tribe are Class II gambling devices.[144] Based on this ruling, the tribe installed fifty-five of the machines. Two months later, on September 14, law enforcement officers of the FBI, the U.S. Marshal's Office, and the Oklahoma Highway Patrol raided the Shawnee Tribe's gaming operations and seized the machines on a federal warrant obtained by Lewis.[145] Tribal records and $3,800 in cash were also seized.[146] The action against the Shawnee facility was part of a broader investigation that resulted in thirty-six non-Indian gambling sites in northeastern Oklahoma and Southeastern Kansas being raided at the same time the warrant was executed against the tribe.[147]

In this environment of adverse court rulings and recalcitrant public officials, Oklahoma tribes successfully negotiated two Class III compacts in 1994 and one in 1995. The Miami and Tonkawa tribes each signed compacts permitting them to operate off-track pari-mutuel simulcast horse wagering. The

Miami and Modoc tribes signed a compact in September 1995 permitting Class III off-track betting at the Miami, Oklahoma, gaming site.[148]

Some Oklahoma tribes have attempted to expand gaming to their aboriginal homelands. Recognizing the unique nature of Oklahoma tribal holdings and history, Congress made it possible through the IGRA for tribes to acquire land noncontiguous to their current holdings and use it for gaming purposes (25 USCS #2719 a). The Eastern Shawnee Tribe operates a bingo hall across the Oklahoma border in Seneca, Missouri. As early as 1984, the Miami Tribe of Oklahoma investigated the possibility of acquiring potential trust land in Cuyahoga County, Ohio, for the purposes of establishing high-stakes bingo games in Oakwood.[149] The Delaware Tribe of Western Oklahoma has several times raised the possibility of opening gaming facilities in New Jersey.[150] In November 1995 the residents of Wildwood, New Jersey, voted 1,081 to 491 to turn over to the tribe a parcel of land being used as a parking lot with the intention of building a tribal casino.[151]

Clearly, Oklahoma gaming tribes have had to fight for their right to offer games of chance on a case-by-case, tribe-by-tribe basis. They have done so in the face of inertia on the part of the state's governors and determined opposition by U.S. Attorneys. Each victory or defeat for an individual tribe directly affects the gaming opportunities of all tribes in the state. Although the tribes have been active in court, they have not been active in the political arena. Individual tribal leaders do become involved in non-Indian political campaigns. Wilma Mankiller and Bill Anoatubby, for example, have been active in the campaigns of various Democratic candidates for office.[152]

THE GAMING ASSOCIATION

Unlike the tribes in New Mexico, but consistent with historic patterns, Oklahoma tribes have not been able to unite effectively and lobby for a unified gaming position. The Oklahoma

Indian Gaming Association (OIGA) was formed after the IGRA was passed, but it has had neither the visibility nor the cohesiveness of the New Mexico Indian Gaming Association. The OIGA succeeded the Oklahoma Indian Gaming Commission, an outgrowth of the United Indian Nations of Oklahoma.[153] OIGA's bylaws were based on those of the National Indian Gaming Association.[154]

The OIGA has periodically served as a conduit for information to the state's gaming tribes,[155] but it has been faulted for lack of leadership and direction.[156] As Gary Pitchlynn has noted, the OIGA reflects "the same old divisiveness."[157] Attendance at meetings has generally been low, and for most of its existence the OIGA has had minimal financial resources with which to mount a sophisticated and sustained gaming strategy. Given the inherent divisions among the state's tribes, the comparatively low economic stakes of Indian gaming in Oklahoma, and the formidable opposition of state and federal authorities, the ineffectiveness of this organization is not surprising.

The response of the OIGA to the casino referendum proposal demonstrated the difficulty the tribes had in developing a unified gaming strategy. As Pitchlynn observed, the tribes were "torn about how to react to" DeBartolo's plan.[158] Some tribal leaders thought a successful referendum would help the tribes achieve Class III gaming. Others believed that should a vote to legalize casino gambling fail, gaming opponents could then argue that Oklahomans clearly favored a public policy of limited legal gambling, thus killing Class III gaming for the tribes. Some leaders, such as Lawrence S. Snake, president of the Delaware Tribe of Western Oklahoma, believed that the tribes should push for their own version of a casino referendum.[159] There was "no consensus position" on DeBartolo's proposal.[160]

Ironically, the OIGA has been active at the national level through participation in the National Indian Gaming Association. Charles Keechi, former president of the Delaware Tribe of Western Oklahoma, served for several years as chairman of the NIGA, and tribal attorneys such as Jess Green and Gary

Pitchlynn have been active on various strategic and tactical planning committees and task forces. According to Green, one of the important contributions of the OIGA has been providing funding for trips to NIGA meetings by Oklahoma tribal leaders. But this is limited, and Green's fees are paid by gaming tribes.

At its October 1995 meeting, the OIGA voted to include tribes from Kansas and Texas in its membership and changed its name to the Southern Indian Nations Gaming Association. According to the Chickasaw Nation gaming commissioner and the organization's new president, the expanded organization will give the Kansas and Texas tribes a voice in the National Indian Gaming Association.[161]

THE LIMITATIONS OF TRIBAL UNIQUENESS

The efforts of Oklahoma tribes to operate gaming have in large measure been through the more traditional avenues available to governmental units: inside lobbying by tribal representatives with government officials and litigation in state and federal courts. Among the former were attempts to follow the IGRA and negotiate compacts with Oklahoma governors. To date this approach has been only partially successful and has not resulted in expanded tribal gaming enterprises in Oklahoma. Similarly, the litigation path has produced conflicting results. While the *Ponca* decision can be generally be considered a success, *Green* and *Cabazon II* were clearly defeats.

The Class III compact process in Oklahoma has demonstrated three crucial points. First, a governor not committed to the process can produce an outcome detrimental to a tribe's interest. Second, the Potawatomi experience demonstrated that the role of the U.S. Attorney can be decisive in the ultimate results of tribal-state negotiations, notwithstanding the absence of a statutory role for the person holding that office. Third, the requirement for one-on-one negotiations can have an adverse impact on tribal unity.

THE ROLE OF ELECTED AND APPOINTED OFFICIALS

Several tribal attorneys who have been involved in Class III negotiations are convinced that the state's chief executives have not negotiated in good faith. Delays and last-minute barriers to completed compacts have derailed efforts by Oklahoma tribes to expand their gaming operations. The appointment of Oklahoma City University law professor Kirke Kickingbird as newly elected Republican Governor Frank Keating's counsel for Indian affairs was a hopeful sign to many tribal leaders.

Possibly more detrimental to tribal gaming in Oklahoma than dilatory tactics by governors has been the aggressive action taken by the state's U.S. Attorneys. These officials have inserted themselves into tribal-state negotiations on Class III gaming issues, issued direct threats to tribes engaging in certain kinds of gaming activities, and evidenced a lack of regard for tribal court processes. As Jess Green has noted about states where tribes and governors have been at odds, "In many areas, United States District Attorneys have recognized the equity problems of such inconsistent positions and have abstained from becoming active forces in Indian gaming."[162] This has been the case in New Mexico but not in Oklahoma.

The discretion of U.S. Attorneys is an area of policy implementation overlooked in the political science literature. Former U.S. Attorney General Griffin B. Bell and Daniel J. Meador have written that this office "is one vested with considerable policymaking implementing responsibility."[163] The significant differences in the actions of these officials in Oklahoma and New Mexico indicate their potential crucial role in some areas of policy. While there is no empirical evidence to support why such differences occur, there are at least two reasons they might. The first is the state's political culture. As Morgan, England, and Humphreys note, "A state's political culture . . . helps to define (1) the structure and functioning of government institutions, (2) the orientations and behavior of political leaders, and (3) public policies made in the name of the people."[164]

Oklahoma's political culture, particularly as it relates to historical questions of Indian-white relations and broader questions of morality, may be expositive. As we have seen, Oklahoma's history of Indian-white relations is marked by ethnic and policy schizophrenia: on the one hand, proud of its historical Indian roots; on the other, obstructionist in permitting the exercise of tribal self-governance. While Indians are the centerpiece of the State Department of Tourism's "Native America" campaign, other state agencies act to deny the existence of a contemporary Indian *political* status.

Oklahoma's political culture has strong individualistic and traditional roots. Pari-mutuel horse racing was not legalized in Oklahoma until 1985, several years before restaurant patrons could buy "liquor by the drink." In the 1994 congressional elections Oklahoma gave the Republican party one of its greatest national victories: the GOP now holds the governor's office, both U.S. Senate seats, and five of the state's six U.S. House seats. The religious right was a significant factor in these results.[165]

An official's ideology, cultural background, political ambition, and familiarity with a policy issue may help to determine how he or she performs the duties of the position. By the nature of the office, a U.S. Attorney is usually a product of the political culture of the state or district in which he or she serves. In his study of U.S. Attorneys, Eisenstein noted that "they belong to and identify with the community in which they serve. . . . Thus, local claims on their attention, time, and policies come to rival the demands of national policy and headquarters' directives."[166]

The ties to Oklahoma politics and culture are clear in the case of the two U.S. Attorneys who have been most opposed to Indian gaming. Stephen Lewis, U.S. Attorney for the Northern District, is a former Speaker of the Oklahoma House as well as the 1992 Democratic candidate for the U.S. Senate. John W. Raley, U.S. Attorney for the Eastern District, was born in Bartlesville and graduated from Oklahoma Baptist University and the University of Oklahoma Law School. A former assistant U.S. Attorney for the Western District of Oklahoma, Raley was appointed to his current position by President Bush in 1990. In

a rare occurrence in the world of partisan presidential appointments, he was reappointed to his position by President Clinton
in September 1993.[167]

The second possible reason for the differences in how U.S.
Attorneys exercise their discretion may be derived from purely
personal traits. Eisenstein noted that "energetic, dynamic U.S.
attorneys make their own opportunities to have a significant
impact." Furthermore, "aggressive U.S. attorneys appear
frequently to believe that they ought to play a major role in
shaping the actions of their office."[168] It would appear that the
actions of the U.S. Attorneys in Oklahoma are the product of
either or both of these factors.

INSIDE LOBBYING: THE COURTS

In their chapter on Oklahoma in Hrebenar and Thomas's
Interest Group Politics in the Midwestern States, England and
Morgan write, "The extent of judicial lobbying in Oklahoma is
a mystery."[169] While this may be true generally of other interests in the state, it is not the case with Indian tribes in Oklahoma. Much of the advancement in the exercise of tribal
authority in the state has resulted from court action either initiated by the tribes or in response to state action against a tribe
or tribal member. Attorneys for Oklahoma tribes have also been
active in the past decade as amici in gaming and nongaming
cases heard by the U.S. Supreme Court.

It is important to put the extent of recent tribal judicial
activism in historical perspective. Some of the significant Indian
law cases have involved Oklahoma tribes, both before and after
their removal from their homelands. *The Cherokee Cases* of the
1830s establishing the governing principles of Indian law
occurred because the Cherokee Nation was resisting the intrusion of Georgia law. *Talton v. Mayes* (1896), a case involving the
reach of Cherokee and federal law in Indian Territory, established that the Bill of Rights did not apply to Indian tribes.
Lone Wolf v. Hitchcock (1903) resulted from the Kiowa Tribe's
contention that allotment violated the Treaty of Medicine Lodge.

The outcome was the Court's holding that Congress could abrogate a prior treaty with the Indians merely by passing new legislation, thus strengthening the plenary power of Congress.

As has been pointed out, the resurgence in tribal government activity in the 1970s began with *Littlechief* and *Harjo*. The innovative arguments of young attorneys set aside seventy years of "misinformed but conventional wisdom"[170] concerning the status of Oklahoma tribal governments and landholdings.[171] Significantly, considering the history of tribal-state relations and notwithstanding the opinions of the Oklahoma Tax Commission, the court decisions recognizing the status of Indian Country in Oklahoma came in Oklahoma courts.

While questions of state criminal jurisdiction were being settled in state court, three of the Five Civilized Tribes won a significant but ultimately unfulfilled victory in the U.S. Supreme Court regarding the Arkansas River bed. In 1966 the Cherokee Nation of Oklahoma brought suit against the state of Oklahoma and a number of oil companies seeking to recover royalties from minerals extracted from the Arkansas River bed. The Cherokee Nation, later joined by the Chickasaw and Choctaw nations, claimed that it owned the land by virtue of the 1830 Treaty of Dancing Rabbit Creek and the 1835 Treaty of New Echota. The Court found in the tribes' favor in 1970 in *Choctaw Nation v. Oklahoma.*

"The cruel irony" as Strickland has written, is that the tribes' Supreme Court victory . . . has not been accompanied by success in Congress."[172] For the past twenty-five years, Congress has failed to settle the financial claims demanded by the three tribes.[173] Even after the Corp of Engineers put a price of $177 million on the riverbed, Congress failed to act, proving once again that a favorable outcome in the courts does not necessarily lead to political success. Strickland draws a parallel to the original *Cherokee Cases* of the 1830s.

> The Cherokees still wait at the pleasure of the Congress for the appropriation of the funds for property the Court found to have been theirs under the terms of the 1835

Treaty of New Echota, the treaty forced on the tribe after the failure to execute the mandate of the Supreme Court in *Worcester v. Georgia.* Once again, the tribe, the court, and the American people have come full circle.[174]

Apart from those legal disputes in which they have a direct interest, attorneys for Oklahoma tribes have filed amicus curiae briefs in major Supreme Court cases involving significant issues of Indian law. In the two Indian gaming cases to come before the Court, *California v. Cabazon Band of Mission Indians* (1987) and *Seminole Tribe of Florida v. Florida* (scheduled for oral arguments in fall 1995), two Oklahoma tribes supported the tribes involved. The Sac and Fox Tribe's attorney, G. William (Bill) Rice, joined a brief filed by other tribes and organizations in *Cabazon;* and Gary Pitchlynn, attorney for the Ponca Tribe in its gaming suit against Oklahoma, joined with attorneys for the Poarch Creek Indians and filed a brief in *Seminole* for the Ponca (the state of Oklahoma filed amicus briefs in these two cases in support of California and Florida). *Seminole* is especially important to the Ponca Tribe because the decision in that case could determine whether the Court will grant Oklahoma's request to hear its appeal of *Ponca v. Oklahoma.*

Several Oklahoma tribes filed briefs in support of the Sac and Fox, Potawatomi, and Chickasaw tribes in their legal battles with the Oklahoma Tax Commission. Bill Rice, attorney for the Sac and Fox Nation in its dispute with the commission, filed briefs on behalf of the tribe in each of the other three cases, including the two involving the Chickasaw Nation. In *Potawatomi* and *Graham* the amici were joined by several other Oklahoma tribes and related organizations. The Inter-Tribal Council of the Five Civilized Tribes also filed amicus briefs in *Potawatomi* and *Graham.* Bob Rabon, attorney for the Chickasaw in *Graham,* filed in the former, while Dennis Arrow, attorney for the tribe in *Chickasaw,* filed the latter.

Oklahoma tribes filing amici in these three cases did not necessarily confine themselves to Oklahoma lawyers. The Boulder, Colorado, based Native American Rights Fund filed

briefs on behalf of the Cheyenne-Arapaho tribes in *Potawatomi,*
Sac and Fox, and *Chickasaw.* The United Indian Nations of Oklahoma joined on the *Potawatomi* brief. Glenn M. Feldman of
Phoenix, Arizona, filed briefs for a number of Oklahoma tribes
in *Graham, Potawatomi,* and *Chickasaw.* Boulder attorney Thomas
Fredericks submitted briefs for the Ponca Tribe and the Ponca
Tax Commission in *Sac and Fox.* The extent of the involvement
of Oklahoma Indian tribes and organizations in these four
cases is presented in the Appendix.

Oklahoma tribes also participated in some of the most significant Indian law cases of the 1980s by means of amicus curiae
briefs. For example, Bill Rice filed in *Duro v. Reina* for the Sac
and Fox Nation, the Kickapoo Tribe, and the Housing Authority of the Sac and Fox Nation; the Cherokee Nation filed in
Yakima County v. Yakima Indian Nation; and Michael Minnis filed
for the Muscogee (Creek) Nation in *New York v. Attea.*

As with similar activity by New Mexico tribes, the success of
these efforts by Oklahoma tribes was mixed. This lobbying
tactic by tribes in Oklahoma again points to deficiencies in the
literature concerning interest group activity in the courts. However, it is also clear that Oklahoma tribes have made considerable use of the court system to achieve their substantive policy
goals. Much of this activity, including the gaming cases, has
involved efforts by the tribes to assert their contentions about
the breadth of tribal sovereignty and the limits of state intrusion in Indian Country. This has been particularly significant
in Oklahoma given the state's historic development and the
subsequent history of tribal-state relations.

GOVERNMENT-TO-GOVERNMENT RELATIONS

At least some Oklahoma tribes have demonstrated that they
are prepared to assert their sovereignty by establishing intergovernmental relations with the state of Oklahoma. Tribal-state
agreements are becoming more common, even among tribes
initially critical of such arrangements. These agreements have
come about for at least two reasons. First, tribal and state officials

have come to recognize the legitimate governing powers of the tribes. As has been shown, this has occurred because of changes in the understanding of the tribes' legal status and because of changes in national policy designed to encourage self-determination and self-governance. The second reason that the tribes and the state are more open to government-to-government agreements is a practical one: it saves time and money and reduces confusion and contention. It is less expensive for tribal and state governments to negotiate than it is to litigate their differences.

It should now be clear that the Oklahoma Tax Commission's arguments about tribal lands and sovereign immunity are doomed in federal court. Even when the commission has won, for example, the applicability of state taxes to non-Indians, enforceability is problematic. Thus the in lieu of taxes agreement kept tribal and state governments out of another round of expensive litigation. A residual benefit of these agreements for the tribes was the recognition by the state of the authority of tribal governments to negotiate sovereign to sovereign.

The cross-deputization agreements also solved a significant practical problem—that of ensuring law and order across jurisdictional lines. These agreements also resulted from and strengthened the legitimacy of the separate status of Indian Country and the consequent lack of state authority therein.

The success of tribal-state agreements in these areas has not been paralleled in gaming. There are at least three reasons for this. First, the state's gaming policy and its enforcement have significantly limited the willingness of the governors to negotiate Class III compacts. Governors have narrowly construed what is permissible under the IGRA, limiting the kind of Class III compact that can be negotiated.[175] Jess Green, a member of the NCAI/NIGA Task Force, has written that "states such as Oklahoma refuse to honor IGRA yet insist that Indian gaming be restricted by the same federal law" and that in Oklahoma "United States Attorneys have become major players in the political process of Indian gaming."[176] While governors may justify their actions on narrow federalism grounds, the actions of U.S. Attorneys in the state have been less understandable.[177]

Second, the state's political culture, while in transition,[178] has not yet reached the point where political leaders have room to accept the tribes' interpretation of the IGRA. The observation of gambling expert William R. Eadington that this kind of activity "is still viewed by many members of society as a questionable, if not immoral, activity that attracts questionable, if not immoral, people" seems particularly true in Oklahoma.[179] There appears to be real conflict among voters on the broad issue of legalized or state-supported gambling. A decade after approving horse racing and pari-mutuel wagering, the lottery referendum was defeated. The immediate opposition that arose to the DeBartolo casino proposal indicates that changing public policy to permit that activity will be difficult.

OUTSIDE LOBBYING: NOT YET

Finally, the inability of the tribes to unite politically has prevented them from competing effectively in the political arena with those opposed to *any* gaming expansion, such as religious groups, or those favoring only those forms of additional gaming that enhance their own economic interest, such as DeBartolo. Although the tribes have come to strongly assert their individual sovereign status, they have not yet reached the point of collective action. The tribes have used the opportunity available to them under the IGRA to pursue their individual gaming interests. This has meant that tribes either litigate or negotiate those interests independent of any joint interests. As has been shown, the general go-it-alone strategy is the result of the historic and cultural differences among the tribes.

Gaming is also a different kind of issue for the tribes than either taxation or cross-deputization. Gaming is potentially a source of additional competition among the tribes for limited leisure dollars. This kind of potential competition has elsewhere resulted in tribes working at cross-purposes politically, with one tribe or group of tribes attempting to expand their gaming while another tribe or group of tribes attempts to prevent it. The same thing could happen in Oklahoma.

The obstacles to expanded gaming have not resulted from the inherent political status of the tribes but from their strategic choices and from Oklahoma's political environment. The latter includes public policy and its interpretation and implementation and the attitudes and levels of responsiveness of Oklahoma public officials.

That Oklahoma tribes have not engaged in outside lobbying and campaign activities to the degree that New Mexico tribes have does not diminish the legitimacy of such actions or call into question the dual status tribes possess. The unique history of Oklahoma tribes and the wide variety of indigenous cultures they represent within the context of Oklahoma's political culture establishes the parameters of tribal options. This can be seen in nongaming issues such as smoke shop and gasoline taxation and cross-deputization. Tribes have attempted to resolve these controversies through direct negotiations and lawsuits. For Oklahoma tribes, inside individual tribal lobbying is the preferred method of achieving political and policy objectives.

While the outcome for Indian gaming is thus far more limited in Oklahoma than it is in New Mexico, the political status of tribes in the two states is not fundamentally different, nor are the fundamental sovereignty questions. Changes in any of the three conditions—public policy, institutional and official attitudes toward Indians, and the degree of cohesion among tribes—could produce results similar to those in New Mexico.

A change in public policy could result if the DeBartolo casino referendum is passed or if a second referendum scheduled for a vote in early 1996 passes. State Question 669 would roll back property taxes and limit future property tax increases. Opponents of the measure have argued that if SQ 669 passes, state and local governments would need to find new sources of revenue. Casino gambling is pointed to as the most likely option. Either of these referenda would expand the Class III gaming opportunities available to Oklahoma tribes.

It is possible that the tribes could become more cohesive and active. One catalyst for this might be the sense of urgency surrounding the cuts made in the 1996 fiscal year BIA budget

(Reeves 1995). Tribes in Oklahoma and around the nation protested these cuts and promised to become active not only to restore funding levels but to oppose those who favor the cuts in the 1996 elections. In late October 1996 Chickasaw Nation governor Bill Anoatubby was proceeding with his plans to organize a statewide Indian political action committee (PAC). At a minimum, he said, the Chickasaw Nation would have a PAC of its own in 1996.[180] Morgan, England, and Humphreys observed that "Indian political activism" has "not been played out in the mainstream political arena" in Oklahoma.[181] This may be about to change.

Absent a change in any of these conditions, it is unlikely that official opposition to expanded Indian gaming will change. However, if such changes did occur, Indian gaming will most assuredly grow in the state. First, a change in public policy would remove the rationale for opposition by both state and local officials. Second, if the state's tribes are able to become actively and effectively involved in supporting public officials who endorse their positions, Oklahoma tribes could have electoral success similar to that of New Mexico tribes.

These factors have individually and in combination affected the strategic choices of Oklahoma tribes and resulted in an Indian gaming environment much more limited than in New Mexico. Several points of comparison can be drawn between tribal efforts in Oklahoma and new Mexico. First, tribes in Oklahoma and New Mexico have very different traditions of intertribal cooperation based in large part on the indigenous status of the tribes within the state. Second, the lack of tribal cohesiveness based on historical and cultural differences has prevented the tribes in Oklahoma from engaging in the kinds of tribal interest group activity utilized by New Mexico tribes, including involvement in political campaigns. Third, gaming tribes in New Mexico coalesced behind the strategic and tactical leadership of such individuals as Kevin Gover. Gover provided the political savvy and leadership that the tribes drew on throughout their struggle. This has been lacking in Oklahoma. Fourth, Gover's strategy and the tribes' commitment would not have been possible without the financial resources made possible by the success of gaming. Gaming revenues provided the war chest that funded the campaign to protect tribal gaming. Fifth, the opposition of state and federal officials has forced Oklahoma tribes into court much more often than New Mexico tribes. Lawsuits have sometimes been initiated by the tribes and sometimes by the state of Oklahoma. Sixth, the active opposition of Oklahoma's U.S. Attorneys has severely and directly curtailed Indian gaming in the state, in dramatic contrast to the position of the U.S. Attorney in New Mexico. The seizure of tribal video machines by the U.S. Attorney for the Eastern District of Oklahoma stands in stark contrast to the "stand-down" agreement reached with New Mexico tribes by that state's U.S. Attorney. Seventh, the ongoing issue of expanded non-Indian gaming in Oklahoma has added a dimension to the efforts of Indian tribes to expand their gaming that is not nearly as evident in New Mexico. The opponents of non-Indian gaming in Oklahoma have come to rely on the specter of expanded Indian gaming as a rhetorical device to bolster their arguments about the potential harmful effects of widespread gambling. Eighth, notwithstanding the issue of Indian gaming, tribal governments in Oklahoma continue to demonstrate their ability to act as sovereigns and, when conditions are ripe, to engage in intergovernmental relationships with the state of Oklahoma.

Conclusion

The ways in which New Mexico and Oklahoma tribes have attempted to protect their gaming interests demonstrate that tribal political status is unique in theory and vulnerable in practice. Tribal governments possess the commonly understood attributes of both sovereigns and interest groups. One aspect of their uniqueness is their ability to flexibly exercise those attributes under certain favorable conditions. The vulnerability of tribal status is apparent when certain other conditions occur, including the political zeitgeist. The struggles of Indian tribes to control and expand gaming in Oklahoma and New Mexico have delineated the strengths and vulnerabilities of the tribes. The specific cases of New Mexico and Oklahoma offer an in-depth look at how some tribes have adapted their unique status in the American political system to meet historic challenges and new exigencies.

The experiences of tribes in these two states provide insights about several discrete aspects of the American political system. First, the filing of amicus curiae briefs by tribal attorneys on gaming and related sovereignty issues expands knowledge and understanding of the role of interest groups in the judicial system. Indian issues provide an intriguing insight into how the judicial system is used to further political and policy goals. This is most clearly seen when tribal and state governments oppose each other on issues involving a clash of sovereign interests. Second, and related to the filing of amicus briefs, is the significant role tribal attorneys play in tribal politics. The range of their involvement in tribal issues not only highlights one aspect of tribal politics but also provides new evidence of the pervasive influence lawyers have in American political life. Third, as demonstrated by the New Mexico and Oklahoma studies, the role of U.S. Attorneys in the policy process is potentially crucial, although largely unexplored by political science. This book builds on the minimal work that has been done in this area of judicial politics. Fourth, Indian gaming demonstrates that an issue of importance to Indian tribes can have an effect on related public policy and politics outside of Indian Country. A significant example is the New Mexico tribes' strategic campaign activities during the 1994 race for governor. Fifth, the circumstances under which the Indian Gaming Regulatory Act were passed shed new light on the significance of federal court decisions in setting the national legislative agenda.

THE STATUS OF TRIBES IN THE AMERICAN POLITICAL SYSTEM

Indian tribes are unmistakably part of the American political system. Their separate sovereign status is recognized in the Indian Commerce Clause of the U.S. Constitution. It is not insignificant that Article 1, section 8, clause 3, gives Congress the power to regulate trade with tribes, states, and foreign nations. Robert N. Clinton has noted of the Indian Commerce Clause, "No power over the Indian tribes was conferred," nor was the new federal government "authorized to manage affairs of the Indians, but rather affairs *with* the Indians."[1] For eighty-two years after George Washington was sworn in as president and the First Congress met in New York, the executive and the national legislature managed Indian affairs through legislation and the constitutional treaty-making power. The latter was a tacit recognition that Indian tribes had a political status that was unlike the states and more resembled that of foreign nations.

The U.S. Supreme Court has continually set and reset the boundaries of tribal sovereignty. It has emphasized the inherent independent political status of tribes while recognizing the power of Congress to exercise its "plenary power" to diminish that status or permit states to intrude on it. Congress in turn has alternately acknowledged the separate sovereign status of tribes and devised policies to terminate that status. The bright line of sovereignty, however, means that tribes have all of their inherent aboriginal sovereignty to the degree that it has not been voluntarily ceded by the tribes or unilaterally extinguished by the Congress.[2]

However, court decisions defining the limits of sovereignty do not fully define the *political* status of tribal governments. The U.S. Constitution, Supreme Court rulings, and historical fact establish the inherent and residual sovereignty of Indian tribes. Congressional policies have vacillated in their emphasis on it, but inherent tribal sovereignty remains. While the modern forms of tribal government are not those of pre-Columbian tribes,[3] they are recognized as legitimate governing entities by the federal government. In fact, the era of self-determination has strengthened tribal self-governance.

Sovereignty alone does not explain the political status of Indian tribes. Tribes do more than legislate, adjudicate, and administer. They also engage in the political processes of state and national governments in order to protect their sovereignty. Tribes often appear to act in ways similar to other arenas of government seeking to influence political institutions and the policy process. For example, elected and appointed tribal leaders testify at legislative hearings, lobby administrative bodies, and file lawsuits or amicus briefs in litigation in which their interests are at stake.

Tribes also act as classic American interest groups, becoming involved in the electoral process. Engaging in these activities takes them out of the realm of traditional intergovernmental lobbying efforts.[4] Many contemporary tribal governments, often fueled by gaming money, make campaign contributions, use the media to garner support for their political goals, and mobilize tribal members and employees to bring pressure on public officials. All of these activities are outside the scope of state, county, and municipal governments and within the scope of interest groups.[5] However, no interest group has constitutional standing that gives Congress sole authority to regulate its activities. While some interest groups have standing to intervene in some discrete issues, none has the sovereign responsibility to govern on behalf of an electorate living on lands that constitute a quasi-national land base. No interest group has aboriginal sovereignty over members; tribal membership is beyond any Olsen-like scheme explaining why people join groups.[6] You do not join a sovereign Indian nation, you are born into it.

Indian tribes increasingly follow a 1991 observation of Senator Inouye to tribal leaders. The then chairman of the Senate Select Committee on Indian Affairs said, "You can maintain and strengthen your sovereignty by *using* the political process of the United States of America."[7] Gaming, as an issue of sovereignty and economic survival, has made it imperative for tribes to use every asset and resource available to them to protect their interests. These include the financial resources generated by tribal gaming and the inherent flexible political status of tribal governments. The results have been increased activity by some tribes in the electoral process as well as in the more traditional intergovernmental lobbying sphere.

This activity is especially evident with respect to the 1996 presidential election. Voter registration drives were conducted throughout Indian Country, including Oklahoma and New Mexico. In New Mexico precincts identified by the secretary of state saw registration climb from 35,982 in 1994 to 37,480 in 1996.[8] According to Gover, national coordinator of the Democratic Native American Steering Committee, "We don't really divide between Republican and Democrat. . . . We divide on whether someone is pro- or anti-Indian. That's the kind of political sophistication we're looking for."[9]

Tribes and tribal enterprises, usually gaming related, also made campaign contributions. The following made significant contributions to the Democratic National Committee: the Oneida Tribe of Wisconsin ($40,000), Mille Lacs Grand Casino ($15,000), the St. Croix Tribal Council ($15,100), and Oklahoma's Cheyenne-Arapaho Business Committee ($100,000).[10] Two years earlier the Sault Ste. Marie Tribe of Chippewa Indians endorsed Republican Governor John Engler and gave the state Republican party $60,000.[11] The Choctaw Nation of Oklahoma made a $5,000 contribution to the congressional campaign of Democrat Darryl Roberts.[12]

These amounts pale when compared to those of the Mashantucket Pequot Tribe of Connecticut, operator of "the Western world's largest and most profitable casino,"[13] and California tribes in the 1994 state attorney general race. Between 1993 and 1995 the Pequots made "soft money" contributions of $465,000 nationwide, $365,000 to various Democratic party committees.[14] In 1994 California tribes, upset with the incumbent attorney general's negative attitude toward Indian gaming, combined to give more than $700,000 to his Democratic opponent.[15]

The fight by Indian tribes in New Mexico and Oklahoma over the past decade to control gaming has demonstrated the strengths and vulnerabilities of their political status. This fight, while over a new and complex issue, has occurred within the context of historic tensions in Indian policy and within the U.S. Constitution itself. Gaming has generated a struggle among sovereigns over the right to control resources and to define the extent of self-government permitted under the Constitution. Historic and fundamental conflict over states' rights in the formulation and implementation of Indian policy are central to this struggle, as are the legal and moral commitments made to Indian tribes through treaties, laws, and court decisions. As seen in the different levels of political activities by New Mexico and Oklahoma tribes, unique historical factors specific to the political environment and Indian-white relations play a role in how tribes in a specific state use their political status. However, even if a given state's tribes are politically inactive or constrained by the historical factors of the political culture, the fundamental political status of tribes is the same. Just as some states are better at presenting their case to Congress, so are some tribes better able to put forward their political agenda.

A UNIQUE BUT VULNERABLE STATUS

That tribes are vulnerable to the political currents and zeitgeist is clearly seen in the attack on Indian gaming coming at the same time as national politicians and the U.S. Supreme Court attempt to devolve more power to the states. As has been seen in gaming and other related tribal state conflicts in Oklahoma and New Mexico, "the federalism debate has always greatly affected Indian tribes—and the field of Indian law—and the renewed debate is no exception."[16]

Conflict over gaming also demonstrates the historical fact that tribes remain at risk in the American political system. Tribes, although more sophisticated in their use of the political tools available to them, must nonetheless be vigilant in responding to the demands of other powerful actors in that system. Indian tribes have always been at risk when the avaricious urges of the nation desired their natural resources, whether they be land, water, minerals from the earth, or gambling.

AMICUS CURIAE BRIEFS IN INDIAN LITIGATION

Increasingly tribes and Indian organizations have been very aggressive in filing amicus curiae briefs in lawsuits before the U.S. Supreme Court involving gaming and other issues relating to tribal sovereignty. The numbers of briefs filed and the tribal resources expended on them demonstrate how the American judicial system is used by those seeking either to establish a favorable policy or prevent an adverse policy from being promulgated. The coordinated manner in which these briefs are filed is illustrative of the common ground tribes find on most issues relating to gaming and sovereignty. In addition, how tribal attorneys decide who files which briefs in a given case indicates a sophisticated system of decision making regarding resources and expertise.

We thus see in tribal amicus activity a clear example of judicial lobbying. When we select discrete litigation pitting states' rights against tribal sovereignty, this phenomenon becomes dramatically clear. Intergovernmental disputes, that is, states versus tribes, illustrate the significant role of the courts. The degree of seriousness with which each side views such questions is demonstrated by the unanimity of tribes on one side of an issue and that of states on the other. In *Seminole Tribe of Florida v. Florida* and the three recent Oklahoma Tax Commission cases, states and tribes clearly delineated their different perspectives in the briefs filed with the court.

Another area of interest in litigation involving tribes and states is the position of the U.S. government as seen in the amicus briefs filed by the U.S. Solicitor General. In recent years the role of the Solicitor in guiding U.S. Supreme Court action has grown. As in other types of lawsuits, the Court will often ask the Solicitor General for the government's position on an Indian issue. One way of determining how a particular administration views Indian sovereignty or states' rights questions is to look at which side the government's briefs support.

THE ROLE OF TRIBAL ATTORNEYS

An issue closely related to the filing of amicus briefs is the general role of tribal attorneys in tribal politics. The examples of tribal attorneys in New Mexico and Oklahoma have shown that they act in at least the following capacities: (1) litigator, (2) lobbyist, and (3) political strategist.

As litigators, tribal attorneys are involved in standard client-attorney relationships. They advise their clients on the legal options and strategies available in any potential law suit, whether as plaintiff or as defendant. They file briefs, offer motions, take depositions—in short, do what all attorneys do when representing a client. The difference is that their client is a sovereign government that has a unique government-to-government relationship with the federal government. Thus tribal attorneys must be familiar with a body of law that is unique in the American judicial system.

While tribal attorneys must have specialized knowledge, they generally have fewer resources available to them than their opposite number representing states or corporations. They sometimes even have fewer resources than individuals they are litigating. For example, the prosecutor of the Navajo Nation does not have access to electronic on-line data bases that nearly all private attorneys have.

As lobbyists, tribal attorneys engage in all of the activities one would expect of professionals advancing the policy goals and interests of their clients. This occurs at national, state, and local levels. A clear example of the role of attorneys as lobbyists is the battle by New Mexico tribes in the state legislature, where at least one attorney drafted legislation to be submitted on behalf of his client tribes. Tribal attorneys are also key advisers in the efforts to amend the Indian Gaming Regulatory Act.

Finally, tribal attorneys have played significant roles in devising the political strategies implemented to promote Indian gaming. Attorneys such as New Mexico's Kevin Gover have been heavily involved in state and national politics and use their expertise and contacts to further tribal policy goals. At the national level, as members of the various National Indian Gaming Association working groups, attorneys provide significant assistance to tribal leaders developing coordinated strategies that will advance tribal gaming interests legislatively, administratively, judicially, and politically.

THE ROLE OF THE U.S. ATTORNEY

Early on it became clear to me that the role of U.S. Attorneys was potentially a crucial variable in the success or failure of tribal attempts to operate gaming enterprises. Arising first in a discussion with Ponca tribal attorney Gary Pitchlynn, the largely independent discretionary authority of U.S. Attorneys became a focus of my research when it became evident that the differences between New Mexico and Oklahoma gaming tribes were in large measure due to the actions of these federal officials. Much of what Eisenstein argued in his excellent *Counsel for the United States* (1978) was found to be true in the case of U.S. Attorneys and Indian gaming. For example, the influence of local political connections, political ambition, and personal experiences can be seen as likely motives for the actions of New Mexico's John Kelly and Oklahoma's Steve Lewis and John Raley. Moreover, the independent nature of their presidential appointments and their relative freedom from control by the attorney general gives them broad latitude in the choices they make about law enforcement.

At least two additional findings regarding the role of U.S. Attorneys emerged in my study. First, these presidential appointees, in exercising their independent discretionary power, play a significant *policy-implementing* role. Absent a clear policy position from the White House or the Justice Department, U.S. Attorneys may choose to implement policy in a variety of ways, none of them necessarily consistent across federal districts. While this has been evident in the diverse actions of U.S. Attorneys in the issue of Indian gaming in New Mexico and Oklahoma, it has also been true *within a single state.* U.S. Attorneys in two separate California districts have made different judgments about enforcing the IGRA within their jurisdictions.[17]

The issue of policy variance across federal districts and states indicates that federalism is an important matter in the discretionary role of U.S. Attorneys. What is significant about Indian gaming and the actions of U.S. Attorneys is that it requires the federal appointee to consider not only federal law, in this case the IGRA and the Johnson Act, but state law as well. It requires U.S. Attorneys to interpret *state* gaming law to determine what kinds of Indian gaming are permissible under *federal* law. As we have seen in New Mexico, John Kelly waited for two state supreme court decisions before taking actions to close the Indian-operated casinos in his state. Similarly, Steve Lewis acted without specific Justice Department clearance and conducted a raid on an eastern Oklahoma Indian tribe based on his interpretation of state gaming law, ignoring a tribal court ruling in the process.

Second, law enforcement in Indian Country clearly has ramifications for federalism issues as well as for the future political ambitions of U.S. Attorneys. Depending on the Indian population and the land base of a given federal district, a U.S. Attorney's office may find itself devoting considerable amounts of its resources to law enforcement in Indian Country. This is certainly the case in New Mexico and Oklahoma but is even more true in states like South Dakota. (Hogen 1996).

Because there are discrete policy and law subfields with the prefix "Indian" attached to them, the assumption is often made that they operate in a vacuum and have little connection to broader areas of public policy and law. The battles over Indian gaming have demonstrated that an Indian policy issue can have a major impact on otherwise unrelated issues and the political process itself.

Indian gaming has presented fundamental questions about federalism and intergovernmental relations. The IGRA and the Supreme Court's *Seminole* decision have done more than define the parameters of Indian gaming; they have played a dramatic role in the redefinition of the federal-state balance of power. By limiting the power of Congress to abrogate state Eleventh Amendment sovereign immunity under the Commerce Clause, the Court has clearly sided with and advanced the current political tide of devolution. The governors and states' rights won and Congress lost.

The political controversies of Indian gaming itself have forced many states to reconsider their own gaming policies, particularly in light of *Cabazon* and the IGRA. In Oklahoma a ballot initiative was begun because supporters of casino gambling in the state claimed that Indians were likely to wind up with a monopoly on Class III gaming if the state did not legalize the activity. We have also seen how Indian gaming issues in New Mexico drastically altered the conventional wisdom of legal gaming in the state. Furthermore, an unanticipated consequence of Indian gaming and the compacts signed by Gov. Gary Johnson and the tribes was a state supreme court ruling sharpening the lines of executive and legislative authority. As demonstrated by the debate over the motor fuel tax in Oklahoma and New Mexico, other issues stemming from the political status or concerns of Indian tribes can find their way onto a state's legislative or political agenda.

The financial resources generated by gaming have enabled some tribes to become significant players in the political process. New Mexico's gaming tribes have demonstrated how a sophisticated political operation can be mounted by tribes with the money, leadership, and determination to do so. Chapters 4 and 5 described the well-organized and generously funded effort mounted by tribes in that state to elect a governor favorable to their cause and then win over public opinion and secure the passage of pro-gaming legislation.

Their efforts in turn have had an impact on state politics, including exacerbating partisan differences between the governor and the legislature and clarifying the conflicting ambitions of some of the state's leading political figures. As the 1996 election year got under way, tribes made strategic decisions concerning which legislative races to become involved in. This helped to determine the composition of the next New Mexico legislature.

New Mexico is not an isolated case. Connecticut's Mashantucket Pequot Tribe, many California tribes, and tribes in Wisconsin and Minnesota have also become active politically because of the gaming issue. Even Oklahoma tribes were making historic efforts in 1996 to become involved in the electoral process, having not only been shut out of expanded gaming opportunities but also having recently engaged in a bitter legislative battle to keep from losing the gains made in *Oklahoma Tax Commission v. Chickasaw Nation of Oklahoma.*

THE ROLE OF FEDERAL COURTS IN SETTING THE NATIONAL LEGISLATIVE AGENDA

The events leading to Congress passing the Indian Gaming Regulatory Act in 1988 were spurred in large measure by federal court rulings handed down in litigation resulting from tribal attempts to expand their gaming enterprises and prevent state governments from exercising any regulatory authority over them. As first lower federal courts and then the Supreme Court itself ruled in favor of the tribes, interest groups opposed to tribal gaming turned to Congress for a remedy and relief. As described in chapter 3, the Schattschneider-like efforts of non-Indian gaming interests and state officials to limit the court-determined rights of tribes to operate gambling ventures led them directly to Congress. While the legislation that resulted has been, at best, a mixed blessing for the tribes, it was fortunate for the tribes that the leading congressional actors—Udall, Inouye, McCain—were pro-Indian. Nevertheless, as the debates and reports indicate, the issue was clearly on the congressional agenda because of the rulings of federal courts over a period of four years.

The battle over Indian gaming has shed considerable light on legislative agenda setting. While Henschen and Sidlow made a contribution to the field much beyond Kingdon, they did not go far enough in their own research. Finally, the actions of tribes, states, and non-Indian gaming interests in moving from the courts to the legislature expand Schattschneider's groundbreaking work on the "scope of conflict" over political and economic issues.

All five of these areas are worthy of additional research. They not only illuminate the study of Indian politics and policy but also expand the knowledge base of political science regarding the entire American political system.

A FINAL WORD ON THE STATUS OF AMERICAN INDIAN TRIBES IN THE AMERICAN POLITICAL SYSTEM AT THE END OF THE TWENTIETH CENTURY

The status of tribes combines sovereignty and interest group activity in ways unique in the American political system. The self-governing powers of tribes rests on aboriginal sovereignty and national policy. Although their status remains "dependent" and they are no longer dealt with through the treaty process, tribes have an evolving place in the American system of federalism. American federalism itself is a dynamic process. As tribes gain governing experience and Congress delegates them governing authority, tribal governments assume a status above local government and increasingly on a level resembling that of states. Administratively and statutorily, for example, tribes have been granted the right to be treated as states in some areas of environmental protection.[18]

States and tribes have contending views of the extent of sovereignty each may exercise. This is classic intergovernmental competition and conflict. Gaming is a striking example of the dynamic nature of federalism, as tribal, state, and federal governments each exercise some amount of sovereignty over gaming in Indian Country. The authority exercised by tribal governments is the result of tribal sovereignty. In passing the IGRA, Congress recognized a state interest in gambling activities, limiting tribal sovereignty and exercising its broad powers in Indian affairs. The *Seminole* decision was an explicit recognition of the federalism question involved in the IGRA; the Court diminished congressional power to abrogate the states' Eleventh Amendment sovereign immunity.

With renewed partisan political emphasis on the Tenth Amendment and the Court's concern about congressional authority under the broad Commerce Clause, federalism is being redefined. Tribes are clearly affected by this process. They are turning to the courts and legislatures to achieve legal and political recognition of their sovereign status. In so doing, they are behaving as other sovereigns in the federal system.

While some of this is not new,[19] the degree of sophistication and resources brought to bear in the process is new. John Echohawk, Native American Rights Fund executive director, noted in 1990, "What's happening is that tribal governments are becoming a permanent part of the fabric of American federalism. . . . You have a federal government, state government and tribal government—three sovereigns in one country."[20]

In the battle over Indian gaming, tribes have also rediscovered and redefined the other aspect of their status, that of interest groups. Their goals in behaving as interest groups include influencing other levels of government. Two major aspects of this activity, however, make Indian tribes as interest groups unique. First, tribal governments and enterprises can become directly involved in electoral politics. Second, the goals of tribal governments resemble those of other groups only superficially. While attempting to get a larger piece of the federal pie, like other interest groups, tribal governments' pleas are based on their status and relationship with the federal government. Treaty obligations and the trust relationship mean tribes have a base from which to approach Congress that states do not have.

How tribes use their status varies widely from tribe to tribe and state to state. Historical, political, and cultural factors impose limits or pose political opportunities for tribes. Individual and cooperative political leadership among the tribes may also be important. While there are examples of effective tribal leaders among Oklahoma tribes, rarely do they form a united front, even on Indian gaming. This is partly the result of tribal and historical differences. Similar factors have had the opposite effect in the tribes' fight for Indian gaming in New Mexico.

However, the differences among the tribes in the two states do not indicate a difference in political status within the political system. All tribes have the same status and exercise it to the degree resources, leadership, and political environment make action possible. Finally, while there is a firmly established tribal-federal state relationship, tribes and states have no formal relationship. It must be constantly established and reestablished, making effective use of tribal political status increasingly imperative.

Epilogue

The culmination of more than a decade of near-victories and near-defeats but no definitive outcome for New Mexico tribes finally occurred in the 1997 legislative session. After a grueling and often emotionally charged effort by tribal gaming advocates, the 43d Legislature passed a bill making legalized Indian gaming possible in the state. Under the new law, tribes signing compacts could operate casino games, including machine and table games, and would bear most of the regulatory oversight of their own games. The compacts were to last for a term of nine years; established a minimum age of twenty-one for both patrons and employees of tribal casinos; required that such benefits as leave, insurance, safety conditions, workers' compensation, and unemployment benefits as well as wage and hour requirements be the same as those for the rest of the state; restricted check cashing and the use of ATMs at gaming facilities; prohibited employment discrimination; established minimum gaming machine specifications and central computerized reporting and auditing systems at all casinos; and prohibited alcoholic beverages from casino gaming areas. Employee background checks were required. Regulatory fees to the state were set at $6,250 per facility per quarter plus an additional $300 per gaming machine and $750 per gaming table.

Another section of the law required tribes to share their gaming revenue with the state. This was set at 16 percent of the net from each tribal facility. This requirement was the most controversial aspect of the new law, and many tribal leaders believed it went beyond what was allowed by the IGRA.

On July 8, 1997, five months after signing the bill into law, Governor Johnson signed ten gaming compacts and revenue-sharing agreements. The signatories were the Tesuque, San Felipe, Pojoaque, Santa Clara, Isleta, Acoma, Taos, Sandia, and Laguna pueblos and the Mescalero Apache Tribe.[1] All but Laguna Pueblo were currently operating casinos.[2] Because of the revenue-sharing agreements, the Interior Department was reluctant to go along with the compacts but Secretary Babbitt allowed them to go into effect without taking any formal action, an option he had under the IGRA.[3] On August 23 Babbitt wrote to Governor Johnson of his concerns about the compacts, which, he said in a press release, "appear to put New Mexico tribes in an untenable position."

> On the one hand, they are expected to agree to a number of burdensome conditions that go well beyond the scope of any of the 161 compacts that are now approved between states and tribes in this country. On the other hand, if tribes do not agree to those conditions or if the compacts are disapproved, existing gaming establishments many be threatened with closure, causing immediate and enormous economic hardship.[4]

Even while the tribes were offering their now-legal games, the 16 percent revenue-sharing agreement remained controversial. Most tribes did not pay the entire amount due to the state. Neither the Mescalero nor Jicarilla Apache Tribe paid anything whatsoever when the first payments were due on October 25, 1997.[5] By the time the New Mexico legislature convened for its biennial sixty-day session in January 1999, only the Pueblo gaming tribes had paid anything to the state.[6]

Once again the legislature became the arena for New Mexico's tribes to achieve what they believed was a fair and level playing field. At least seven bills dealing with the tribal-state compacts were introduced. Tribal leaders and Rep. Roger Madalena of Jemez Pueblo pushed for an outright reduction in the revenue-sharing amount, to an average of about 9 percent annually per tribe.[7] Madalena's bill passed the House by a vote of 43 to 22 but died in the Senate. What finally did pass both Houses was a bill sponsored by Democratic Senate President Pro Tem Manny Aragon that provided for a process by which a new compact could be negotiated. Under the provisions of the new law, after a compact is negotiated between a tribe and the governor it is submitted to the Legislative Services Council for review. If the council approves, it sends it on to the legislature for a final vote.[8]

As it had in the past legislative sessions, the New Mexico Indian Gaming Association had taken a key role in getting the 1997 legislation passed. Four months after the compacts were signed, Kevin Gover was nominated to the position of assistant secretary of the interior for Indian affairs.

OTHER BATTLES, OTHER ARENAS

The clash of interests and the maneuvering for position in the most appropriate arena of conflict that took place in New Mexico and Oklahoma also occurred throughout the 1990s in California. However, the fight over the scope of tribal sovereignty was not limited to state capitols. Some of the most crucial and divisive struggles took place in the ultimate arena of American politics, Washington, D.C.

CALIFORNIA

In the years following *Cabazon* and passage of the IGRA, California gaming tribes prospered at the same time that they continued to face opposition on several fronts. First, Republican Governor Pete Wilson refused to sign Class III gaming compacts with those tribes that had expanded their gaming operations. Second, U.S. Attorneys in California's three federal districts continually threatened to seize tribal casino equipment, which they considered to be in violation of the Johnson Act and California gaming statutes through forfeiture lawsuits. Third, non-Indian gaming interests in Nevada increasingly saw the expansion of tribal gaming in California as a threat to their own interests. These three points of opposition were intertwined and, in 1998, led to a division among the tribes and a heightening of the political conflict over gaming in the state.

Although certain Class III games are legal in California—state lottery, pari-mutuel horse racing, card clubs, and charitable gaming—Governor Wilson refused to sign compacts with the tribes during the first six years of his two terms in office. In the face of this reality, most of the state's tribes—without compacts—began to offer various kinds of video gambling devices, which they argued were similar to the kind used by the California state lottery. Wilson contended that these devices were in violation of state law. When seven tribes requested negotiations with the state under the IGRA for specific kinds of games, Wilson refused to negotiate. His position was that the IGRA does not *require* tribal-state negotiations; that the law violated the Tenth Amendment; and that the games proposed by the tribes violated state law. The difference between the tribes and Wilson on the last issue raised again the question of what was the permitted scope of gaming under the IGRA.

As occurred in New Mexico, both the state and the tribes agreed to seek a judicial determination of whether California was obligated to negotiate compacts with the tribes. The federal district court ruled in favor of the tribes, finding that most of the games the tribes proposed to operate were within the scope of negotiations.[9] On appeal, the Ninth Circuit reversed the district court, holding that "with the possible exception of slot machines in the form of video lottery terminals, California has no obligation to negotiate with the Tribes on the Proposed Gaming Activities."[10] In a strongly worded dissent, Judge William C. Canby, Jr., calling *Rumsey* "a case of major significance in the administration of the Indian Gaming Regulatory Act," wrote that "this ruling effectively frustrates IGRA's entire plan governing Class III gaming." The U.S. Supreme Court refused to hear the case in 1997.

While the U.S. Attorneys in the three California districts believed that the games the tribes offered were illegal, they agreed to wait for the outcome of the judicial process and did not begin forfeiture proceedings against the allegedly offending tribes. After the Supreme Court refused to hear *Rumsey,* the U.S. Attorney for the Southern District asked the tribes in his district to begin reducing the number of gaming machines. Several years earlier the tribes and the U.S. Attorney had agreed to a set number of machines until the scope of gaming issue was litigated. The so-called San Diego Agreement was originally made "on the basis of a handshake."[11] The U.S. Attorney again held off any further action against the tribes in his district after the Pala Band of Mission Indians began what appeared to be serious negotiations with the state in fall 1996. The proposed compact that was being negotiated was controversial among most of the state's tribes and led to a shift in the battleground from the courts to the legislature and to the voters of California. The wait-and-see attitude of the California U.S. Attorneys was similar to the position adopted by John Kelly in the early years of the New Mexico gaming conflict.

To add confusion to an already confused gaming situation, the California Supreme Court had ruled in June 1996 that California's State Keno Lottery was illegal. Western Telcon and the California Horsemen's Benevolent and Protective Association sought a declaration in the trial court that the game was illegal. The court permitted the California-Nevada Indian Gaming Association (CNIGA) to intervene as a defendant. The court of appeals upheld the trial court's ruling. The Supreme Court, however, reached a different conclusion about the California State Keno Lottery, declaring that it was, "as a matter of law, not an authorized lottery game."[12] The decision spurred the tribes to seek a legislative solution to the scope of gaming issue.

Five months after the *Western Telcon* decision Governor Wilson, for the first time since his election in 1990, began serious negotiations with a California tribe. According to Pala Band of Mission Indians chairman Timothy Smith, Wilson agreed to negotiate with his tribe because the band had no current gaming operations, was a large tribe "by California standards," and had a stable government.[13] After nearly a year and a half of negotiations, Wilson signed a 132-page compact with the Pala Band on March 6, 1998. Compacts with eleven tribes, including the Pala Band, were overwhelmingly approved by the California legislature in August 1998.[14]

The success of the Pala Band and the other tribes that signed the compact was not universally supported by the rest of California's tribes. Most viewed the compact's provisions to be generally punitive and restrictive. For example, the compact did not allow slot machines, tribes were restricted to lottery devices deemed legal by the state, and other tribes had sixty days to indicate their intention to join the compacts. After the sixty days had passed, according to Wilson, "U.S. Attorneys will take immediate enforcement actions against all other tribes out of compliance."[15] California Attorney General Dan Lungren, like Wilson a longtime critic of Indian gaming, said after the signing, "The Pala compact is innovative and unprecedented in that it provides for a form of legal Indian gaming that is permitted under California law. Banked games and slot machines are still illegal in California."[16] Most objectionable to the tribes opposing the compact, however, was the provision that established a statewide limit on the number of gambling devices. A total of 19,900 devices would be allowed, with each tribe restricted to 199 unless one tribe licensed additional devices from other tribes, to a maximum of 975 devices.[17]

In an interesting twist that had statewide political overtones, the compact required that tribal gaming employees be covered by the state's workers' compensation law. Further, in a reversal of Wilson's long-held attitudes about organized labor, the compact extended collective bargaining rights to tribal service employees. As Bill Ainsworth of the *San Diego Union-Tribune* wrote on April 13, 1998, the compact's "major provisions seem to call for everything that the governor dislikes—more unions, more lawsuits, and redistributing wealth from prosperous to impoverished tribes."[18] On August 25 the newspaper reported that the Viejas Band of Kumeyaay Indians, which signed the Pala compact, reached an agreement with the Communications Workers of America permitting the union to organize the tribe's casino workers.

In April 1998 a coalition of forty gaming tribes that had not engaged in negotiations with Wilson on the Pala Band compact submitted petitions containing 800,000 signatures to place a pro-gaming initiative on the fall ballot.[19] If enacted, the proposition would authorize tribal-state compacts; allow tribes currently operating gaming facilities to continue to offer their existing games; and only allow Indian gaming on Indian lands. The gambling currently legal under California law would continue. Las Vegas-style games and banked games would not be permitted. The proposition further established uniform standards for Indian gaming facilities and gave the state the right to inspect tribal gaming facilities and records. The tribes would reimburse the state for all costs related to regulating the casinos. Up to 6 percent of the net machine revenues would be used to support housing, medical, and social services for all Californians.[20]

The coalition responsible for the Proposition, calling itself Yes on 5: Californians for Indian Self-Reliance, alleged that the Pala compact was the result of "a secret backroom deal negotiated with a single Tribe." "The only real winners from the proposed Wilson/Pala Compact," the coalition contended, "would be Nevada and its rich Las Vegas casino owners."[21] Anthony Pico, chairman of the Viejas Band, told a hearing held in San Diego by the National Gambling Impact Study, "After eight years of court battles, legislative fights and divisive political rhetoric, the governor brought us a compact to sign—a compact that we were never a party to—a compact that exacted a very dear price: a piece of our sovereignty."[22]

The subsequent campaign seemed to bear out the coalition's view of the Nevada gambling interests' concerns about the proposition. But Nevada gaming interests were joined in their opposition to Proposition 5 by Governor Wilson, Republican candidate for governor Dan Lungren, labor unions, church groups, and other interest groups, including the Traditional Values Coalition. The major organized opposition to Proposition 5 was led by a group called the Coalition Against Unregulated Gaming comprising Nevada gaming interests, several labor unions, and Indian tribes. As of October 17, 1998, the coalition listed contributions of $26,203,010, 44 percent from entities donating $10,000 or more. Five contributions were $1 million or more: $8 million from Mirage Resorts/Bellagio of Las Vegas; $6.5 million from Circus Circus Enterprises, Las Vegas; $6.5 million from Hilton Hotels Corp., Beverly Hills; $1.7 million from W. G. Bennett, Chairman, Sahara Gaming Corporation, Las Vegas; and $1 million from Caesar's ITT, Las Vegas.[23]

While these amounts are impressive, the contributions made by pro-Proposition 5 tribes were extraordinary. Contributions listed by Californians for Indian Self-Reliance as of October 17 amounted to $59,715,205; of these, 99.9 percent were for at least $10,000. Five tribes contributed more than $1 million: San Manuel Tribal Administration, $26.7 million; Viejas Band, $10.2 million; Morongo Band of Mission Indians, $10 million; Pechanga Band of Mission Indians, $8.6 million; and Agua Caliente Band of Cahuilla Indians, $1.5 million. Nine other tribes gave more than $100,000 to the campaign.[24] By the end of the campaign, more than $100 million were spent for and against Proposition 5.[25]

Proposition 5 overwhelming passed by a little over five million votes to a little over three million votes (62.4 to 37.6%).[26] However, the implementation of the referendum was threatened by two lawsuits, one filed by the Employees and Restaurant Employees International Union and another by an individual citizen. The state's labor unions had been divided on Proposition 5 during the election, although most opposed passage. The plaintiffs argued that the proposition violates the California constitution's prohibition on Nevada- and New Jersey-style casinos as well as the U.S. Constitution's Supremacy Clause, as it violates the IGRA. The California Supreme Court granted the plaintiffs' motion to delay implementation pending arguments. Governor Wilson, due to leave office in January 1999, and outgoing Attorney General Lungren supported the lawsuit. When the newly elected Democratic attorney general, Bill Lockyer, took office, he was granted permission by the Supreme Court to withdraw Lungren's written arguments in favor of the lawsuit.[27] Governor Gary Davis, who defeated Lundgren in November, and Lockyer indicated that they wanted to be neutral in the dispute, but Davis also indicated his desire to enter negotiations with the tribes.

The saga of the California tribes has all of the elements found in similar conflicts by tribes in New Mexico and Oklahoma. The significance of U.S. Attorney discretion; the attitudes of individual governors and how a change in the occupant of the state house can dramatically and swiftly alter the dynamics of the process; intertribal divisions;[28] the interplay of interest groups and political parties; and the ability of courts to help set the political and policy agenda are all as evident in California as they were in New Mexico and Oklahoma. The shortcomings of the Indian Gaming Regulatory Act were also clear almost from the beginning in California. Governor Wilson's refusal to negotiate and the confusion over the scope of gaming, both results of deficiencies and ambiguities in the IGRA, clearly exacerbated the situation in the state. Finally, the dual role of tribes as interest groups and sovereigns was readily and significantly apparent in California, particularly their activities in lawsuits and in the debate over Proposition 5 as they, and their opponents, sought the arena most favorable to their position.[29]

INDIAN COUNTRY UNDER ATTACK

With Indian gaming profits increasing and tribal political activities changing the face of politics in many states, tribal sovereignty came under growing attacks in the national arenas of conflict from governors and members of Congress. Near the end of the decade Indian tribes were experiencing the most direct assault on their sovereignty in nearly forty years. The federal trust relationship with the tribes was under the greatest attack since the termination era. These pressures were occurring at the same time that federalism was undergoing a historic transformation. Devolution of power and program administration to the states was supported by both the Democratic president and Republicans in Congress and state houses across the country. Tribes faced determined opposition to their sovereign status on at least three fronts: gaming, funding, and tribal sovereign immunity.

Legislation was introduced in every newly elected Congress to curtail Indian gaming. Anti-Indian gaming members of Congress were spurred by the 1996 *Seminole* decision. In declaring unconstitutional the provision of the IGRA that gave tribes the right to sue states in federal court, the Court had opened the door to potential unilateral action by the secretary of the interior. Amendments to the 1998 and 1999 Interior Department appropriations bills prevented the secretary from approving Class III gaming for tribes without compacts. Sen. Michael B. Enzi (R-Wy.), introducing his amendment to the 1999 bill, declared that its purpose was "to ensure that the rights of this Congress and all 50 States are not trampled on by an unelected Cabinet official."[30] A six-month suspension was ultimately agreed to. Reintroducing the bill in March 1999, this time as an amendment to the Emergency Supplemental Appropriations Act for 1999, Enzi stressed the need for the status quo so that the IGRA could be given comprehensive consideration. The amendment passed the Senate by a voice vote on March 19, 1999.[31]

Another approach to limit the impact of Indian gaming was Rep. Bill Archer's (R-Tex.) effort to tax the proceeds of tribal enterprises. The chairman of the House Ways and Means Committee argued that as Indian gaming grows, it competes for money that would have been spent on taxable goods and services. Legislation taxing Indian gaming profits passed the House in 1996 but was killed in the Senate. The following year, a similar proposal was overwhelming defeated notwithstanding

Archer's argument that his bill would raise $1.9 billion in revenue by 2002.[32] A concerted lobbying effort by the tribes as well as strong Republican opposition to Archer's proposal on the committee contributed to its defeat.

Rep. Ernest J. Istook (R-Okla.) sought to limit the expansion of Indian gaming through an amendment to the 1998 Interior Department appropriations bill that would have sharply limited the ability of the secretary of the interior to take new land into trust for a tribe wanting to offer gaming under the IGRA. Arguing that "all people should be equal under the law," Istook charged that the tribes "are marketing the tax evasion to their customers."[33] His "fair play amendment" would have required that any new land taken into trust for tribes or individual Indians be taxed by states.[34]

Slade Gorton (R-Wash.), a longtime foe of tribal sovereignty, launched two simultaneous attacks on the tribes. Drawing on a widely held misconception that all Indian tribes were doing well financially under Indian gaming, Gorton proposed means testing of some federal appropriations to tribes. As Assistant Secretary Gover told the National Congress of American Indians in October 1998, "Our adversaries have used the illusion of rich Indians to justify cutting BIA and IHS [Indian Health Service] budgets to the bone and reducing funds available to even the neediest tribes."[35] Gorton proposed, and the Interior Appropriations Subcommittee he chaired passed, a needs-based means test for tribal priority allocations (TPA) money. TPA funds local units of tribal governments and, as Gover told the Senate Committee on Indian Affairs, "supports the goals of Indian self-determination by providing Tribes with the choice of programs provided as well as the means of delivery, either by the Tribe or by the Bureau."[36] The BIA was directed to devise a formula "taking into account each tribe's tribal business revenues from all business ventures, including gaming."[37] TPA funds accounted for $700 million in the 1998 budget, more than half the BIA's funding for that year.

Meetings among Senators Gorton, Campbell, Inouye, Stevens, Domenici, McCain, and Gover led to a compromise version of

Gorton's proposal. The compromise set a minimum level of TPA funding at $160,000. Remaining funds would be allocated to tribes according to the recommendations of a new task force consisting of two representatives from each of the BIA areas.[38] This was to address what Gorton said was the purpose of his so-called Robin Hood proposal, that is, the unequal distribution of federal funds that left some small and poor tribes receiving an inadequate amount of TPA funds. The compromise, as passed in the appropriations bill, resulted in $16.5 million being distributed to 310 tribes and Alaska Native villages.[39]

Gorton's second attack on the tribes was directed at their sovereign immunity from lawsuits. The Washington Republican introduced this proposal as an amendment to the Interior Department appropriations bill for 1998, along with his "Robin Hood" means testing plan. As approved by his subcommittee, the bill would have required any tribe that received TPA funds to waive its sovereign immunity and subject tribes that did so to the jurisdiction of federal courts.[40] Working with the same group that developed the means test compromise, Gorton agreed to withdraw the subcommittee's amendment in exchange for a promise that hearings would be held in the next Congress.

After withdrawing a similar proposal in 1997 on the guarantee of hearings the next year, Gorton introduced S. 1691, The American Indian Equal Justice Act, in February 1998. The bill would "uphold the principle that no government should be above the law" and declared that sovereign immunity "is incompatible with the rule of law in democratic society."[41] One of the bill's prime and most controversial features would have required tribes to impose state excise, use, and sales taxes in Indian Country. To enforce this provision, states were given the right to sue in federal court. Gorton's bill also provided that federal courts would have jurisdiction over civil actions or claims against a tribe. Section 2692 of the bill would make tribes "liable, relating to tort claims, in the same manner, as a private individual or corporation under like circumstances." In a crippling blow to tribal sovereignty, the bill gave consent "to institute a civil cause of action against an Indian tribe in a court of general jurisdiction of the State, on a claim arising within the State, including a claim arising on an Indian reservation or Indian Country." This section effectively repealed the 1968 amendments to P.L. 280 and extended P.L. 280 to all states in Indian Country.

The chairman of the Senate Committee on Indian Affairs, Ben Nighthorse Campbell (R-Colo.), began the first of three days of hearings on the legislation by saying that Gorton's bill "is arguably the most meaningful legislation since the Termination Era of the 1940s and 1950s. In fact, some have suggested that this bill is a 1990s version of termination."[42] Senator Inouye pointed out that tribes and states were increasingly turning to negotiated compacts to resolve differences. He went on to say, "Having reviewed the written testimony submitted to the committee for today's hearing, let us also be clear that what some would seek from this body, is not an alternative means of collecting state taxes, but rather action by the federal government to assure that commercial activities conducted on Indian lands are rendered incapable of competing in [the] free market place."[43] The bill faced enormous opposition from Indian Country. Although it was marked up by the Senate Committee on Indian Affairs in May 1998, it died with the close of the 105th Congress.

The nation's governors remained committed to revising the IGRA and asserting more state influence over Indian gaming and supported some of the broader efforts to limit tribal sovereignty. At its winter 1999 meeting, the National Governors Association (NGA) reaffirmed its policy on Indian gaming, first adopted at its winter 1997 meeting.[44] Among the NGA's concerns were the scope of gaming; the meaning of "good faith"; regulatory oversight; the interior secretary's rule-making authority in light of *Seminole;* trust land acquisition; federal enforcement; and state and local taxation of new trust lands. The NGA policy paper argued that Indian gaming has an impact on what happens in the rest of the state. The governors also wanted the IGRA's "good faith" requirement be applied to the tribes. Echoing one of the major themes of Indian politics of the

1990s, the NGA expressed its concern about the cost to state revenues when lands were withdrawn from the tax roles and placed in trust for Indians. The NGA's director, Raymond C. Scheppeach, was a frequent witness at Capitol Hill hearings on Indian issues, especially gaming.

The National Indian Gaming Association and the NIGA/NCAI Task Force continued to work with the Senate Committee on Indian Affairs to resolve contentious issues involving the IGRA. As NIGA's chairman, Rick Hill, told the committee in March 1999, "Indian Country has consistently not been able to support legislation that does not contain a fix for the problem created by the U.S. Supreme court in the *Seminole* case. . . . Without a *Seminole* fix, states will continue to make unconscionable demands for the limited revenue generated from tribal governmental gaming."[45]

INDIAN POLITICS AT THE MILLENNIUM

As the United States and Indian Country approached the twenty-first century, many of the issues concerning Indian/non-Indian relations are fundamentally the same as those that existed since before the nineteenth century. The reasons for this are found in the history of those relations and in the American political system. All disputes involving tribes must be resolved with that system and in the context of history. Indian people remain generally the most economically disadvantaged in the United States. Racism in border towns near Indian reservations continues.

But there have been twists to the flowing stream of history. In the current era of self-determination and self-governance, there is little doubt that tribal governments have begun to take their place in the American system of federalism. This constitutional and political fact was further emphasized when President Clinton issued Executive Order 13084 in May 1998 requiring the federal government to consult and coordinate with Indian tribal governments, an order nearly identical to one issued the same day regarding federal-state relations. The historic political conflict between tribal and state sovereignty continues as vigorous as ever because the tribes have greater resources than at any time since they were a military power courted by European nations and new colonists alike. Tribes are asserting their inherent sovereignty in whatever arenas are politically and legally appropriate. Gaming has provided the economic opportunity to fight these battles, but the battles are being led and fought by Indians. The great political leaders and warriors such as Pope, Tecumseh, John Ross, and Crazy Horse have been replaced by the likes of Wilma Mankiller, Frank Chaves, Gary Pitchlynn, Rick Hill, and Kevin Gover.

Oklahoma Indian Tribes with Class III Compacts, April 8, 1998

Tribe	Type of Compact
Choctaw Tribe of Oklahoma	Off-Track Pari-mutuel Simulcast Horse Wagering
Citizen Band of Potawatomi Nation	Off-Track Pari-mutuel Simulcast Horse Wagering
Iowa Tribe of Oklahoma	Off-Track Pari-mutuel Simulcast Horse Wagering
Miami Tribe of Oklahoma	Off-Track Pari-mutuel Simulcast Horse Wagering
Miami-Modoc Tribe of Oklahoma	Off-Track Pari-mutuel Simulcast Horse Wagering
Otoe-Missouria Tribe of Oklahoma	Off-Track Pari-mutuel Simulcast Horse Wagering
Tonkawa Tribe of Oklahoma	Off-Track Pari-mutuel Simulcast Horse Wagering

Information from the National Indian Gaming Commission, April 8, 1998.

Notes

INTRODUCTION

1. This book will not consider at any length the place of American Indian tribes in the international arena. This is a fascinating and important line of inquiry that is beyond my scope here.

CHAPTER 1

1. Wilkinson, *American Indians, Time and the Law*, ix.
2. Harring, *Crow Dog's Case*, 2.
3. Strickland, "Genocide-at-Law."
4. O'Brien, *American Indian Tribal Governments*, 14.
5. Deloria, *God Is Red*, 76.
6. Hagan, "Private Property, the Indian's Door to Civilization," 127.
7. Sando, *Nee Hamish*, 16.
8. Washburn, *Red Man's Land/White Man's Law*, 143.
9. Lowi, *The End of the Republican Era*, 5.
10. Ibid., 4.
11. The significance of John Locke for American Indian politics in the American political system is the ideological basis it has provided in guiding policy and establishing normative goals. Clearly, other political thinkers had significant influence on the Founders in their deliberations, most significantly Montesquieu.

12. Locke, *Second Treatise of Government,* 29.

13. Grant, *John Locke's Liberalism,* 160.

14. Williams, *The American Indian in Western Legal Thought,* 248.

15. Rogin, *Ronald Reagan, the Movie, and Other Episodes in Political Demonology,* 135.

16. Johnson & Graham Lessees v. McIntosh, 21 U.S. 543 (1823). Quotations from Marshall that follow are from this decision.

17. Deloria, *Behind the Trail of Broken Treaties,* 105–6.

18. Deloria and Lytle, *The Nations Within,* 2.

19. Kickingbird, "Way Down Yonder in the Indian Nations, Rode My Pony Cross the Reservation," 308.

20. Norgren, *The Cherokee Cases,* 47.

21. State v. George Tassels, 1 Dudley 229 (1830).

22. Norgren, *The Cherokee Cases,* 97.

23. Cherokee Nation v. Georgia, 30 U.S. 1 (1830). Quotations in this paragraph and the next are from this decision.

24. Worcester v. Georgia, 31 U.S. 515 (1832). Quotations in this paragraph and the next are from this decision.

25. Robert V. Remini, *Andrew Jackson and the Course of American Freedom,* 2:34.

26. Ibid., 33.

27. Ibid., 279.

28. Strickland, "A Tale of Two Marshalls," 114.

29. 68 Stat. 674.

30. Parman, *Indians and the American West in the Twentieth Century,* 1.

31. O'Brien, *American Indian Tribal Governments,* 76.

32. U.S. v. Clapox, et al., 35 F. 575 (1888).

33. *Federal Register,* vol. 62, no. 205, pp. 55270–75, October 23, 1997. The list included 330 federally acknowledged tribes in the lower 48 states and 225 Alaska Native villages.

34. U.S. Congress, Senate, Special Committee on Investigations of the Select Committee on Indian Affairs, *Final Report and Recommendations,* 5.

35. Ibid.

36. Calbom, "Prepared Statement of Linda M. Calbom, Director, Civil Audits Accounting and Information Management Division, United States General Accounting Office, Before the House Committee Task Force on Indian Trust Fund Management; Echohawk, "Prepared Testimony of John E. Echohawk, Executive Director, Native American Rights Fund, before the House Resources Committee Task Force on Trust Management Re: Oversight Hearing on Management of Indian Trust Funds."

37. McCain, "McCain Releases New Study Confirming Gross Mismanagement of Indian Trust Funds by BIA."

38. Calbom, "Prepared Statement." A class action lawsuit was filed by the Native American Rights Fund on behalf of IIM account holders in June 1996.

39. Jeff Barker, "Audit: BIA 'Lost' $2 Billion; Unable to Account for Tribal Trust Funds," *Arizona Republic,* April 8, 1996 (Lexis-Nexis). In a play on the Clinton administration's Whitewater scandal, some Indians have termed the BIA scandal "Redwater." Adrianne Flynn, "McCain to Probe BIA Losses; $2.4 Billion Shortage of Trust Confirmed," *Arizona Republic,* May 4, 1996 (Lexis-Nexis).

40. Morris, "Termination by Accountants."

41. Hertzberg, "Reaganomics on the Reservation."

42. Deloria, "The Evolution of Federal Indian Policy Making," 255.

43. Slade Gorton, "Indians Are Getting a Fair Shake," *Washington Post,* September 18, 1995 (Lexis-Nexis).

44. Oliphant v. Suquamish Indian Tribe, 435 U.S. 191 (1978).

45. Van Biema, "Bury My Heart in Committee."

46. U.S. Congress, Senate, *Congressional Record* S11976, 105th Cong., 1st sess., 1995.

47. U.S. v. Kagama, 118 U.S. 375 (1886); Lone Wolf v. Hitchcock, 187 U.S. 553 (1903).

48. The Crow Dog and Spotted Tail families agreed on a resolution to the incident that involved the former paying $600 and giving eight horses and one blanket to the latter. Harring.

49. Ex parte Crow Dog, 109 U.S. 556 (1883).

50. Harring, *Crow Dog's Case,* 101.

51. 23 Stat. 385.

52. Harring, *Crow Dog's Case,* 147.

53. Prucha, *The Great Father,* 65.

54. 24 Stat. 388–391.

55. Cohen, *Handbook of Federal Indian Law* (1982), 130.

56. 34 Stat. 182.

57. Prucha, *The Great Father,* 227.

58. Cohen, *Handbook of Federal Indian Law* (1982), 136.

59. 60 Stat. 1049.

60. The commission was expanded to five members in 1967.

61. Prucha, *The Great Father,* 342.

62. Ibid., 343.

63. 67 Stat. B132.

64. In 1947 BIA Commissioner William Zimmerman testified before a Senate committee that services could be withdrawn from tribes based on a three-tier rating: those tribes that could have services withdrawn immediately; those that would be ready in ten years; and those that would need more than ten years. Prucha, *The Great Father,* 343.

65. Cohen, *Handbook of Federal Indian Law* (1982), 811.
66. Ibid.
67. Ibid., 813.
68. 67 Stat. 588–90.
69. Fixico, *Termination and Relocation*, 111.
70. In 1958 the new state of Alaska was added as a mandatory P.L. 280 state. 72 Stat. 545.
71. Ten states subsequently assumed some type of jurisdiction over at least some of the tribes located in their borders: Arizona, Florida, Idaho, Iowa, Montana, Nevada, North Dakota, South Dakota, Utah, and Washington. Cohen, *Handbook of Federal Indian Law* (1982), 362–63 n.125.
72. 82 Stat. 73.
73. Prucha, *The Great Father,* 355.
74. 76 Stat. 429.
75. 102 Stat. 431.
76. 92 Stat. 246.
77. Valencia-Weber, "Shrinking Indian Country," 1281.
78. According to Clinton, "Each opinion was rated as a tribal win or loss depending on the manner in which the Court's opinion affected *tribal,* rather than individual, Indian interests." Robert Clinton, "The Dormant Commerce Clause," 1057 n.2.
79. Ibid., 1057.
80. Monette, "A New Federalism for Indian Tribes."
81. 104 U.S. 621 (1881).
82. 435 U.S. 191 (1978).
83. 450 U.S. 544 (1981).
84. 495 U.S. 676 (1990); 492 U.S. 408 (1989).
85. Prucha, *American Indian Treaties,* 1.
86. Ibid., 2.
87. Washburn, *Red Man's Land/White Man's Law,* 57.
88. Deloria, *Behind the Trail of Broken Treaties,* 108.
89. Ibid., 108–109.
90. Oklahoma and Alaska were not included in the IRA. For a discussion of law extending most of the IRA's provisions to Oklahoma tribes, the Oklahoma Indian Welfare Act, see chapter 5 below.
91. Cohen, *Handbook of Federal Indian Law,* 147.
92. Prucha, *The Great Father,* 324–25.
93. Carmack, "A New Approach to Indian Affairs."
94. 88 Stat. 2203.
95. 92 Stat. 3069.
96. 105 Stat. 1278.
97. The participating tribes were the Hoopa Valley tribe of California, the Lummi Indian Nation, the Jamestown S'Kallam tribe,

and the Quinault Indian Nation, all located in Washington; the Mille Lacs Band of Chippewa Indians of Minnesota; the Absentee Shawnee Tribe of Oklahoma and the Cherokee Nation of Oklahoma.

98. 108 Stat. 4250.

99. Office of Self-Governance, "Background; Annual Growth of Self-Governance."

100. Michael H. Trujillo, "Director's Keynote Address: 1998 Tribal Self-Governance Joint Department of the Interior and Indian Health Service Fall Conference," Palm Springs, California, November 16–19, 1998. http://www.ihs.gov/publicinfo/director/sg98.asp.

101. 358 U.S. 217 (1959).

102. 411 U.S. 104 (1973).

103. 436 U.S. 49 (1978).

104. 435 U.S. 313 (1978).

105. Josephy, *The Patriot Chiefs.*

106. Viola, *Diplomats in Buckskin.*

107. 43 Stat. 253.

108. 112 U.S. 94 (1884).

109. Cohen, *Handbook of Federal Indian Law,* 267.

CHAPTER 2

1. Goodman, *The Luck Business,* 59.

2. National Gaming Survey, "National Gaming Survey: The Newsletter of the National Gaming Industry," *Casino Journal* (April 22, 1996) 2–3. http://www.intersphere...player.summary/sample.

3. GAO, *Money Laundering—Rapid Growth of Casinos Make Them Vulnerable.*

4. "Some Statistics on Gambling in the United States," Gannett News Service, August 17, 1995 (Lexis-Nexis).

5. Ibid.; GAO Report, 1996.

6. "National Gaming Survey," 1.

7. Goodman, *The Luck Business,* 105.

8. U.S. Congress, Senate, Committee on Indian Affairs, *Amending the Indian Gaming Regulatory Act, and for Other Purposes: Report to Accompany S487.*

9. Ibid.

10. Gannett News Service.

11. GAO, *Tax Policy: A Profile of the Indian Gaming Industry* (Letter Report, 05/05/97, GAO/GGD-97-91.http://frwebgate.access.gpo.gov/cgi-bin...7091.txt&directory=diskb/wais/data/gao,1.

12. Gannett News Service.

13. GAO, *Tax Policy,* 1.

14. Schattschneider, *The Semisovereign People.*

15. Kingdon defines an agenda as "the list of subjects or problems to which governmental officials, and people outside of government closely associated with those officials, are paying some serious attention at any given time." John W. Kingdon, *Agendas, Alternatives, and Public Policies,* 4. The second edition, published in 1995, also fails to mention the role of courts as political agenda setters.

16. Ibid., 16.

17. Henschen and Sidlow, "The Supreme Court and the Congressional Agenda-setting Process."

18. Beers, introduction to *New Federalism Intergovernmental Reform from Nixon to Reagan,* xi.

19. Wolf, "Killing the New Buffalo," 67.

20. Seminole Tribe of Florida v. Butterfield, 491 F.Supp. 1015 (1979).

21. Ibid., 658 F.2d 310.

22. 426 U.S. 373 (1976).

23. See Oneida Tribe of Wisconsin v. Wisconsin, 518 F.Supp. 712, decided by the Western District Court of Wisconsin in July 1981; and Barona Group of Capitan Grande Band of Mission Indians v. Duffy, 649 F.2d 1185, decided by the Ninth Circuit Court of Appeals in 1982.

24. DeDominics, "Betting on Indian Rights."

25. Joint Appendix, *California v. Cabazon Band of Mission Indians,* No. 85-1708 (1985) (Lexis-Nexis).

26. Ibid.

27. Cabazon Band of Mission Indians v. City of Indio, 694 F.2d 634.

28. Joint Appendix, *California v. Cabazon Band of Mission Indians.*

29. Cabazon Band of Mission Indians v. County of Riverside, 783 F.2d 906 (1986).

30. 18 U.S.C. 1955.

31. Brief of Appellants, *California v. Cabazon Band of Mission Indians.*

32. Ibid.

33. Brief of Appellees, *California v. Cabazon Band of Mission Indians.*

34. Ibid.

35. Ibid.

36. California v. Cabazon Band of Mission Indians, 400 U.S. 202 (1987). The following quotations in the text are taken from this decision.

37. Henschen and Sidlow, "The Supreme Court," 686.

38. Rose, "The Indian Gaming Act and the Political Process," 3.

39. Udall, "The Indian Gaming Act and the Political Process," 26.

40. Santoni, "The Indian Gaming Regulatory Act," 395.

41. Ducheneaux, Prepared Statement of Franklin Ducheneaux (Ducheneaux, Taylor & Associates) before the Senate Indian Affairs Committee on *Seminole v. Florida*.

42. Reid, "Indian Gaming and the Law," 17.

43. U.S. Congress, House, Representative Morris Udall of Arizona, 98th Cong., 1st sess., *Congressional Record*, November 18, 1983, H 34184–34185.

44. U.S. Congress, House, Representative Norman David Shumay of California, 98th Cong., 2d sess., *Congressional Record*, October 3, 1984, H 11018.

45. U.S. Congress, Senate, Senator Dennis DeConcini of Arizona, 99th Cong., 1st sess., *Congressional Record*, April 4, 1985, S. 4124. Representative Shumay reintroduced his bill from the 98th Congress a month later. U.S. Congress, House, Representative Norman David Shumay of California, 99th Cong., 1st sess., *Congressional Record*, May 8, 1985, E 2004.

46. Schattschneider, *The Semisovereign People*, 10.

47. U.S. Congress, House, Committee on Interior and Insular Affairs, *Indian Gaming Regulatory Act*, 263–64.

48. U.S. Congress, Senate, Select Committee on Indian Affairs, *Establishing Federal Standards and Regulations for the Conduct of Gaming Activities within Indian Country*, 609.

49. Ibid., 365.

50. U.S. Congress, House, Committee on Interior and Insular Affairs, *Indian Gaming Regulatory Act*, 381.

51. Ibid., 113.

52. Ibid., 114.

53. Select Committee on Indian Affairs, *Establishing Federal Standards and Regulations for the Conduct of Gaming Activities within Indian Country*, 205.

54. Committee on Interior and Insular Affairs, *Indian Gaming Regulatory Act*, 159.

55. Bureau of Indian Affairs, Office of Public Information, "Tribal Consultation Will be Key to BIA Task Force on Bingo."

56. Bureau of Indian Affairs, "BIA Supports Tribes, Expresses Concerns at Bingo Consultation Session."

57. Committee on Interior and Insular Affairs, *Indian Gaming Control Act*, 16.

58. Ibid., 17–18.

59. "U.S. Indian Affairs Director Says Bingo Halls Send Wrong Signal," *Chicago Tribune*, December 23, 1985 (Lexis-Nexis). As principal chief of the Cherokee Nation, Swimmer vetoed a Tribal Council resolution that would have permitted tribal-sponsored bingo.

60. "Indian Economic Growth Stressed," UPI, October 16, 1985 (Lexis-Nexis).

61. Committee on Interior and Insular Affairs, *Indian Gaming Regulatory Act.*

62. Ibid.

63. U.S. Congress, Senate, Select Committee on Indian Affairs, *Indian Gaming Regulatory Act: Report Together With Additional Views,* 22.

64. Ibid., 23.

65. Reid, "Indian Gaming and the Law," 17.

66. Ducheneaux, Prepared Statement.

67. Ibid.

68. Congress, Senate, Report 100-446, 4.

69. The Court granted a writ of certiorari on June 10, 1986.

70. House, Representative Morris K. Udall of Arizona, 99th Cong., 2d sess., *Congressional Record,* April 21, 1986, H 2012.

71. House, Representative John McCain of Arizona, 99th Cong., 2d sess., *Congressional Record,* April 21, 1986, H 2012.

72. U.S. Congress, Senate, Senator Mark Andrews of North Dakota, 98th Cong., 2d sess., *Congressional Record,* October 6, 1986, S 15390.

73. Ducheneaux, Prepared Statement.

74. U.S. Congress, Senate, Daniel Inouye of Hawaii, 100th Cong., 2d sess., *Congressional Record,* September 15, 1988, S 12654.

75. Ibid.

76. U.S. Congress, Senate, Senator Tom Daschle of South Dakota, 100th Cong., 2d sess., *Congressional Record,* September 15, 1988, S 12657.

77. U.S. Congress, Senate, Senator Daniel Inouye of Hawaii, 100th Cong., 2d sess., *Congressional Record,* September 15, 1988, S 12651.

78. U.S. Congress, Senate, Senator Daniel Evans of Washington, 100th Cong., 2d sess., *Congressional Record,* September 15, 1988, S 12651.

79. U.S. Congress, Senate, Senator John McCain of Arizona, 100th Cong., 2d sess., *Congressional Record,* September 15, 1988, S 12653. McCain was elected to the Senate in 1986 after serving fourteen years in the House.

80. U.S. Congress, House, Representative Morris K. Udall of Arizona, 100th Cong., 2d sess., *Congressional Record,* September 26, 1988, H 8153.

81. Ibid.

82. U.S. Congress, House, Roll Call Vote on S. 555, *Congressional Record,* September 27, 1988, H 8426.

83. Santoni, "The Indian Gaming Regulatory Act," 404.

84. "High Stakes Bingo to Continue: Congress Clears Legislation to Regulate Indian Gambling," *Congressional Quarterly Weekly*, October 1, 1988, 2730.

85. Reid, "Indian Gaming and the Law," 19.

86. Allen, Written Statement of W. Ron Allen.

87. Hill, Statement of Rick Hill, 3.

88. U.S. Congress, Senate, Senate Committee on Indian Affairs, *Amending the Indian Gaming Regulatory Act, and For Other Purposes: Report to Accompany S487*, 104th Cong., 2d sess., March 14, 1996, Report 104–241, 7.

89. Cheyenne River Sioux Tribe v. South Dakota, 3 F.3d 273 (1993); Spokane Tribe of Indians v. Washington, F.3d (1994); Ponca Tribe of Oklahoma v. Oklahoma, 37 F.3d 1422 (1994).

90. Seminole Tribe of Florida v. Florida, 11 3d 1016 (1994).

91. National Governors Association, NGA Policy: EC-1. Indian Gaming, adopted Winter Meeting 1993; reaffirmed Winter Meeting 1995.

92. Ibid.

93. Cigler, "Not Just Another Interest Group," 140.

94. Ibid.

95. NIGA, Fact Sheet: NIGA, National Indian Gaming Association, Washington, D.C., n.d.

96. NIGA, *Annual Report 1994*.

97. NIPC, "Tribal Representation in Washington, D.C."

98. Ibid., 5.

99. NIGA, *Annual Report 1994*, 6.

100. Gary Pitchlynn, interview by author, Norman, Oklahoma, March 27, 1995.

CHAPTER 3

1. Nostrand, *The Hispano Homeland*.

2. WPA, *New Mexico: A Guide to the Colorful State*.

3. Elazar, *The American Partnership*, 142.

4. Ibid.

5. Hrebenar and Thomas, *Interest Group Politics in the American West*.

6. Ibid.

7. Ibid.

8. Nostrand, *The Hispano Homeland*, 3.

9. WPA, *New Mexico: A Guide to the Colorful State*, 4.

10. Waters, *Masked Gods*, 18.

11. 36 Stat. 557.

12. Cohen, *Handbook of Federal Indian Law* (1941), 383.

13. Sando, *Pueblo Nations,* 21.

14. Cohen, *Handbook of Federal Indian Law* (1941), 396.

15. United States v. Joseph, 94 U.S. 614 (1876).

16. United States v. Sandoval, 231 U.S. 28 (1913).

17. Ibid.

18. Ibid.

19. Sando, *Pueblo Nations,* 122.

20. Cohen, *Handbook of Federal Indian Law* (1941), 391.

21. Gordon-McCutchan, *Taos Indians and Battle for Blue Lake.*

22. Wunder, *Retained by the People.*

23. In a surprise move in late August 1999, Zah announced he was changing his party registration from Democrat to Republican and endorsed Arizona Senator John McCain for the Republican party presidential nomination in 2000. Maniaci, "Senator McCain Meets with Tribal Leaders."

24. Sando, *Pueblo Nations,* 122.

25. Winters v. United States, 207, U.S. 564 (1908).

26. Sando, *Pueblo Nations,* 123.

27. New Mexico v. Aamodt, 537 F.2d 1102 (1976).

28. Merrion v. Jicarilla Apache Tribe, 455 U.S. 130 (1982).

29. Petroleum Corporation v. New Mexico, 490 U.S. 163 (1989).

30. New Mexico v. Mescalero Apache Tribe, 462 U.S. 324 (1983).

31. McCool, "Indian Voting," 111–12.

32. Trujillo v. Garley, U.S. Dist. Ct., Vic.A. No. 1353 (1948).

33. Montoya v. Bolack, 70 N.M. 196, 372 P.2s 387 (1962).

34. Ibid.

35. Ibid.

36. Prince v. Board of Education of Central Consolidated Independent School District No. 22, 88 N.M. 548, 543 P.2d 1176 (1975).

37. Montoya v. Balock, 70 N.M. 196, 372 P.2s 387 (1962).

38. Amicus brief of the state of New Mexico, *Cotton Petroleum v. New Mexico,* 1988.

39. Class I gaming, consisting of traditional Indian games of chance, are under the sole regulatory authority of individual tribes.

40. 30-19-5, NMSA.

41. NMIGA, New Mexico Indian Gaming Association Charter and Bylaws.

42. Oklahoma News Briefs, UPI, March 10, 1983 (Lexis-Nexis).

43. Ibid.

44. Brief of Appellees, *California v. Cabazon Band of Mission Indians.*

45. Ibid.

46. By this time Sandia, Isleta, Acoma, and Tesuque pueblos and the Mescalero Apache Tribe were operating bingo halls.

47. Frank Chaves, Interview by author, March 17, 1995, Santa Fe, New Mexico.

48. Ibid.; Regis Pecos, interview with author, Santa Fe, New Mex., January 19, 1988.

49. Ibid.; Chronology of Events, New Mexico Indian Gaming Association, 1996.

50. John Yaeger, "Odds Favor Video Gambling for 2 Tribes," *Albuquerque Journal*, October 1, 1991.

51. Regis Pecos, interview with author, Santa Fe, New Mex., January 19, 1996.

52. Ibid.

53. NMSA 29-8-1; NMSA 11-1-6.

54. New Mexico Indian Association, Gaming Chronology of Events, 1996.

55. Ibid.

56. Jackie Jadrnak, "King Wants Agreements Made Public," *Albuquerque Journal*, December 12, 1991.

57. The Jicarilla Apache Tribe and San Juan, Pojoaque, and Isleta pueblos each filed similar lawsuits in October 1994, as did Acoma and Tesuque pueblos in early November.

58. John Hume, "Feds Challenge Tribal Gaming Operations," *Albuquerque Journal*, May 3, 1992.

59. John Yaeger, "Odds Favor Video Gambling for 2 Tribes."

60. New Mexico Indian Gaming Association, Charter and Bylaws, 1993.

61. Chaves, A Briefing for the Representative of the Navajo Nation."

62. New Mexico Indian Gaming Association, Charter and Bylaws, 1993.

63. New Mexico Indian Gaming, Association Charter and Bylaws, 1993.

64. Frank Chaves, letter to author, January 2, 1997.

65. Harris and Harris, "American Indians and Tribal Governments."

66. Hain and Garcia, "Voting, Elections, and Parties."

67. Ray Powell, telephone interview with author, Albuquerque, New Mex., August 22, 1994.

68. McCool, "Indian Voting."

69. Ray Powell, Chairman, New Mexico Democratic party, telephone interview by author, August 22, 1994, Albuquerque, New Mexico.

70. Gover's law partner, Cate Stetson, was defeated by one vote in her campaign to become the new state Democratic Party chair in May 1995.

71. Powell, telephone interview.

72. "Casino Planned at Pueblo," *Albuquerque Journal,* July 12, 1995.

73. Zack Van Eyck, "King Vows to Fight Tesuque Poker, Blackjack Plans," *New Mexican,* July 19, 1994; Zack Van Eyck, "San Juan Casino Dealing Poker," *New Mexican,* July 20, 1994.

74. Zack Van Eyck, "Tribes Agree to Toe the Line on Gaming," *New Mexican,* July 19, 1994.

75. Thom Cole, "King May OK Gaming: Compact Could Be Signed by November Vote," *Albuquerque Journal,* December 25, 1994.

76. Mark Oswald, "King, Zah Discuss Gambling Compact," *New Mexican,* August 25, 1994.

77. Ibid.

78. Zack Van Eyck, "King Won't Sign Gaming Compacts," *New Mexican,* September 17, 1994.

79. Ibid.

80. John Robertson, "President Gives King Hand, Meets with Luna," *Albuquerque Journal,* October 18, 1994.

81. Gover and Cooney, "Cooperation between Tribes and States in Protecting the Environment."

82. Karen Peterson, "Johnson Holds Slight Edge in Battle of the Billfold," *New Mexican,* November 4, 1994.

83. "The Governor's Race Q & A," *Albuquerque Journal,* November 6, 1994.

84. "Navajo President Vetoes Gambling: Zah Wants Tribe to Vote on Casinos," *Albuquerque Journal,* August 6, 1994.

85. Zack Van Eyck, "Johnson, Mondragon will Negotiate," *New Mexican,* September 21, 1994.

86. Ponca Tribe of Oklahoma v. Oklahoma, 834 F.Supp. 1341 (1992).

87. Zack Van Eyck, "Pojoaque Pueblo Goes for Johnson," *New Mexican,* September 23, 1994.

88. Governor King received personal endorsements from some Indian leaders, including Santa Ana Pueblo governor Andrew Gallegos, Santo Domingo Pueblo governor Ernie Lovato, and Navajo Nation vice president Marshall Plummer.

89. King raised $916,556 for the general election; Mondragon raised $47,062.

90. In a January 31, 1995, referendum, the Mescalero Apache Tribe voted 490 to 362 to reject the proposed nuclear waste storage facility.

91. Tribal financial support for Johnson continued after the election. Postelection contributions were received from Pojoaque Gaming ($30,000), Isleta Bingo ($10,000), Acoma Pueblo ($5,000), Santa Ana Pueblo ($5,000), and Santo Domingo Pueblo ($500). Brenda Norrell, "Tribes Contribute to New Mexico Governor," *Indian Country Today,* May 12, 1995.

92. John Robertson, "'Favors' Focus of Debate: King Blasts Johnson for Tribal Donations," *Albuquerque Journal,* October 27, 1994.

93. Frank Chaves and Greg Histia, "Gaming Is an Answer to the Poverty That's Hurting Pueblos," *Albuquerque Journal,* September 22, 1994.

94. Ibid.

95. Karen Peterson, "Johnson Ends King Era," *New Mexican,* November 9, 1994.

96. Thom Cole, "King May OK Gaming: Compact Could Be Signed by November Vote," *Albuquerque Journal,* August 9, 1994.

97. Tom Arviso, Jr., "People Choose Hale-Atcitty," *Navajo Times,* November 10, 1994.

98. King, *Cowboy in the Roundhouse,* 327.

99. John Robertson, "Negotiator Named for Indian Gambling: Gov. Elect Wants to Move Quickly," *Albuquerque Journal,* December 16, 1994.

100. State ex rel. Clark, No. 22,489 (1995) N.M. Lexis 4.

101. Ibid., 7.

102. Hain and Folmar, "The Legislature." The Legislative Council is one of the permanent "interim committees" that meet when the legislature is not in formal session. It consists of eight members from each house, including the Speaker of the House, Senate President Pro Tempore, and each House's minority leaders.

103. Thom Cole, "Johnson Hires Gaming-Pact Case Lawyer: Firm Donated to Campaign," *Albuquerque Journal,* May 3, 1995.

104. Barry Massey, "Gaming Easily the Top Lobby," *New Mexican,* January 16, 1996.

105. The Associated Press reported that lobbyists for gaming interests spent about 25 percent of all reported lobbying expenditures during the first half of 1995.

106. Johnson signed a compact with Nambe Pueblo on March 1 and with San Ildefonso Pueblo in early April.

107. Gary Johnson, Testimony, June 22, 1995.

108. Compact, A Compact Between the Pueblo of _____ and the State of New Mexico Providing for the Conduct of Class III Gaming. Santa Fe, February 13, 1995.

109. Agreement, Tribal-State Revenue Sharing Agreement, February 13, 1995, 3, 4–5.

110. Richard B. Archuleta, "Tribes Don't Tell Whole Story in Gambling Controversy," *Albuquerque Journal,* February 6, 1995.

111. Rosalyn North, Secretary, New Mexico Senate Select Committee on Gaming, interview by author, March 14, 1995, Santa Fe, New Mexico.

112. The account of these events is based on notes made by the author at the time they occurred on March 17, 1995.

113. Rex Hackler, interview with author, Santa Fe, New Mex., January 18, 1996; and telephone interview with author, January 20, 1996.

114. "Indians: State Should Run Gambling," *New Mexican*, March 5, 1995.

115. Thom Cole, "Approval of Compacts Signed by Nambe and Acoma Pueblos Was Delayed Due to Their Late Submission to the Interior Department," *Albuquerque Journal*, May 3, 1995.

116. Tina Griego, "Tribes Consider Some Changes," *Albuquerque Tribune*, March 17, 1995.

117. Frank Chaves, interview with author, Santa Fe, New Mex., March 17, 1995.

118. Schattschneider, *The Semisovereign People*.

119. Garcia and Thomas, New Mexico: Traditional Interest in a Traditional State."

120. Cigler and Loomis, "Organized Interests and the Search for Certainty."

121. Morehouse, *State Politics, Parties and Policy;* Zeigler, *Politics in the American States;* Thomas, *Interest Group Politics in the American West.*

122. John J. Kelly, letter to Governor Ernest Lujan, Pueblo of Santa Ana, from John J. Kelly, United States Attorney, District of New Mexico, Albuquerque, December 14, 1995.

123. Chaves, interview.

124. Richard Hughes, telephone interview with author, October 27, 1995.

125. Eisenstein, *Counsel for the United States*.

126. Sando, *Pueblo Nations*.

127. "Shouldn't Economic Development Also include Native Americans?" *New Mexico Business Journal* (June 1995) (Lexis-Nexis).

128. Rosenthal, *The Third House*.

129. Cigler, Not Just Another Special Interest," 132.

130. Ibid.

131. Reed and Fort, "The Fragmented Executive System."

132. Letter of Bruce King to Dale Mason, December 28, 1993. Emphasis added.

133. Bruce King, interview with author, New Mexico State Capitol, Santa Fe, March 14, 1995.

134. Wolf, "Killing the New Buffalo."

135. Ibid., 53.

136. Gary Johnson, Testimony, June 22, 1995.

137. Frank Chaves, interview with author, Albuquerque, New Mex., August 23, 1994.

138. Gary Johnson, Testimony, June 22, 1995.

139. Epstein and Rowland, "Interest Groups in the Courts."

140. Ibid.

141. O'Connor, "The Rise of Conservative Interest Group Litigation"; O'Connor and Epstein, "Amicus Curiae Participation in U.S. Supreme Court Litigation"; Shapiro, "Amicus Briefs in the Supreme Court"; Bradley and Gardner, "Underdogs, Upperdogs, and the Use of the Amicus Brief."

142. O'Connor and Epstein, "Amicus Curiae Participation in U.S. Supreme Court Litigation"; Hedman, "Friends of the Earth and Friends of the Court."

143. Frank Chaves, interview by author, March 17, 1995, Santa Fe, New Mexico.

144. Karen Peterson, "Two Lawmakers Challenge Gaming Compacts," *New Mexican,* April 21, 1995 (Lexis-Nexis).

145. NMIGA, New Mexico Indian Gaming Tribes Position Statement on Indian Gaming, April 1993.

146. Rosenthal, *The Third House.*

147. Ibid.

148. "Indian Gaming Group Defends U.S. Attorney: Gambling Critic Is after Tribes, Statement Says," *New Mexican,* September 16, 1995.

149. Paul Swazo, "Gambling: For many Tribes, No Other Choice," *New Mexican,* December 1, 1994.

150. Cigler, "Not Just Another Special Interest," 131–53.

CHAPTER 4

1. Michael Hartranft, "Casino to Open Sunday; San Felipe Goes Ahead Despite Uncertain Pacts," *Albuquerque Journal,* November 11, 1995.

2. Vince Lujan, interview with author, Santa Fe, N. Mex., February 3, 1996.

3. Karen Peterson, "Tribes Made $46 Million, Panel Told," *New Mexican,* January 18, 1996.

4. The tribes and their Indian employees are not subject to either of these state taxes; however, non-Indian employees must pay state income taxes and firms doing business with the casinos are subject to gross receipts taxes.

5. The quoted figures from Chaves and Robertson are from notes I took while observing the hearings on January 17 and February 3, 1996, respectively.

6. NMIGA, *Indian Gaming.*

7. Jake Viarrial, interview with author, Pojoaque Pueblo, New Mex., January 19, 1996; NMIGA, *Indian Gaming.* As part of its economic development plan, Pojoaque Pueblo also purchased the Downs at

Santa Fe racetrack in September 1995. Tommy Trujillo, "Pojoaque Pueblo to Buy the Downs; Horsemen Differ on What Effect the Sale Will Have on Horse Racing in Santa Fe," *New Mexican*, September 30, 1995 (Lexis-Nexis).

8. Vince Lujan, interview.

9. 1995 N.M. Lexis; 904 P.2d 11 (1995).

10. New Mexico is the second of three states where the separation of powers issue has been an issue in connection with Class III compacts. In 1992 the Kansas Supreme Court held that while the governor had the power to negotiate a Class III compact with the Kickapoo Tribe, she had "no power to bind the State to the terms thereof" absent specific legislative delegation (Kansas ex rel. Stephan v. Finney, 251 Kan. 559; 836 P.2d 1169; 1992 Kan. Lexis 130). See also Burr, "Broken Promises Revisited," for background. Similarly, in November 1995, on the day after the New Mexico Supreme Court decided *Citation Bingo,* the Rhode Island Supreme Court held that the state's governor had authority to negotiate a Class III compact with the Narragansett Tribe, but, "absent specific authorization from the General Assembly," he had "no express or implied constitutional right or statutory authority to finally execute and bind the state to such a compact by his execution thereof" (Narragansett Indian Tribe of Rhode Island v. Rhode Island 1995 R.I. Lexis 267).

11. New Mexico ex rel. Clark v. Johnson, 1995 N.M. Lexis; 904 P.2d. 11 (1995).

12. NMSA 1978, 11-1-1 to 11-1-7.

13. Ibid., 29-8-1 to 29-8-3.

14. Clark v. Johnson.

15. "Text of Supreme Court Order on Indian Gambling," *Albuquerque Journal,* August 5, 1995.

16. NMSA 1978, 30-19-6.

17. Clark v. Johnson.

18. Reed and Fort, "The Fragmented Executive System."

19. Kevin Gover, interview with author, Santa Fe and Tesuque Pueblo, New Mex., February 3, 1996.

20. Thom Cole, "Tribes Still Honoring Pacts; Ruling Voided Deals, Attorney General Says," *Albuquerque Journal,* July 15, 1995.

21. Michael Hartranft, John J. Lumpkin, and Mike Gallagher, "Court: Gaming Pacts Illegal; Area Pueblos Won't Close Their Casinos," *Albuquerque Journal,* July 14, 1995.

22. Thom Cole, "Court: Gaming Pacts Illegal; Govern Claims Deals Are Valid," *Albuquerque Journal,* July 14, 1995.

23. Cole, "Tribes Still Honoring Pacts."

24. Thom Cole, "Feds OK 11 of 13 Gambling Compacts; Agency's Decision Pending on Last 2," *Albuquerque Journal,* March 17, 1995.

25. Barry Massey, "Montoya's Casino Policy Faulted; State Shouldn't Keep Money, Udall Says," *Albuquerque Journal,* August 11, 1995.

26. Barry Massey, "State to Return Gaming Funds; Treasurer Cites High Court Ruling," *Albuquerque Journal,* August 22, 1995; Barry Massey, "Gaming Easily the Top Lobby," *New Mexican,* January 16, 1996.

27. Eisenstein, *Counsel for the United States.*

28. Thom Cole, "Johnson Urged to Fix Gaming Dispute Quickly; Feds Encourage Special Session," *Albuquerque Journal,* July 28, 1995.

29. "Johnson's Compacts Face Renegotiation," *Albuquerque Journal,* July 28, 1995.

30. Thom Cole, "Gov. May Negotiate on Casinos; Tribes Not Willing to Rework Compacts," *Albuquerque Journal,* July 27, 1995.

31. Thom Cole, "Johnson Folds on Gaming; Lawmakers, Tribes Asked to Fix It," *Albuquerque Journal,* August 3, 1995.

32. Citation Bingo, Ltd. v. Otten, 1995 N.M. Lexis 426.

33. The court cited the sections of the IGRA that classified "electronic or electromechanical facsimiles of any game of chance" as Class III but "electronic, computer, or technological aids" as Class II.

34. Infinity Group, Inc. v. Manzagol, N.M. 632, 884, P.2d. 523 (1994).

35. Ibid.

36. Mike Taugher and John Robertson, "State Raids Gaming Clubs; Agents Find Most Machines Unplugged," *Albuquerque Journal,* December 7, 1995.

37. Thom Cole, "Kelly Says Slots Out for Tribes; U.S. Attorney Cites Ruling," *Albuquerque Journal,* December 1, 1995.

38. Thom Cole, Scott Sandlin, and Michael Hartranft, "Tribes: Kelly Seeks Casino Closings; Voluntary Shutdown Doesn't Seem Likely," *Albuquerque Journal,* December 8, 1995.

39. Richard W. Hughes, telephone interview with author, December 15, 1995.

40. U.S. Attorney, District of New Mexico, "News Release: U.S. Attorney Sets Deadline for Tribes to Halt Gaming," Albuquerque, December 14, 1995.

41. Kelly, letter to Governor Ernest Luhan.

42. Hughes, telephone interview.

43. Shutiva, letter to U.S. Attorney John J. Kelly.

44. Lucero, letter to U.S. Attorney John J. Kelly.

45. Peter Eichstaedt and Thom Cole, "Pueblo May Block Roads; Others Urge Peaceful End to Gaming Feud," *Albuquerque Journal,* December 21, 1995.

46. CNN, "Native American Casinos Face Legal Threats," January 6, 1996 (Lexis-Nexis).

47. Pueblo of Santa Ana, et al. v. Kelly, et al., Stipulation 1996, 2, 2–3.

48. At least one pueblo governor, Jake Viarrial, believed that the road blockade threats led Kelly to back away from the forfeiture action. Interview with author, Pojoaque Pueblo, January 19, 1996.

49. Judge Vasquez approved the stipulation and rejected Marshall's intervention petition.

50. Odis Echols, interview with author, Santa Fe, New Mex., February 2, 1996.

51. Ibid.

52. Gover, interview with author.

53. Echols, interview with author.

54. Rex Hackler, interview with author, Santa Fe, New Mex., February 2, 1996.

55. Ibid.

56. Toward the end of the session Frank Chaves told the *New Mexican* that joining forces with the other gaming interests might have been a mistake. Karen Peterson, "Late Decisions, Absent Governor Killed Gambling," *New Mexican,* February 15, 1996.

57. Gover, interview with author; Ron Shutiva, interview with author, Santa Fe, New Mex., February 2, 1996.

58. Thom Cole, "Indian Casino ATMs Targeted; Lawyer Asks State to Revoke OK," *Albuquerque Journal,* January 18, 1996.

59. Richard W. Hughes, telephone interview with author, October 27, 1995; and interview, Santa Fe, New Mex., January 18, 1996.

60. I informed Hughes of Oklahoma's Tribal-State Relations Act and provided him with a copy of it in the early stages of his work on the New Mexico bills. Following the *Finney* decision nullifying the Kickapoo compacts, the Kansas legislature passed a statute creating a provision for legislative approval of Class III compacts negotiated by the governor. As of September 1995 two Kansas tribes had ratified Class III compacts under this law. The Kansas statute was deemed more consistent with the New Mexico Constitution than the Oklahoma statute and thus served as the model for the bill drafted by Hughes.

61. "Tribal Lawyer Pushes 'Content-Neutral' Gambling Legislation," *New Mexican,* February 4, 1996.

62. A cartoon in the July 19, 1996, *Albuquerque Journal* captured the problem: two Indian men stand in front of a wall that has lines leading downward from the words "New Mexico State Government" to three windows marked "Executive," "Legislative," and "Judicial." In the windows are the heads of Johnson, Aragon, and Chief Justice Baca, over which appear, respectively, the words "Yes!" "Maybe . . ." and "No!" One of the Indian men holds a piece of paper marked

"Indian Gaming Compacts"; the other comments, "It's the same old story—white man speak with forked tongue . . ."

63. Hughes, telephone interview, December 15, 1995.

64. "There Was Plenty of Bluster on Final Day," *New Mexican*, February 16, 1996 (Lexis-Nexis).

65. Michael Olguin, "Session Faced Barrage of Issues," *Albuquerque Journal*, February 23, 1996.

66. Ibid.

67. Hackler, telephone interview with author, March 15, 1996.

68. Leonard Tsosie, interview with author, January 17, 1996.

69. Barry Massey, "96 Legislative Session Was Struggle for Power," *New Mexican*, February 18, 1996.

70. Karen Peterson, "Tribes Already Looking at Elections," *New Mexican*, February 14, 1996.

71. Gover, interview with author, February 3, 1996.

72. Regis Pecos, interview with author, Santa Fe, New Mex., January 19, 1996.

73. Louis Sahagun, "10 N.M. Tribes Reject U.S. Order to Close Casinos; Gaming: Ultimatum Follows Ruling Banning Gambling and Voiding State-Tribal Compacts; Indians Cite Financial Stakes, Issue of Sovereignty," *Los Angeles Times*, December 23, 1995 (Lexis-Nexis).

74. Hackler, telephone interview with author, March 15, 1996.

75. Thom Cole, "Losers Sue Casino Banks; Gamblers, Spouses Want Bets Repaid," *Albuquerque Journal*, January 3, 1996.

76. Thom Cole, "Kelly, Tribes Settle; But Judge Hasn't OK'd Casino Deal," *Albuquerque Journal*, January 20, 1996.

77. Tom Day, "Corrales Dentist Becoming a Force in Gambling Dispute," *Rio Grande Sun*, January 18, 1996.

78. Leslie L. Linthicum, "Gaming Foes Hammer Ads: Group Lodges Complaints with FCC, Secretary of State," *Albuquerque Journal*, January 4, 1996.

79. Rosenthal, *The Third House*, 89.

80. Hackler, interview with author, February 2, 1996.

81. Tsosie, interview with author.

82. It is the nature of participant observation that bits and pieces of interviews, conversations, and observations sometimes provide tantalizing information that leads not to a smoking gun but to the sound of gunfire. The role of Indian gaming in the override attempts is a high priority for further research.

83. Rosenthal, *The Third House*, 25.

84. Ibid., 155.

85. Ibid.

86. Eisenstein, *Counsel for the United States*, 196.

87. Ibid., 197.

88. Hughes, telephone interview with author, December 15, 1996; Gover, interview with author, February 3, 1996.

89. Herbert A. Becker, telephone interview with author, March 15, 1996.

90. Hughes, telephone interview; Frederick Vigil, interview with author, Santa Fe, New Mex., January 17, 1996.

91. "Chino: Roadblocks No Way to Solve Problem," *Rio Grande Sun,* January 18, 1996.

92. Viarrial, interview with author, January 17, 1996.

93. Gover, interview with author.

94. Documents submitted in March 1996 as evidence in the upcoming federal litigation showed that several tribes contributed $150 per tribal slot machine to the pro-gaming efforts. Karen Peterson, "Slot Machine 'Tax' Funded '94 Contributions," *New Mexican,* March 29, 1996 (Lexis-Nexis).

95. The exception was once again Chino, Mescalero Apache president. His tribe joined neither the pueblos' motion for a preliminary injunction nor the stipulation with Kelly. Instead the Mescaleros asked the Federal District Court for the District of Columbia for a restraining order against Babbitt and Reno. The court refused and sent the tribe's motion back to the Federal District for New Mexico to be joined with the pueblos' case. See "Mescalero Suit Back to N.M.; Judge: Combine Case with 9 Other Tribes," *Albuquerque Journal,* February 7, 1996; and Bill Hume, "Mescalero Stealth Attack Blunted," *Albuquerque Journal,* February 11, 1996.

96. "Gambling Bill Lures Corruption, Chino Says," *Albuquerque Journal,* February 7, 1996.

CHAPTER 5

1. Morgan, England, and Humphreys, *Oklahoma Politics and Policies,* 35.

2. Elazar, series introduction to Morgan, England, and Humphreys, *Oklahoma Politics and Policies,* xxiii, xxxiii.

3. Elazar, *American Federalism,* 140.

4. Hrebenar and Thomas, *Interest Group Politics and the American West,* 5.

5. Morgan, England, and Humphreys, *Oklahoma Politics and Policies,* 3, 15.

6. Strickland, *The Indians of Oklahoma,* xi.

7. Debo, *A History of the Indians of the United States,* 408.

8. Gibson, *America's Exiles,* 14.

9. Debo, *And Still the Waters Run,* 10.

10. Kickingbird, "'Way Down Yonder in the Indian Nations,'" 309.

11. Cohen, *Handbook of Federal Indian Law* (1982), 784–85.

12. 34 Stat. 267.

13. Two recent books, one fiction and one nonfiction, recount the corruption and murder accompanying the oil strike on Osage lands: McAuliffe, *The Deaths of Sybil Bolton;* and Hogan, *Mean Spirit.*

14. Blend, "The American Indian Federation"; Clark, "The New Deal for Indians."

15. Clark, "The New Deal for Indians," 79.

16. Wright, *A Guide to the Indian Tribes of Oklahoma,* 25.

17. Clark, "The New Deal for Indians," 79.

18. Debo, *A History of the Indians of the United States,* 371.

19. Ibid.; Carmack, "A New Approach to Indian Affairs"; Carmack, interview with author, Norman, Okla., November 18, 1991, and February 24, 1992.

20. Strickland, *The Indians of Oklahoma,* 79.

21. Pipestem, "The Journey from *Ex parte Crow Dog* to *Littlechief,*" 4.

22. Phillip Lujan, interview with author, Norman, Okla., April 15, 1995; Bill Anoatubby, interview with author, Ada, Okla., July 3, 1995; Lawrence S. Snake, telephone interview with author, July 19, 1995.

Divisions among the state's Indian tribes may reflect similar divisions in the state generally. In "'The More Things Change . . . ,'" 200, Danney Goble has noted that the geographic areas encompassing the two former territories comprising the state remain economically and culturally "distinct."

23. Phillip Lujan, interview.

24. Ibid., Snake, interview.

25. Anoatubby, interview, July 3, 1995.

26. Rennard Strickland, interview with author, Norman, Okla., April 13, 1995.

27. Robert R. Stephens, telephone interview with author, August 5, 1995.

28. Jess Green, telephone interview with author, August 4, 1995.

29. O'Brien, "The Government-Government and Trust Relationships."

30. Wright, *A Guide to the Indian Tribes of Oklahoma.*

31. Strickland, interview.

32. Kelly Haney, interview with author, Oklahoma City, Okla., February 28, 1995.

33. Gary S. Pitchlynn, interview with author, Norman, Okla., March 27, 1995.

34. Kirke Kickingbird, interview with author, Oklahoma City, Okla., April 18, 1995.

35. "Tribes, State Stand Behind Historic Compact," *Cherokee Advocate*, July/August 1992.

36. "15 Tribes Join Protest of 'Smoke Shop' Bill," *Sac and Fox News*, June 3, 1992.

37. "Tribal Leaders Unite to Oppose Bill," *Sac and Fox News*, July 1, 1992.

38. David McCullough, telephone interview with author, July 31, 1995.

39. In addition to the tribes mentioned, the following have signed the tobacco compacts: Iowa, Apache, Shawnee, Osage, Quapaw, Tonkawa, Kickapoo, Wyandotte, Sac and Fox, and Potawatomi.

40. Debo, *And Still the Waters Run*, 20.

41. Gover, "Oklahoma," 150.

42. Kickingbird, "'Way Down Yonder in the Indian Nations,'" 303.

43. Pipestem and Rice, "The Mythology of the Oklahoma Indians," 259.

44. Gover, "Oklahoma," 151–52, 152.

45. Pipestem, "The Journey from *Ex parte Crow Dog* to *Littlechief*," 25; Kickingbird, "'Way Down Yonder in the Indian Nations,'" 330.

46. Kickingbird, "'Way Down Yonder in the Indian Nations,'" 330.

47. Gover, "Oklahoma," 139, 141.

48. Kickingbird, "'Way Down Yonder in the Indian Nations,'" 331.

49. 84 Stat. 1091.

50. Harjo v. Kleppe, 420 F.Supp. 1110 (D.D. Case 1976).

51. Strickland, *The Indians of Oklahoma*, 75.

52. *Muscogee (Creek) Nation v. Hodel* (1988).

53. Pipestem, "The Mythology of the Oklahoma Indians Revisited," 1.

54. *U.S. v. Littlechief* (1977).

55. Derryberry, Oklahoma Attorney General Opinion.

56. Strickland, *The Indians of Oklahoma*, 76.

57. Ibid.; Arrow, "Oklahoma's Tribal Courts."

58. Arrow, "Oklahoma's Tribal Courts," 7.

59. 12 Okla. St. #728 (1995).

60. Julie Rorie, telephone interview with author, July 25, 1995.

61. McCullough, "Intergovernmental Agreements under the State-Tribal Relations Act," 54.

62. Derryberry, Oklahoma Attorney General Opinion. Lexis-Nexis.

63. Turpin, Oklahoma Attorney General Opinion. Lexis-Nexis.

64. McCullough, "Intergovernmental Agreements under the State-Tribal Relations Act," 56.

65. Hammons, "Cross-Deputization in Oklahoma's Indian Country," 108.

66. 74 Okla. St. #1221–1223 (1995).

67. 74 Okla. St. #1221.B.

68. The debate on Haney's bill in and out of the legislature demonstrated the deep anti-Indian sentiment of some state officials. Tax Commission secretary Don Kilpatrick asked, presumably rhetorically, "Does it mean that every time the Legislature passes a bill, we have to negotiate with every tribe in Oklahoma . . . ? If they are sovereign, how can they vote in our elections?" Chuck Ervin, "Legislation on Indian Sovereignty Causes Concern," *Tulsa World,* May 7, 1985. During floor debate, Rep. Ken Harris (D-Lawton) referred to the "guerrilla warfare" of western Oklahoma tribes. Jim Myers, "House Approves Indian Tribes Bill," *Tulsa World,* March 15, 1985.

69. 74 Okla. St. #1221.

70. Ibid., #1221.C, D.

71. Wilson to Senator John McCain, Chairman, Senate Comiteee on Indian Affairs, June 12, 1995.

72. Gover, "Oklahoma," 153.

73. Robert Reinhold, "Bingo Issue Pits Creek Indians against Oklahoma," *New York Times,* December 13, 1985.

74. Gover, "Oklahoma," 161.

75. Oklahoma Tax Commission, "Oklahoma Tax Commission's Position on State Tax Law Compliance by Tribally Owned Businesses," Sovereignty Symposium II, Oklahoma City, May 30–June 1, 1989, 1–6.

76. Oklahoma Tax Commission, *Oklahoma Tax Commisson v. Graham,* No. 99-266, brief, 1988.

77. Oklahoma Tax Commission, *Oklahoma Tax Commission v. Citizen Band Potawatomi Indian Tribe of Oklahoma,* No. 89–1322, brief, 1990.

78. The Sac and Fox Tribe imposed its own income tax on tribal employees, whether or not they were tribal members. The tribe also imposed a tax on motor vehicles.

79. Oklahoma Tax Commission, *Oklahoma Tax Commission v. Sac and Fox Nation,* No. 92–259, brief, 1992.

80. Oklahoma Tax Commission, *Oklahoma Tax Commisson v. Chickasaw Nation,* No. 94–771, brief, 1995.

81. Anoatubby, interview with author, Oklahoma City, Okla., April 21, 1995; and Ada, Okla., July 3, 1995.

82. 47 Okla. St. #1136 (1995); Anoatubby, interview, July 3, 1995.

82. Anoatubby, interview, July 3, 1995.

83. Ibid.

84. *Oklahoma Tax Commission v. Sac and Fox Nation* (1993).

85. Morgan, England, and Humphreys, *Oklahoma Politics and Policies*, 32.

86. Loving, Oklahoma Attorney General Opinion No. 93–1.

87. Epperly, "Class III Gaming," 439.

88. 21 Okla. St. #965.

89. 21 Okla. St. #941.

90. 21 Okla. St. #949.

91. 3 Okla. St. #220, 205; 21 Okla. St. #1051.

92. Edmondson, Oklahoma Attorney General Opinion No. 95–6.

93. Mark A. Hutchingson and Lillie-Beth Sanger, "Gambling Raid Hits Shawnee Elks Lodge," *Sunday Oklahoman*, April 16, 1995.

94. Organized opposition to State Question 658 was led by Oklahomans Against the Lottery and Horsement Against the Lottery Threat (HALT). The *Daily Oklahoman* was also editorially opposed to the referendum.

95. Forrest A. Claunch, "Point of View: SQ 658: Claunch Makes His Case," *Daily Oklahoman*, May 8, 1994.

96. Don Nickles, "Lottery Could Legalize Casino Gambling on Indian Lands," *Daily Oklahoman*, May 8, 1994.

97. Jess Green, telephone interview with author, August 1, 1995.

98. John Greiner, "Politicians Don't Expect New Lottery Anytime Soon," *Daily Oklahoman*, May 15, 1994.

99. Paul English and Mick Hinton, "Racing Group Wants Casinos in Oklahoma," *Daily Oklahoman*, June 27, 1995.

100. There are anecdotal accounts of high stakes bingo and casino games being operated by individuals on tribal land in western Oklahoma in the late 1970s. However, according to a confidential source, the games were quietly closed down after an investigation by state and local law enforcement agencies.

101. Senate, Select Committee on Indian Affairs, *Establishing Federal Standards and Regulations for the Conduct of Gaming Activities within Indian Country*, 125.

102. Ibid., *Gaming Activities on Indian Reservations and Lands*, 106.

103. United Press International, "Oklahoma News Briefs," March 10, 1983 (Lexis-Nexis).

The sheriff also shut down the Picher, Oklahoma, Volunteer Fire Department's Sunday bingo game for violating the state law prohibiting such games.

104. State ex rel. May v. Seneca-Cayuga Tribe of Oklahoma, 711 P.2d 77 (1985).

105. Griff Palmer, "Indian Tribe's Bingo Operations Expected to Persist Unimpeded," *Daily Oklahoman*, July 27, 1985.

106. Seneca-Cayuga Tribe of Oklahoma v. Oklahoma ex rel. Thompson, 874 F.2d 709 (1989).

107. Indian Country, U.S.A., Inc. v. Oklahoma ex rel. Oklahoma Tax Commission.

108. Indian Country, U.S.A., Inc. v. Oklahoma Tax Commission, 829 F.2d 967 (1987).

109. Kickingbird, interview.

110. Lorbiecki, "Indian Sovereignty versus Oklahoma's Gambling Laws."

111. Senate, Select Committee on Indian Affairs, *Establishing Federal Standards and Regulations for the Conduct of Gaming Activities within Indian Country*, 562–79.

112. John Klein, "New Regulations Expect to Help Indian Gaming Industry Flourish," *Tulsa World*, November 28, 1990 (Lexis-Nexis).

113. Wayne Singleterry, "Attorneys Ask Court to Resolve Bingo Squabble," *Daily Oklahoman*, September 14, 1988.

114. Mark A. Hutchison, "Caddo Tribe Appealing Denial of Bingo Contract," *Daily Oklahoman*, July 1, 1992.

115. United Press International, untitled, December 23, 1981 (Lexis-Nexis).

116. "Bingo Vetoed, Grants to FRU Halted," *Cherokee Advocate*, September 1984.

117. "Council Approves Code of Ethics, Not Commission," *Cherokee Advocate*, May 1989.

118. "October Council Approves Bingo Operation," *Cherokee Advocate*, December 1989.

119. The Cherokee Nation later opened two more bingo halls: the Outpost in Catoosa, a suburb of Tulsa, in September 1993 and another in West Siloam Springs in April 1994. "Cherokee Nation Bingo Outpost, Inc. Plans Expansion," *Cherokee Advocate*, July 1994.

120. The court first disposed of the state's contention that the United Keetoowah Band of Cherokee Indians was not a "tribe" for the purposes of federal court jurisdiction. The court pointed out that the band was a federally recognized tribe incorporated under the Oklahoma Indian Welfare Act.

121. *United Keetoowah Band of Cherokee Indians v. Oklahoma ex rel. Moss* 1176.

122. Kickingbird, interview.

123. Michael McNutt, "Lack of Interest, Money Puts Rein on Ponca Track," *Daily Oklahoman*, October 1, 1992.

124. The proposal appeared to have new life in early September 1995. The Black Hawk Gaming & Development Company announced that the Anadarko BIA area director had approved its application to place a parcel of land in trust for the Sac and Fox Nation to operate high stakes bingo.

125. Epperley, "Class III Gaming," 443–44.

126. Rob Martindale, "Tonkawas Shut Down Casino Gambling Operation," *Tulsa World,* October 1, 1991.

127. Rob Martindale, "Casino Uses Bingo to Shield Other Games," *Tulsa World,* February 16, 1992.

128. Paul English, "Governor Signs Pack OK'ing Video Gaming," *Daily Oklahoman,* July 11, 1992.

129. Ridgeway, "The Potawatomi/Oklahoma Compact of 1992," 537.

130. Paul English, "Ex-Assistant Attorney General Hired for Negotiations," *Daily Oklahoman,* February 19, 1992.

131. Ridgeway, "The Potawatomi/Oklahoma Compact of 1992," 526.

132. Ibid., 527.

133. Michael Minnis, telephone interview with author, July 27, 1995. Although the U.S. Attorney for the Eastern District of Oklahoma disputed the alleged threat, the Tenth Circuit cited it in its *Green* decision: "Oklahoma negotiated for this condition because the U.S. Attorney had informed the state that the importation of VLTs under the Compact could subject both Oklahoma and the Tribe to liability under the Johnson Act." *Citizen Band Potawatomi Indian Tribe of Oklahoma v. Green* (1993).

134. Tribal-State Class III Gaming Compact Between the Citizen Band Potawatomi Indian Tribe of Oklahoma and the State of Oklahoma, Oklahoma Secretary of State, July 6, 1992. Author's files.

135. David McCullough, telephone interview with author, July 31, 1995.

136. Ponca Tribe of Oklahoma v. Oklahoma, 834 F.Supp. 1341 (1992).

137. Ponca Tribe of Oklahoma v. Oklahoma, 37 F.3d 1422 (1994). The appeals court combined the *Ponca* case with those involving the Kickapoo Tribe and the State of Kansas; Sandia Pueblo and the State of New Mexico; and the Mescalero Apache Tribe and the State of New Mexico. The district court in the *Kickapoo* case, unlike courts in the other three cases, had found that the IGRA did waive Eleventh Amendment sovereign immunity.

138. Other tribes involved in the lawsuit was the Eastern Band of Cherokees, the Poarch Band of Creeks, Isleta Pueblo, Rumsey Rancheria, the San Manuel Band of Mission Indians, and the Spokane Tribe. Alabama, Arizona, California, Colorado, Connecticut, Florida, Idaho, Kansas, Michigan, Mississippi, Nebraska, North Dakota, South Dakota, Wisconsin, and Wyoming intervened as defendants.

139. Cabazon Band of Mission Indians, et al. v. National Indian Gaming Commission, 827 F.Supp. 26 (1993).

140. Green, "Indian Gaming 1994," 7.

141. Cabazon Band of Mission Indians, et al. v. National Indian Gaming Commission, 14 F.3d 633 (1994), commonly referred to as *Cabazon II.*

142. Jess Green, interview with author, Ada, Okla., August 4, 1995.

143. Green, "Indian Gaming 1995," 11.

144. Captain v. Ross, Case No. CIV-95-01, Miami Agency (1995).

145. It is unclear why the Oklahoma Highway Patrol participated in the raid, since, as Jess Green told me, the state had no jurisdiction in the matter.

146. "Eastern Shawnees Promise Battle over Seizure of Tribal Property in Gaming Dispute," press release, Eastern Shawnee Tribe of Oklahoma, September 18, 1995.

147. "U.S. Attorney Announces Joint Federal and State Investigation of Illegal Gambling in Northeastern Oklahoma and Southeastern Kansas," press release, U.S. Attorney, Eastern District of Oklahoma, September 14, 1995.

148. "Butler Gets Oklahoma Approval for Gaming," Reuters, September 15, 1995 (Lexis-Nexis).

149. United Press International, "Indian Bingo Plan under Study," April 15, 1984 (Lexis-Nexis).

150. Ray Romano, "3 Indian Tribes Stir Casino Fears," *New York Times,* August 1, 1993 (Lexis-Nexis); "Block Wildwood Casino; Indian Gambling Would Circumvent N.J. Law," *Asbury Park Press,* August 30, 1995 (Lexis-Nexis).

151. Evelyn Nieves, "Casino Plan May Not Be a Pipe Dream," *New York Times,* November 10, 1995.

152. "Mankiller Endorses Synar for Re-election," *Cherokee Advocate,* July/August 1992; Anoatubby, interview, July 3, 1995.

153. Fixico, *Termination and Relocation.*

154. Robert R. Stephens, telephone interview with author, August 5, 1995.

155. Gary S. Pitchlynn, interview with author, Norman, Okla., March 27, 1995; Stephens, telephone interview.

156. Pitchlynn, interview, March 27, 1995; Lawrence S. Snake, telephone interview with author, July 19, 1995; McCullough, telephone interview, July 31, 1995.

157. Pitchlynn, interview, March 27, 1995.

158. Ibid.

159. Snake, interview, July 19, 1995.

160. Pitchlynn, interview, March 27, 1995.

161. Tracy Burris, telephone interview with author, October 23, 1995.

162. Green, "Indian Gaming 1995," 3.

163. Bell and Meador, "Appointing United States Attorneys," 255.

164. Morgan, England, and Humphreys, *Oklahoma Politics and Policies*, 8.

165. Bednar and Hertzke, "Oklahoma."

166. Eisenstein, *Counsel for the United States*, x.

167. Judicial Staff Directory, "Rayel, John W."

168. Eisenstein, *Counsel for the United States*, 196, 192.

169. England and Morgan, "Oklahoma," 275.

170. Kickingbird, "'Way Down Yonder in the Indian Nations,'" 303.

171. See Pipestem and Rice, "The Mythology of the Oklahoma Indians"; and Pipestem, "The Journey from *Ex parte Crow Dog* to *Littlechief.*"

172. Strickland, "A Tale of Two Marshalls," 111.

173. Arkansas Riverbed Authority, "As Long as Rivers Flow . . ."; Strickland, "A Tale of Two Marshalls."

174. Strickland, "A Tale of Two Marshalls," 125–26.

175. Ridgeway, "The Potawatomi/Oklahoma Compact of 1992."

176. Green, "Indian Gaming 1995," 3.

177. Gary S. Pitchlynn, interview with author, February 3, 1995.

178. England and Morgan, "Oklahoma"; Morgan, England, and Humphreys, *Oklahoma Politics and Policies*, 17.

179. Eadington, *Indian Gaming and the Law*, vi.

180. Anoatubby, interview, October 23, 1995. In mid-December 1995 an intertribal group began to organize an Indian PAC, including the selection of officers and coordinators. "Indian Leaders Forming Political Action Committee," *Daily Oklahoman*, December 14, 1995.

181. Morgan, England, and Humphreys, *Oklahoma Politics and Policies*, 143.

CONCLUSION

1. Clinton, "The Dormant Indian Commerce Clause," 1156–57.

2. Cohen, *Handbook of Federal Indian Law*.

3. O'Brien, "The Government-Government and Trust Relationships."

4. Cigler, "Not Just Another Special Interest Group."

5. While unionized public employees are often active lobbyists and campaigners, they do so independently of any sanction or direction from the government entity that they work for.

6. Olsen, *The Logic of Collective Action*.

7. Inouye, "Address to Tribal Leaders," 7.

8. "Indian Voters Register This Year," *Gallup Independent*, September 9, 1996.

9. Ibid.

10. Brian Ford, "Tribes Protest $100,000 Expenditure," *Tulsa World,* July 12, 1996.

11. George Weeks, "Whatever Engler Wagers to Do on Gaming, He'll Be Among Friends," *Detroit News,* April 30, 1995 (Lexis-Nexis).

12. "Choctaw Money for Candidate Questioned by Republicans," *Indian Country Today,* September 2–9, 1996.

13. Kenan Pollack, "Mashantucket Pequots: A Tribe That's Raking It In," *U.S. News & World Report,* January 15, 1996.

14. Meredith O'Brien, "Gaming Executives Have a Lot at Stake in Washington," *Hartford Courant,* July 12, 1996.

15. "Umberg Crosses the Line," *Fresno Bee,* November 4, 1994 (Lexis-Nexis).

16. Monette, "New Federalism for Indian Tribes," 618.

17. Becker, telephone interview, March 15, 1996.

18. Gover and Cooney, "Cooperation between Tribes and States," 36.

19. See Viola, *Diplomats in Buckskin;* Norgren, *The Cherokee Cases.*

20. W. John Moore, "Tribal Imperatives," *National Journal,* June 9, 1990 (Lexis-Nexis).

EPILOGUE

1. After first refusing to do so, the Jicarilla Apache Tribe later signed the compact and argeement.

2. Press Release, for Immediate Release, July 8, 1997, contact Diane Kinderwater. http://164.64.43.1/hotissues/news/Gaming_7-7-97.htm.

3. U.S. Department of the Interior, "Media Advisory: Department of the Interior to Allow New Mexico Indian Gaming Compacts to Take Effect, 22 August 1997." http://www.doi.gov/news/indnmst.html.

4. Office of the Secretary, "Statement of Secretary of the Interior Bruce Babbitt on the New Mexico Gaming Compacts, 23 August 1997." http://www.doi.gov/news/indnmcom.html. See also attached letter to New Mexico Governor Bruce Johnson.

5. The Mescalero Tribe still had not paid anything to the state when its president, Wendell Chino, died on October 30, 1998, after serving in tribal office for more than thirty years.

6. "Tribal Gaming Payments," *Albuquerque Tribune,* February 10, 1999.

7. Wren Propp, "Panel Axes Casino Rate Bill: Revenue Sharing Plan Sought Cut," *Albuquerque Journal,* March 20, 1999.

8. New Mexico Legislature, Senate Bill 737, 44th Legislature, 1st Sess., 1999. The Bill passes the Senate 25-11 and the House 49-7.

9. The district court held that the proposed banking and percentage card games using traditional casino game themes were outside the scope of negotiation.

10. Rumsey Indian Rancheria of Wintun Indians v. Wilson, 64 F.3d 1250 (1994).

11. Office of the United States Attorney, Southern District of California, "News Release: United States Files Suit against Slot Machines Operated by Sycuan and Barbona Tribes, San Diego, Calif., 14 May 1998." http://www.usdoj.gov/usao/cas/pr/cas80514.1.html.

12. Western Telcon, Inc. v. California State Lottery, 96 C.D.D.S. 4645 (1996).

13. Testimony of Robert Smith, Chairman of the Pala Band of Mission Band Indians, before the National Gambling Impact Study Commission, 29 July 1998. http://standup.quicknet.com/statements/robert_smith_1998_july_29.html.

14. Mary Lynne Vellinga, "Tribes' Gambling Pacts Ratified by Lawmakers," *Sacramento Bee,* August 28, 1998.

15. Pete Wilson, "Governor Pete Wilson's Statement Pala Band Compact, 6 March 1998." http://www.ca.gov/t/governor/compactp.html.

16. Dan Lungren, "Lungren, Tribal Leaders and Local Law Enforcement Discuss Implementation of Landmark Indian Gaming Compact, Sacramento, California, 9 March 1998." http://caag.state.ca.us/press/98-036.htm

17. The assistant secretary of the interior for Indian affairs approved the Pala compact on April 25. In a press release Gover said, "Our approval of this compact can not and does not mean that the State meets its obligation of good-faith negotiating merely by offering identical compacts to other tribes." "U.S. Department of the Interior, Bureau of Indian Affairs Approves Gaming Compact and Preserves the Right of Other Tribes to Negotiate Their Own Compacts, 25 April 1998." http://www.doi.gov/bia/news98/palanews.htm.

18. Bill Ainsworth, "Wilson Has a New Tune for Indian Gaming Pact," *San Diego Union-Tribune,* April 13, 1998.

19. James P. Sweeney, "Tribes Gather 800,000 Names for Gaming Vote," *San Diego Union-Tribune,* April 21, 1998.

20. Yes on 5, "Summary of Key Provisions, Yes on 5: Californians for Indian Self-Reliance." http://www.cisr.org/Summary2.html.

21. Yes on 5, "Is Proposition 5 Better for California Indians and Our State than the Indian Gaming Proposal developed by Governor Wilson and Promoted by Las Vegas Casino Interests?" Yes on 5: Californians for Indian Self-Reliance, http://yeson5.org/q14.html.

22. Jeff Gorman, "California Tribes Turn Up Volume," *Las Vegas Sun*, July 30, 1998.

23. Informed Voter, http://www.informedvoter.org/topcon.html.

24. Ibid.

25. Dave Berns, "Californians Pass Gaming Prop," *Las Vegas Review Journal*, November 4, 1998.

26. "Statement of Vote: 1998 General Election, November 3, 1998." http://Vote98.ss.ca.gov/Final/Statement_of_Vote.htm.

27. "State Changes Position on Indian Gaming," *San Francisco Chronicle*, January 8, 1999.

28. Those tribes that eventually signed Pala compacts opposed Proposition 5. By election day, eighty-eight California tribes *supported* Proposition 5.

29. On August 23, 1999, the California Supreme Court handed down a six to one decision in *Hotel Employees & Restaurant Employees International Union v. Davis* holding Proposition 5 unconstitutional. The court ruled that the type of gaming legalized by Proposition 5 was prohibited by the California constitution. In an environment closely resembling that in New Mexico after that state's supreme court struck down the 1994 gaming referendum and again after the New Mexico court held the tribal-state compacts unconstitutional, California tribal leaders and the state's political leaders searched for a way to preserve Indian gaming in the state. Tribes had been preparing a constitutional amendment in anticipation of an adverse ruling by the court, and after the court's decision, Governor Davis and legislative leaders appeared ready to support an early referendum on an amendment clearing the way for tribal-state compacts. Robert Salladay, "Davis, indian Tribes Work to Save Casinos: Temporary Deal May Allow Time to Place New Measure on Ballot," *San Francisco Examiner*, August 26, 1999; Dan Smith, "Analysis: Gambling Proposal Could Resolve Issue," *Sacramento Bee*, August 28, 1999.

30. Congress, Senate, Senator Michael B. Enzi of Wyoming, 105th Cong., 2d sess., *Congressional Record*, September 15, 1998, S. 10356.

31. Congress, Senate, Voice Vote on Amendment 111, 106th Cong., 1st sess., *Congressional Record*, S. 2985.

32. David Stafford, "Proposal to Tax Native American Tribal Businesses Crushed—For Now," LEGI-SLATE News Service, June 13, 1997. http://www.legislate.com/nn/news/970613.html.

33. Congress, House, Representative Ernest J. Istook of Oklahoma, 105th Cong., 1st sess., *Congressional Record*, July 15, 1997, H. 5220, H. 5223.

34. Ibid., H. 5221.

35. Kevin Gover, Kevin Gover, Assistant Secretary—Indian Affairs—Department of the Interior before the 55th Annual National

Congress of American Indians, Myrtle Beach, S.C., October 20, 1998, 7. http://www.doi.gov/bia/ncaikg4.htm.

36. Kevin Gover, Senate Committee on Indian Affairs, "Opening Statement of Kevin Gover, Assistant Secretary—Indian Affairs on the FY 2000 Budget Request for the Bureau of Indian Affairs before the Committee on Indian Affairs, United States Senate" (February 24, 1999). http://www.senate.gov/~scia/1999hrgs/FY00bdgt/gover224.pdf.

37. Congress, Senate, H.R. 2710, sec. 118(b), 105th Cong., 1st sess., *Congressional Record* (September 16, 1997), S. 9389.

38. Congress, Senate, H.R. 2710, Amendment 1197 to sec. 118, 105th Cong., 1st sess., *Congressional Record* (September 16, 1997), S. 9389.

39. U.S. Department of Interior, Bureau of Indian Affairs, "BIA Delivers New Funds to Small and Needy Tribes to Strengthen Tribal Governments and Operations," Washington, D.C., December 11, 1997. http://www.doi.gov.bia/press/small.htm.

40. Congress, Senate, H.R. 2710, secs. 120(1) and (2), 105th Cong., 1st sess., *Congressional Record* (September 16, 1997), S. 9397.

41. Congress, Senate, S. 1691, secs. 1(B) and (b)(3), 105th Cong., 2nd sess., *Congressional Record* (February 27, 1998), S. 1155.

42. Congress, Senate, Senate Committee on Indian Affairs, Prepared Statement of Senator Ben Nighthorse Campbell, Chairman, Senate Committee on Indian Affairs, Hearing on Tribal Sovereign Immunity, March 11, 1998, 1. http://www.senate.gov/~scia/1998/0311_cm.htm.

43. Daniel K. Inouye, Senate Committee on Indian Affairs, Statement of Senator Daniel K. Inouye, Vice Chairman, Committee on Indian Affairs, before the March 11, 1998, Hearing on the Sovereign Authorities and Immunities of Tribal Governments as They Relate to Actions Arising Out of Contracts and the Collection of State Taxes, March 11, 1998, 2. http://www.senate.gov/~scia/1998hrgs/0311_vc.htm.

44. National Governors Association, EDC-6. The Role of States, the Federal Government, and Indian Tribal Governments with Respect to Indian Gaming. http://www.nga.org/Pubs/Policies/EDC/edc06.asp.

45. Congress, Senate, Senate Committee on Indian Affairs, Rick Hill, Chairman, National Indian Gaming Association, S. 399, the Indian Gaming Regulatory Act of 1999 Testimony before the Senate Committee on Indian Affairs, March 24, 1999. http://www.senate.gov/~scia/1999hrgs/igra3.24/hill.pdf.

Bibliography

INTERVIEWS

Anoatubby, Bill (Chickasaw). Governor, Chickasaw Nation. Oklahoma City, Okla., April 21, 1995; Ada,Okla., July 3, 1995; Norman, Okla., October 23, 1995.

Becker, Herbert A. Director, Office of Tribal Justice, U.S. Department of Justice, Washington, D.C.Telephone, March 15, 1996.

Bellmard, Ken. Ponca City, Okla. Attorney, Miami, Tonkawa, Modoc, and Otoe/Missouria tribes. Telephone, October 20, 1995.

Beverly, Anne Marie. Casino Host, Santa Ana Star Casino, Santa Ana Pueblo, New Mex. Santa Fe, New Mex., January 18, 1996.

Burris, Tracy (Chickasaw/Choctaw). Chairman, Oklahoma Indian Gaming Association; Chickasaw Gaming Commissioner. Telephone, October 23, 1995, and March 28, 1996.

Carmack, William. Professor Emeritus of Communication, University of Oklahoma; former Administrative Assistant, U.S. Senator Fred R. Harris; former Assistant Commissioner of Indian Affairs; former Director, National Council on Indian Opportunity, Norman, Okla., November 18, 1991, and February 24, 1992.

Chaves, Frank (Sandia Pueblo). Co-chairman, New Mexico Indian Gaming Commission. Telephone, August 23, 1994; Albuquerque, New Mex., March 17, 1995; Santa Fe, New Mex., March 17, 1995.

Cissell, James C. Clerk of Courts, Hamilton County, Cincinnati, Ohio; U.S. Attorney, Southern District of Ohio, 1977–81. Telephone, September 27, 1995.

Echols, Odis. President, Echols Enterprises, Albuquerque, New Mex.; Registered Lobbyist for Sandia Pueblo and New Mexico Indian Gaming Association. Santa Fe, New Mex., February 2, 1996.

Gover, Kevin (Pawnee). Attorney, Gover, Stetson & Williams, Albuquerque, New Mex.; attorney, Pojoaque Pueblo. Santa Fe and Tesuque Pueblo, New Mex., February 3, 1996.

Gover, Lisa (Pawnee). Attorney, Albuquerque; staff, New Mexico Indian Gaming Association. Santa Fe and Tesuque Pueblo, New Mex., February 3, 1996; Tulsa, Okla., June 5, 1996; telephone, July 13, 1996.

Green, Jess (Chickasaw/Choctaw). Attorney, Ada, Okla.; attorney, Oklahoma Indian Gaming Association and tribes. Telephone, August 1, 1995; Ada, Okla., August 4, 1995; Telephone, October 11, 1995.

Hackler, Rex. Hackler, Rivera, Inc., Bernalillo, New Mex. Santa Fe, New Mex., January 18, 1996; telephone, January 20, 1996; Santa Fe, New Mex., February 2, 1996; telephone, March 15, 1996.

Haney, Enoch Kelly (Seminole). Oklahoma State Senator. Oklahoma City, Okla., February 28, 1995.

Harris, Fred R. Professor of Political Science, University of New Mexico; former U.S. Senator from Oklahoma. Albuquerque, New Mex., August 22, 1994.

Harris, LaDonna. President, Americans for Indian Opportunity. Santa Ana Pueblo, New Mex., August 25, 1994.

Hogen, Phillip (Oglala Lakota). Commissioner, National Indian Gaming Commission; former U.S. Attorney for South Dakota. Telephone, May 6, 1996.

Hughes, Richard W. Santa Fe. Attorney, Santa Ana and San Felipe pueblos. Telephone, October 27, 1995, and December 15, 1995; Santa Fe, New Mex., January 18, 1996; telephone, July 25, 1996.

Huntly, Web (Chickasaw). Manager, Chickasaw Gaming Center, Thackerville, Okla. Telephone, October 20, 1995.

Jojola, Ray (Isleta Pueblo). Member, Isleta Pueblo Tribal Council. Isleta Pueblo, New Mex., January 15, 1996.

Kickingbird, Kirke (Kiowa). Professor of Law and Director, Native American Legal Resource Center, Oklahoma City University College of Law; Counsel to Oklahoma Governor Keating for Indian Affairs. Oklahoma City, Okla., April 18, 1995.

King, Bruce. Former Governor of New Mexico. Santa Fe, New Mex., March 14, 1995.

Lopez, Ronald P. Public Affairs Officer, U.S. Attorney's Office, Albuquerque, New Mex. Telephone, March 14, 1996.

Lucero, Stanley (Laguna Pueblo). Lieutenant Governor, Laguna Pueblo. Santa Fe, New Mex., Janaury 16, 1996.

Lujan, Phillip (Kiowa-Taos). Professor of Communication, University of Oklahoma; Tribal Court Judge. Norman, Okla., April 7, 1995.

Lujan, Vince (Taos Pueblo). Member, Taos Pueblo Council. Santa Fe, New Mex., February 2, 1996.

McCullough, David. Attorney, Minnis & Associates, Oklahoma City; attorney, Citizen Band Potawatomi Tribe. Telephone, July 31, 1995.

McLoughlin, Charles. Assistant U.S. Attorney, Eastern District of Oklahoma, Tulsa. Telephone, November 13, 1995.

Minnis, Michael. Attorney, Minnis & Associates, Oklahoma City; attorney, Citizen Band Potawatomi Tribe. Telephone, July 27, 1995.

North, Rosalyn. Secretary, New Mexico Senate Select Committee on Gaming. Santa Fe, New Mex., March 14, 1995.

Pecos, Regis (Cochiti Pueblo). Executive Director, New Mexico Office of Indian Affairs, Santa Fe, New Mex. Santa Fe, January 19, 1996.

Pinto, John (Navajo). New Mexico State Senator. Santa Fe, New Mex., January 19, 1996.

Pitchlynn, Gary (Choctaw). Attorney, Pitchlynn, Odom, Morse & Ritter, Norman, Okla. Oklahoma City, Okla., February 9, 1995; Norman, Okla., March 27, 1995; telephone, July 20, 1995, and March 28, 1996.

Powell, Ray. Chairman, New Mexico Democratic Party. Telephone, August 22, 1994.

Rice, G. William (Cherokee-Pawnee). Cushing, Okla. Attorney General, Sac and Fox Nation; Professor of Law, University of Tulsa Law School. Telephone, October 27, 1995.

Rorie, Julie. Staff Attorney, Administrative Office, Oklahoma Supreme Court. Telephone, July 25, 1995.

Salazar, Teresa. Legislative Analyst, New Mexico State Representative Linda Lovejoy (Navajo). Santa Fe, New Mex., January 17, 1996.

Sando, Joe S. (Jemez Pueblo). Indian Pueblo Cultural Center Archives, Albuquerque, New Mex. Albuquerque, March 13, 1995.

Shutiva, Ron (Acoma Pueblo). Governor, Acoma Pueblo. Santa Fe, New Mex., February 2, 1996.

Snake, Lawrence S. (Delaware), President, Delaware Nation of Western Oklahoma, Anadarko. Telephone, July 19, 1995.

Stephens, Robert R. (Chickasaw). Purcell, Okla. Former Chairman and Vice Chairman, Oklahoma Indian Gaming Association; former Gaming Commissioner, Chickasaw Nation. Telephone, August 5, 1995.

Strickland, Rennard (Cherokee-Osage). Dean, Oklahoma City University College of Law. Norman, Okla., April 13, 1995.

Teegarden, Tom. Director, Taos Pueblo Office of Community and Economic Development, Taos Pueblo, New Mex. Santa Fe, New Mex., February 2, 1996.

Thorpe, Grace (Sac and Fox). President, No Nuclear Waste on Indian Lands (NECONA); member, Sac and Fox Nation Health Commission. Guthrie, Okla., February 19, 1996.

Tsosie, Leonard (Navajo). New Mexico State Senator. Santa Fe, New Mex., January 17, 1996, and February 3, 1996.

Viarrial, Jake (Pojoaque Pueblo). Governor, Pojoaque Pueblo, New Mex. Pojoaque Pueblo, January 19, 1996.

Vigil, Frederick (Tesueque Pueblo). Governor, Tesueque Pueblo. Santa Fe, New Mex., January 17, 1996.

Warner, Barbara (Ponca). Director, Oklahoma Indian Affairs Commission. Telephone, October 20, 1995.

Williams, Susan (Sisseton-Whapaton). Attorney, Gover, Stetson & Williams. Albuquerque, New Mex., August 25, 1994.

Williams-Teller, Verna (Isleta Pueblo). Former Governor, Isleta Pueblo; Public Gaming Research Institute, Albuquerque, New Mex. Isleta Pueblo, New Mex., January 15, 1996.

Wilson, Curtis. Muscogee Area BIA, Contract Office, Norman, Okla. Telephone, September 13, 1995.

BOOKS AND ARTICLES

Ahola, Amber J. "Call It The Revenge of the Pequots, or How American Indian Tribes Can Sue States under the Indian Gaming Regulatory Act without Violating the Eleventh Amendment." *University of San Francisco Law Review* 27 (Summer 1993): 907–58.

Allen, W. Ron. Written Statement of W. Ron Allen, President National Congress of American Indians, to the Senate Committee on Indian Affairs Regarding the Impact of the U.S. Supreme Court's Recent Decision in *Seminole Tribe of Florida v. State of Florida*. Federal Document Clearing House. (Lexis-Nexis). May 9, 1996.

Almond, Gabriel, and Sidney Verba. *The Civic Culture*. Boston: Little, Brown, 1965.

Angle, Martha. "High-Stakes Bingo to Continue: Congress Clears Legislation to Regulate Indian Gambling." *Congressional Quarterly Weekly Report*, October 1, 1988, 2730.

Anton, Thomas J. 1989. *American Federalism and Public Policy: How the System Works*. New York: Random House.

Arkansas Riverbed Authority. nd. "As Long as Rivers Flow . . ." Tahlequah, Okla.: Authority, n.d.

Arrow, Dennis W. "Oklahoma's Tribal Courts: A Prologue, the First Fifteen Years of the Modern Era, and a Glimpse at the Road Ahead." *Oklahoma City University Law Review* 19 (1994): 5–80.

Barbrook, Alec, and Christine Bolt. *Power and Protest in American Life.* New York: St. Martin's Press, 1980.

Bardakjy, Eugene Neimy. "Is There a Lucky Seven in Florida's Future?" *Nova Law Review* 18 (Winter 1994): 1065–97.

Barsh, Russell Lawrence. "Felix S. Cohen's *Handbook of Federal Indian Law,* 1982 Edition." *Washington Law Review* 57 (1982): 799–811.

———. "The Nature and Spirit of North American Political Systems." *American Indian Quarterly* (Summer 1986): 181–98.

Barsh, Russell Lawrence, and James Youngblood Henderson. *The Road: Indian Tribes and Political Liberty.* Berkeley: University of California Press, 1980.

Beck, Warren A., and Ynez D. Haase, *Historical Atlas of New Mexico.* Norman: University of New Mexico Press, 1969.

Bee, Robert L. "Riding the Paper Tiger." In *State and Reservation: New Perspectives on Federal Indian Policy,* edited by George Pierre Castile and Robert L. Bee. Tucson: University of Arizona Press, 1992.

———. "The Washington Connection: American Indian Leaders and American Indian Policy: The Manipulation of Policy in Indian Affairs." *Indian Historian* 12 (1979): 1–11, 36.

Beer, Samuel H. *New Federalism: Intergovernmental Reform from Nixon to Reagan.* Washington, D.C.: The Brookings Institution, 1988.

Bell, Griffen B., and Daniel J. Meador. "Appointing United States Attorneys." *Journal of Law and Politics* 9 (1993): 247–55.

Belliveau, James J. "Casino Gambling under the Indian Gaming Regulatory Act: Narragansett Tribal Sovereignty versus Rhode Island Gambling Laws." *Suffolk University Law Review* 27 (1993): 388–423.

Bentley, Arthur F. *The Process of Government: A Study of Social Pressure.* Chicago: University of Chicago Press, 1908.

Biolsi, Thomas. *Organizing the Lakota: The Political Economy of the New Deal on the Pine Ridge and Rosebud Reservations.* Tucson: University of Arizona Press, 1992.

Bisset, William T. "Tribal-State Gaming Compacts: The Constitutionality of the Indian Gaming Regulatory Act. *Hastings Constitutional Law Quarterly* 21 (Fall 1993): 71–93.

Blend, Benay. "The American Indian Federation." In *Between Two Worlds: The Survival of Twentieth Century Indians,* edited by Arrell Morgan Gibson, 84–104. Oklahoma City: Oklahoma City Historical Society, 1986.

Bradley, Robert C., and Paul Gardner. "Underdogs, Upperdogs and the Use of the Amicus Brief: Trends and Explanations." *Justice System Journal* 10 (1985): 78–96.

Brief of Appellants. *California v. Cabazon Band of Mission Indians,* No. 85–1708. August 8, 1986. (Lexis-Nexis).

Brief of Appellees. *California v. Cabazon Band of Mission Indians,* No. 85–1708. September 24, 1986. (Lexis-Nexis).

Brief of Appellees State of New Mexico, et al. *Cotton Petroleum Corporation v. New Mexico.* No. 87–1327. August 31, 1989.

Briggs, Charles L. *Learning How to Ask: A Sociolinguistic Appraisal of the Role of the Interview in Social Science.* Cambridge: Cambridge University Press, 1989.

Browne, William P. "Organized Interests and Their Issue Niches: A Search for Pluralism in a Policy Domain." *Journal of Politics* 52 (1990): 477–509.

Bureau of Indian Affairs. Office of Public Information Staff. "BIA Supports Tribes, Expresses Concerns at Bingo Consultation Session." *Indian News Notes* 7, no. 28, August 19, 1983.

Burr, Lance W. "Broken Promises Revisited: A Story of the Kickapoo Nation–Kansas Gaming Compact." *Washburn Law Journal* 32 (1992): 16–34.

Burton, Jeffrey. *Indian Territory and the United States, 1866–1906: Courts, Government, and the Movement for Oklahoma Statehood.* Norman: University of Oklahoma Press, 1995.

Calbom, Linda M. Prepared Statement of Linda M. Calbom Director, Civil Audits Accounting and Information Management Division United States General Accounting Office Before the House Resources Committee Task Force on Indian Trust Fund Management. *Federal News Service,* June 18, 1996. (Lexis-Nexis).

Camire, Dennis. "Former Top Republican Takes Over as Head of Gaming Lobby." Gannett News Service, May 26, 1995. (Lexis-Nexis).

———. "Panel OKs Bill That Would Heighten Regulation of Indian Gambling Operations. Gannett News Service, August 9, 1995 (Lexis-Nexis).

———. "Supreme Court Decision Spurs Confusion on Indian Gaming." Gannett News Service, May 9, 1996 (Lexis-Nexis).

Carmack, William R. "A New Approach to Indian Affairs." In *Between Two Worlds: The Survival of Twentieth-Century Indians,* edited by Arrell Morgan Gibson, 205–35. Oklahoma City: Oklahoma City Historical Society, 1986.

Castile, George Pierre, and Robert L. Bee. *State and Reservation: New Perspectives on Federal Indian Policy.* Tucson: University of Arizona Press, 1992.

———. *To Show Heart: Native American Self-Determination and Federal Indian Policy, 1960–1975.* Tucson: University of Arizona Press, 1998.

Cater, Douglass. *Power in Washington: A Critical Look at Today's Struggle to Govern in the Nation's Capital.* New York: Random House, 1964.

Chaves, Frank. "A Briefing for the Representative of the Navajo Nation, December 9, 1993, Pueblo of Tesuque." In *Legislative Council Subcommittee on Gaming; Session Two Informational Packet; January 11, 1995.* Compiled by the Legislative Council Service, Santa Fe, January 23, 1995.

Cigler, Allan J., and Burdett A. Loomis. *Interest Group Politics,* 4th ed. Washington, D.C.: Congressional Quarterly Press, 1995.

———. "Organized Interests and the Search for Certainty." In *Interest Group Politics,* 3d ed., edited by Allan J. Cigler and Burdett A. Loomis, 385–98. Washington, D.C.: Congressional Quarterly Press, 1991.

Cigler, Beverly A. "Not Just Another Special Interest: Intergovernmental Representation." In *Interest Group Politics,* 4th ed., edited by Allan J. Cigler and Burdett A. Loomis, 131–53. Washington, D.C.: Congressional Quarterly Press, 1995.

Clark, Carter Blue. "The New Deal for Indians." In *Between Two Worlds: The Survival of Twentieth-Century Indians,* edited by Arrell Morgan Gibson, 72–83. Oklahoma City: Oklahoma City Historical Society, 1986.

Clinton, Robert N., Nell Jessup Newton, and Monroe E. Price. *American Indian Law, Cases and Materials,* 3d. ed. Charlottesville, Va.: Michie, 1991.

———. "The Dormant Indian Commerce Clause." *Connecticut Law Review* 27 (1995): 1055–249.

Cohen, Felix. *Handbook of Federal Indian Law.* Washington, D.C.: Government Printing Office, 1941. Rev. ed. Charlottesville, Va.: Michie, 1982.

Conference of Western Attorneys General. *American Indian Law Deskbook,* 2d ed. Niwot: University Press of Colorado, 1998.

"A Compact between the Pueblo of (blank) and the State of New Mexico Providing for the Conduct of Class III Gaming." Santa Fe, February 13, 1995.

Conlan, Timothy. *New Federalism: Intergovernmental Reform From Nixon to Reagan.* Washington: The Brookings Institution, 1988.

Congressional Quarterly. "Gambling Boom: Will the Gaming Industry's Growth Hurt Society?" *CQ Researcher* 4 (March 18, 1994).

Dahl, Robert A. *Preface to Democratic Theory.* Chicago: University of Chicago Press, 1956.

———. *Who Governs?* New Haven: Yale University Press, 1961.

Debo, Angie. *And Still the Waters Run: The Betrayal of the Five Civilized Tribes.* Norman: University of Oklahoma Press, 1984.

————. A *History of the Indians of the United States*. Norman: University of Oklahoma Press, 1970.

DeDominics, Carla. "Betting on Indian Rights." *California Lawyer* 3 (September 1983): 28–33.

Deloria, Vine, Jr. *Behind the Trail of Broken Treaties: An Indian Declaration of Independence*. Austin: University of Texas Press, 1985.

————. *Custer Died for Your Sins: An Indian Manifesto*. Norman: University of Oklahoma Press, 1969.

————. "The Evolution of Federal Indian Policy Making." In *American Indian Policy in the Twentieth Century*, edited by Vine Deloria, Jr., 239–56. Lincoln: University of Oklahoma Press, 1985.

————. *God Is Red*. New York: Dell.

Deloria, Vine, Jr., ed. *American Indian Policy in the Twentieth Century*. Norman: University of Oklahoma Press, 1985.

Deloria, Vine, Jr., and Clifford Lytle. *American Indians, American Justice*. Austin: University of Texas Press, 1983.

————. *The Nations Within: The Past and Future of American Indian Sovereignty*. New York: Pantheon Books, 1984.

Derryberry, Larry. Oklahoma Attorney General Opinion. 1978 Okla. AG LEXIS 178; 10 Op. Atty Gen. Okla. 464. January 4, 1978.

Dexter, Lewis Anthony. *Elite and Specialized Interviewing*. Evanston: Northwestern University Press, 1970.

Doyle, James E. Prepared Testimony of James E. Doyle Attorney General of the State of Wisconsin before the Senate Indian Affairs Committee. Federal News Service, May 9, 1996 (Lexis-Nexis).

Drew, Elizabeth. *Showdown: The Struggle between the Gingrich Congress and the Clinton White House*. New York: Simon & Schuster, 1996.

Ducheneaux, Franklin. Prepared Statement of Franklin Ducheneaux (Ducheneaux, Taylor & Associates) before the Senate Indian Affairs Committee on *Seminole v. Florida*. Federal News Service, May 9, 1996 (Lexis-Nexis).

Dye, Thomas R. *American Federalism: Competition among Governments*. Lexington, Mass.: D. C. Heath, 1990.

Eadington, William R., ed. *Indian Gaming and the Law*. Reno: College of Business Administration, University of Nevada, Reno, 1990.

Echohawk, John E. Prepared Testimony of John E. Echohawk, Executive Director, Native American Rights Fund, before the House Resources Committee Task Force on Trust Management Re: Oversight Hearing on Management of Indian Trust Funds. *Federal News Service*, June 16, 1996. (Lexis-Nexis).

Edmondson, Drew. Oklahoma Attorney General Opinion No. 95–6. March 30, 1995. (Lexis-Nexis)

Eisenstein, James. *Counsel for the United States: U.S. Attorneys in the Political and Legal Systems*. Baltimore: Johns Hopkins University Press, 1978.

Elazar, Daniel. *American Federalism: A View From the States,* 3d ed. New York: Harper & Row, 1984.

——. *The American Partnership: Intergovernmental Cooperation in the Nineteenth-Century United States.* Chicago: University of Chicago Press, 1962.

——. "Changing Conceptions of Rights in the United States." *Publius* 22 (1992): 5–18.

Emerson, Robert T. *Contemporary Field Research: A Collection of Readings.* Prospect Heights, Ill.: Waveland Press, 1983.

England, Robert E., and David R. Morgan. "Oklahoma: Group Power in Transition." In *Interest Group Politics in the Midwestern States,* edited by Ronald J. Hrebenar and Clive S. Thomas, 263–84. Ames: Iowa State University Press, 1993.

Epperley, Linda A. "Class III Gaming: An overview of Federal Caselaw and State Statutes." Paper presented at the In Sovereignty Symposium V: "The Year of the Indian," Oklahoma City, June 9–11, 1992.

Epstein, Leo, and C. K. Rowland. "Interest Groups in the Courts: Do Groups Fare Better?" In *Interest Group Politics,* 2d ed., edited by Allan J. Cigler and Burdett A. Loomis, 275–88. Washington, D.C.: Congressional Quarterly, 1986.

Federal Register. Request for Comments on Establishing Departmental Procedures to Authorize Class III Gaming on Indian Lands When a State Raises an Eleventh Amendment Defense to Suit under the Indian Gaming Regulatory Act. 61 Federal Register No. 21394, May 10, 1996.

Fenno, Richard F., Jr. *Congress in Committees.* Boston: Little, Brown, 1973.

——. *Watching Politicians: Essays on Participant Observation.* Berkeley: Institute of Governmental Studies, University of California Press, 1990.

——. *When Incumbency Fails: The Senate Career of Mark Andrews.* Washington, D.C.: Congressional Quarterly, 1992.

Final Report and Legislative Recommendations. A Report of the Special Committee on Investigations of the Select Committee on Indian Affairs United States Senate. Report No. 101-216. 101st Cong., 1st sess.

Fixico, Donald Lee. *Termination and Relocation: Federal Indian Policy in the 1950s.* Norman: University of Oklahoma Press, 1980.

——. *Termination and Relocation: Federal Indian Policy, 1945–1960.* Albuquerque: University of New Mexico Press, 1986.

Forbes, Jack D. *Native Americans and Nixon: Presidential Politics and Minority Self-Determination, 1969–1972.* Los Angles: American Indian Studies Center, University of California, 1981.

Foreman, Christopher H., Jr. "Grassroots Victim Organizations: Mobilizing for Personal and Public Health." In *Interest Group Politics,* 4th ed., 35–53. Washington, D.C.: Congressional Quarterly Press, 1995.

Freeman, J. Leiper. *The Political Process: Executive Bureau– Legislative Committee Relations.* Garden City, N.Y.: Doubleday, 1995.

———. *The Political Process: Executive Bureau–Legislative Committee Relations.* Rev. ed. New York: Random House, 1965.

French, T. Barton, Jr. "The Indian Gaming Regulatory Act and the Eleventh Amendment: States Assert Sovereign Immunity Defense to Slow the Growth of Indian Gaming." *Washington University Law Quarterly* 71 (Fall 1993): 735–72.

Furber, Bradley B. "Two Promises, Two Propositions: The Wheeler-Howard Act as a Reconciliation of the Indian Law Civil War." *University of Peugeot Sound Law Review* 14 (1991): 211–73.

GAO. "Money Laundering—Rapid Growth of Casinos Make Them Vulnerable." GAO/GGD-96-28, January 4. Federal Documents Clearing House, February 14, 1996 (Lexis-Nexis).

Garcia, Jose, and Clive S. Thomas. "New Mexico: Traditional Interest in a Traditional State. In *Interest Group Politics in the American West,* edited by Ronald J. Hrebenar and Clive S. Thomas, 93–103. Salt Lake City: University of Utah Press, 1987.

Getches, David H., Charles F. Wilkinson, and Robert A. Williams. *Cases and Materials on Federal Indian Law.* St. Paul: West/Wadsworth, 1998.

Gibson, Arrell Morgan, ed. *America's Exiles: Indian Colonization in Oklahoma.* Oklahoma City: Oklahoma Historical Society, 1976.

———. *Between Two Worlds: The Survival of Twentieth-Century Indians.* Oklahoma City: Oklahoma Historical Society, 1986.

Goble, Danney. "'The More Things Change . . .': Oklahoma since 1945." In *Politics in the Postwar American West,* edited by Richard Lowitt, 185–202. Norman: University of Oklahoma Press, 1995.

Goodman, Robert. *The Luck Business: The Consequences and Broken Promises of America's Gaming Explosion.* New York: Free Press, 1995.

Gordon-McCutchan, R. C. *The Taos Indians and the Battle for Blue Lake.* Santa Fe, N. Mex.: Red Crane Books, 1991.

Gover, Kevin. 1976. "Oklahoma." In *Report on Trust Responsibilities and the Federal-Indian Relationship; including Treaty Review. Task Force One: Trust Responsibilities and the Federal-Indian Relationship; including Treaty Review. Final Report to the American Indian Policy Review Commission.* Washington, D.C.: GPO.

Gover, Kevin, and James B. Cooney. "Cooperation between Tribes and States in Protecting the Environment." *NR & E* (Winter 1996): 35–78.

Gover, Stetson and Williams. "Tribal-State Dispute Resolution: Recent Attempts." *South Dakota Law Review* 36 (1991): 277–98.

Grant, Ruth W. *John Locke's Liberalism.* Chicago: University of Chicago Press, 1987.

Green, Jess. "Indian Gaming 1994." Paper presented at Sovereignty Symposium VII: "Full Faith and Credit," Tulsa, Okla., June 6–9, 1994.

―――. "Indian Gaming 1995." Paper presented at Sovereignty Symposium VIII: "Looking Ahead—Looking Back." Tulsa, Okla., June 5–8, 1995.

Griffith, Ernest. *Impasse of Democracy.* New York: Harrison-Hilton Books, 1939.

Grodzins, Morton. "Centralization and Decentralization in the American Federal System." In *Nation of States: Essays on the American Federal System,* edited by Robert A. Goldwin, 1–23. Chicago: Rand McNally, 1963.

Gross, Emma, R. *Contemporary Federal Indian Policy toward American Indians.* New York: Greenwood Press, 1989.

Guth, James L., John C. Green, Lyman A Kellstedt, and Corwin E. Smidt. "Onward Christian Soldiers: Religious Activist Groups in American Life." In *Interest Group Politics,* 4th ed., edited by Allan J. Cigler and Burdett A. Loomis, 55–76. Washington, D.C.: Congressional Quarterly Press, 1995.

Hagan, William T. "Private Property, the Indian's Door to Civilization." *Ethnohistory* 3 (1956): 126–37.

―――. *Theodore Roosevelt and Six Friends of the Indian.* Norman: University of Oklahoma Press, 1997.

―――. *United States–Comanche Relations: The Reservation Years.* Norman: University of Oklahoma Press, 1990.

Hain, Paul L., and Richard H. Folmar. "The Legislature." In *New Mexico Government,* 3d ed., edited by Paul L. Hain, F. Chris Garcia, and Gilbert K. St. Clair, 35–68. Albuquerque: University of New Mexico Press, 1994.

Hain, Paul L., and F. Chris Garcia. "Voting, Elections, and Parties." In *New Mexico Government,* 3d ed., edited by Paul L. Hain, F. Chris Garcia, and Gilbert K. St. Clair, 233–50. Albuquerque: University of New Mexico Press, 1994.

Hamm, Ruth E. "Patterns of Influence among Committees, Agencies, and Interest Groups." *Legislative Studies Quarterly* 8 (August 1983): 379–426.

Hammons, A. Diane. "Cross-Deputization in Oklahoma's Indian Country: How the Office of the Attorney General Has Addressed the Question." Paper presented at the Sovereignty Symposium IV: "The Circle of Sovereignty," Oklahoma City, June 10–12, 1991.

Harring, Sidney. *Crow Dog's Case: American Indian Sovereignty, Tribal Law, and United States Law in the Nineteenth Century.* New York: Cambridge University Press, 1994.

Harris, Fred R., and LaDonna Harris. "American Indians and Tribal Governments." In *New Mexico Government,* 3d ed., edited by Paul L.

Hain, F. Chris Garcia, and Gilbert K. St. Clair, 187–206. Albuquerque: University of New Mexico Press, 1994.

Hedman, Susan. "Friends of the Earth and Friends of the Court: Assessing the Impact of Interest Group *Amici Curiae* in Environmental Cases Decided by the Supreme Court." *Virginia Environmental Law Journal* 10 (1991): 187–212.

Helco, Hugh. "Issue Networks and the Executive Establishment." In *The New American Political System*, edited by King, 87–124. Washington, D.C.: American Enterprise Institute, 1978.

Henschen, Beth M., and Edward I. Sidlow. "The Supreme Court and the Congressional Agenda-setting Process." *Journal of Law and Politics* 5 (1989): 685–724.

Hertzberg, Hazel W. "Reaganomics on the Reservation." *New Republic*, (November 22, 1982): 15–18.

Hertzke, Allen D. "American Religion and Politics: A Review Essay." *Western Political Quarterly* 41 (1988): 825–38.

———. *Representing God in Washington: The Role of Religious Lobbies in the American Polity.* Knoxville: University of Tennessee Press, 1988.

Hertzke, Allen D., and Ronald M. Peters. *The Atomistic Congress: An Interpretation of Congressional Change.* New York: M. E. Sharpe, 1992.

Hill, Rick. *Statement of Rick Hill, Chairman National Indian Gaming Association to the Senate Committee on Indian Affairs: Oversight Hearing on Supreme Court Decision in Seminole v. State of Florida.* Thursday, May 9, 1996. Washington D.C.: National Indian Gaming Association, 1996.

———. "Task Force Changes Position and Opposes Provisions of S. 487." *Indian Gaming* (September 1995): 5.

Hogan, Linda. *Mean Spirit.* New York: Ivy Press, 1992.

Hrebenar, Ronald J. "Interest Group Politics in the American West: A Comparative Perspective." In *Interest Group Politics in the American West*, edited by Ronald J. Hrebenar and Clive S. Thomas, 3–11. Salt Lake City: University of Utah Press, 1987.

Hrebenar, Ronald J., and Clive S. Thomas, eds. *Interest Group Politics in the American West.* Salt Lake City: University of Utah Press, 1987.

Hyde, George W. "The Indian Gaming Regulatory Act of 1988: Did Congress Forget about the Other Commerce Clause?" *Thomas M. Cooley Law Review* 10 (1993): 665–96.

Inouye, Daniel K. "Address to Tribal Leaders." In *Toward a National Indian Legislative Agenda for the 1990s: A Report on National and Regional Tribal Leaders Forums*, 7–11. Oakland, Calif.: American Indian Resource Institute, 1992.

Johansen, Bruce, and Roberto Maestas. *Wasi'chu: The Continuing Indian Wars.* New York: Monthly Review Press, 1979.

Johnson, Cathy Marie. "Conflict or Consensus: The Relationships between Executive Agencies and Congressional Committees in the United States National Government." Ph.D. diss., University of Michigan, 1986.

Johnson, N. B. "The National Congress of American Indians." *Chronicles of Oklahoma* 30 (Summer 1952): 140–48.

Johnson, Gary. "News Conference: 2/13/95 Compact Signing: Remarks prepared for Delivery by Governor Johnson." Santa Fe, New Mexico.

———. Testimony Gary F. Johnson for the State of New Mexico Senate Indian Affairs Gaming. Federal Document Clearing House, June 22, 1995 (Lexis-Nexis).

———. *State of the State Address.* Gary E. Johnson, Governor. State of New Mexico, 1996.

Joint Appendix. *California v. Cabazon Band of Mission Indians,* No. 85-1708, 1996. (Lexis-Nexis).

Jones, Eric D. "The Indian Gaming Regulatory Act: A Forum for Conflict among the Plenary Power of Congress, Tribal Sovereignty, and the Eleventh Amendment." *Vermont Law Review* 18 (Fall 1993): 127–72.

Josephy, Alvin, Jr. *Now That the Buffalo's Gone: A Study of Today's American Indian.* Lincoln: University of Nebraska, 1984.

———. *Red Power: The American Indian's Fight for Freedom.* Lincoln: University of Nebraska Press, 1971.

Jucidial Staff Directory. "Raley, John W. Biographies of Judges and Staff." Career Library, JUDDIR File, 1995 (Lexis-Nexis).

Kading, Linda King. "State Authority to Regulate Gaming within Indian Lands: The Effect of the Indian Gaming Regulatory Act." *Drake Law Review* 451 (1992): 317–38.

Kelly, John J. Testimony before the New Mexico State Legislature of United States Attorney John J. Kelly on the Subject of Gambling in New Mexico January 13, 1995. In *Legislative Council Subcommittee on Gaming; Session Two Informational Packet; January 13, 1995.* Compiled by the Legislative Council Service, Santa Fe, January 23, 1995.

Kelly, Joseph. "American Indian Gaming Law. *New Law Journal:* 143 (November 26, 1993): 1672–3.

Kickingbird, Kirke. "American Indians, Bingo and the Law." *American Indian Journal* 9 (1986): 14–19.

———. "'Way Down Yonder in the Indian Nations, Rode My Pony Cross the Reservation!' From 'Oklahoma Hills' by Woody Guthrie." *Tulsa Law Journal* 29 (1993): 302–43.

Kincaid, John. "Constitutional Federalism: Labor's Role in Displacing Places to Benefit Persons." PS (June 1993): 172–77.

————. "From Cooperative to Coercive Federalism." *ANNALS* 509 (1990): 139–52.

Kingdon, John W. *Agendas, Alternatives, and Public Policies.* New York: HarperCollins, 1984.

————. *Agendas, Alternatives, and Public Policies.* 2d ed. New York: HarperCollins, 1995.

La Potin, Armand S. *Native American Voluntary Organizations.* New York: Greenwood Press, 1987.

Latham, Earl. *The Group Basis of Politics.* Ithaca: Cornell University Press, 1952.

Laurence, Robert. "The Indian Commerce Clause." *Arizona Law Review* 23 (1981): 203–61.

Letgers, Lyman Howard, ed. *American Indian Policy: Self-Governance and Economic Development.* Westport, Conn.: Greenwood Press, 1994.

Legters, Lyman Howard, and Fremont J. Lyden, eds. *Native Americans and Public Policy.* Pittsburgh: University of Pittsburgh Press, 1992.

Levitan, Sar A. *Programs in Aid of the Poor,* 6th ed. Baltimore: Johns Hopkins University Press, 1990.

Levitan, Sar A., and William B. Johnson. *Indian Giving: Federal Programs for Native Americans.* Baltimore: Johns Hopkins University Press, 1975.

Littman, Jonathan. "And the Dealer Stays: Indian Gaming Is a 1990s Gold Rush, with Lawyers Leading the Charge." *California Lawyer* (January 1993) 44–52.

Locher, Leah L. "States Rights, Tribal Sovereignty, and the "White Man's Firewater": State Prohibition of Gambling on New Indian Lands." *Indian Law Journal* 69 (Winter 1993): 255–74.

Locke, John. *Second Treatise of Government.* Edited by C. B. Macpherson. Indianapolis: Hackett, 1980.

Loomis, Burdett A. A New Era: Groups and the Grass Roots. In *Interest Group Politics,* edited by Allan J. Cigler and Burdett A. Loomis, 169–90. Washington, D.C.: Congressional Quarterly Press, 1983.

Lorbiecki, Stephanie A. "Indian Sovereignty versus Oklahoma's Gambling Laws." *Tulsa Law Journal* 20 (1985): 605–33.

Loving, Susan B. Oklahoma Attorney General Opinion No. 93-1. 1993 Okla. AG LEXIS 6. May 21, 1993.

Lowi, Theodore J. "American Business, Public Policy, Case-Studies, and Political Theory." *World Politics* 16 (1964): 677–715.

————. *The End of Liberalism: Ideology, Policy and the Decline of Public Authority.* New York: W. W. Norton, 1969.

————. *The End of Liberalism: The Second Republic of the United States,* 2d ed. New York: W. W. Norton, 1979.

————. *The End of the Republican Era.* Norman: University of Oklahoma Press, 1995.

————. "Four Systems of Policy, Politics, and Choice." *Public Administration Review* (1972): 298–310.

Lunch, William M. *The Nationalization of American Politics.* Berkeley: University of California Press, 1987.

Lunner, Chet. "Governors Plan Vote on Indian Gaming." Gannett News Service, February 1, 1993.

————. "New House Panel to Deal Only with Indian Affairs." Gannett News Service, January 6, 1993.

Lyman, Stanley David. *Wounded Knee 1973: A Personal Account by Stanley David Lyman.* Edited by Floyd A. O'Neil, June K. Lyman, and Susan McKay. Lincoln: University of Nebraska Press, 1991.

McAuliffe, Dennis, Jr. *The Deaths of Sybil Bolton: An American History.* New York: Random House, 1994.

McCain, John. "McCain Releases New Study Confirming Gross Mismanagement of Indian Trust Funds By BIA". *Congressional Press Releases.* Federal Document Clearing House. May 3, 1996 (Lexis-Nexis).

McCay, Nancy. "The Meaning of Good Faith in the Indian Gaming Regulatory Act." *Gonzaga Law Review* 27 (1991–92): 471–86.

McConnell, Grant. *Private Power and American Democracy.* New York: Knopf, 1966.

McCool, Daniel. *Command of the Waters: Iron Triangles, Federal Water Development, and Indian Water.* Berkeley: University of California Press, 1987.

————. "Indian Voting." In *American Indian Policy in the Twentieth Century,* edited by Vine Deloria, Jr., 105–34. Norman: University of Oklahoma Press, 1985.

————. "Indian Water Settlements: The Prerequisites of Successful Negotiation." *Policy Studies Journal* 21 (1993): 227–42.

————. "Intergovernmental Conflict and Indian Water Rights: An Assessment of Negotiated Settlements." *Publius* 23 (1993): 85–101.

McCory, Leila Melanie. "Agenda Setting by Minority Political Groups: A Case Study of American Indians." Ph.D. diss., University of North Texas, 1990.

McCoy, Jonathan T. "Update on Current Litigation under the Indian Gaming Regulatory Act." Paper presented at the North American Gaming Regulators Association Conference, Portland, Oregon, May 9, 1994.

McCulloch, Anne Merline. "Perspectives on Native Americans in Political Science." *Teaching Political Science* 16 (1989): 92–98.

McCullough, David. "Intergovernmental Agreements under the State-Tribal Relations Act." Paper presented at the Sovereignty Symposium V: "The Year of the Indian." Presented by the Oklahoma

Supreme Court, the Sovereignty Symposium, Inc., and the Oklahoma Indian Affairs Commission, Oklahoma City, June 9–11, 1992.

McFarland, Andrew S. "Interest Groups and Theories of Power in America." *Journal of Politics* 17 (1987): 129–47.

Magnuson, Jon. "Casino Wars: Ethics and Economics in Indian Country." *Christian Century*, February 16, 1994, 169–71.

Maniaci, Jim. "Senator McCain Meets with Tribal Leaders: Zah Changes Registration to Republican." *Gallup Independent*, August 28, 1999.

Mason, W. Dale. "The Carl Albert Collection: Resources Relating to Indian Policy, 1963–1968." *Oklahoma Chronicles* 71 (1994): 422–37.

———. 1994. "Can Interest Group Theory Explain the Indian Policy Domain?" Paper presented at the Western Social Sciences Conference, Albuquerque, 1994.

———. "Indian Policy: The Nixon Years." Paper prepared for the Southwestern Political Science Association, Austin, 1992.

———. "Interest Group Federalism: Indian Gaming and the Place of Indian Tribes in the American Political System." Ph.D. diss., University of Oklahoma, 1996.

———. 1998. "Tribes and States: A New Era in Intergovernmental Affairs." *Publius* 28 (Winter 1998): 111–30.

———. "'You Can Only Kick So Long': American Indian Movement Leadership in Nebraska, 1972–1979." *Journal of the West* 23 (1984): 21–31. Reprinted in *Indian Leadership*, edited by Walter Williams. Manhattan, Kan.: Sunflower University Press, 1984.

Matthiessen, Peter. *In the Spirit of Crazy Horse*. New York: Viking Press, 1983.

Means, Russell. *Where White Men Fear to Tread: The Autobiography of Russell Means*. New York: St. Martin's Press, 1995.

Meredith, Howard. *Modern Indian Tribal Government and Politics: An Interdisciplinary Study*. Tsaile, Ariz.: Navajo College Press, 1993.

Mills, C. Wright. *The Power Elite*. New York: Oxford University Press, 1959.

Minnis, Michael. "Judicially Suggested Harassment of Indian Tribes: The Potawatomis Revisit *Moe* and *Colville*." *American Indian Law Review* 16 (1991): 289–318.

———. "Oklahoma's Joint Committee on Tribal-State Relations: An Unrealized Potential for Improving State-Tribal Relations." Paper presented at the Sovereignty Symposium VI: The Word of the People," Tulsa, June 8–10, 1993.

Mitchell, William C., and Michael C. Munger. "Economic Models of Interest Groups: An Introductory Survey." *American Journal of Political Science* 35 (1991): 512–46.

Moe, Terry C. "Toward a Broader View of Interest Groups." *Journal of Politics* 43 (1991): 531–43.

Monette, Richard A. "A New Federalism for Indian Tribes: The Relationship between the United States and Tribes in Light of Our Federalism and Republican Democracy." *University of Toledo Law Review* 25 (1994): 617–72.

Monypenny, Phillip. "Federal Grants-in-Aid to State Governments: A Political Analysis." *National Tax Journal* 13 (1960): 11–16.

Moore, W. John. "Tribal Imperatives." *National Journal,* June 9, 1990 (Lexis-Nexis).

———. "A Winning Hand?" *National Journal,* July 17, 1990, 1796–1800.

Morehouse, Sarah McCally. *State Politics, Parties and Policy.* New York: Holt, Rinehart and Winston, 1981.

Morgan, David R., Robert E. England, and George M. Humphreys. *Oklahoma Politics and Policies: Governing the Sooner State.* Lincoln: University of Nebraska Press, 1991.

Morris, C. Patrick. "Termination by Accountants: The Reagan Indian Policy." *Policy Studies Journal* 16 (1988): 731–50.

Morrison, C. Randall. "The Indian Gaming Regulatory Act and Its Impacts on the Status of Indian Tribes." Paper presented at the Western Social Sciences Conference, Albuquerque, 1994.

Motion for Leave to File Brief Amici Curiae and Brief Amici Curiae of the Pueblo of Sandia, the Pueblo of Acoma, the Pueblo of Tesuque, and the Pueblo of San Juan in Support of the Position of Appellees. *California v. Cabazon,* No. 85–1798. September 24, 1985.

Mulvihill, Henry N. "Indian Casino Gaming in Oklahoma." Paper presented at the Sovereignty Symposium VI: "The Word of the People," Tulsa, Okla., June 8–10, 1993.

Nagel, Joanne. "American Indian Mobilization: Tribal, Intertribal, and Supratribal Strategic Political Action. In *American Mosaic: Selected Readings on America's Multicultural Heritage,* edited by Young I. Song and Eugene C. Kim, 3–14. Englewood Cliffs, N.J.: Prentice-Hall, 1993.

National Gaming Survey. "National Gaming Survey. The Newsletter of the National Gaming Industry." *Casino Journal,* April 22, 1996. http://www.intersphere...player/summary/sample.

National Indian Gaming Commission. *Tribal-State Compact List: Tribal Information for Those with Approved Tribal-State Compacts as of December 14, 1995.* Washington, D.C.: National Indian Gaming Commission.

Newton, Nell Jessup. "Federal Power over Indians: Its Sources, Scope, and Limitations." *University of Pennsylvania Law Review* 122 (1984): 195–287.

———. "Let a Thousand Policy-Flowers Bloom: Making Indian Policy in the Twenty-first Century." *Arkansas Law Review* 46 (1993): 25–75.

Nice, David C. *Federalism: The Politics of Intergovernmental Relations.* New York: St. Martin's Press, 1987.

Nichols, David A. *Lincoln and the Indians: Civil War Policy and Politics.* Columbia: University of Missouri Press, 1978.

NIGA. *Annual Report 1994.* Washington, D.C.: National Indian Gaming Association, 1994.

NIPC. *Reservation-based Gaming.* Washington, D.C.: National Indian Policy Center, n.d.

———. *Resolving Tribal State Tax Conflicts.* Washington, D.C.: National Indian Policy Center, n.d.

———. *Tribal Representation in Washington, D.C.: Its Past and Future Role in Executive Branch and Congressional Policy-making.* Washington, D.C.: National Indian Policy Center, n.d.

———. "Tribal Representation in Washington, D.C.: Its Past and Future Role in Executive and Congressional Policy-making (a Three-Part Paper)." Washington, D.C.: National Indian Policy Center.

NMIGA. "The Economic and Fiscal Impact of Indian Reservation Gaming in New Mexico." Prepared for the New Mexico Indian Gaming Association by the Center for Applied Research. Denver, November 8. In *Legislative Council Subcommittee on Gaming; Session Two Informational Packet; January 11, 1995.* Compiled by the Legislative Council Service, Santa Fe, January 23, 1995.

———. *Indian Gaming: Working for New Mexico.* Santa Fe: New Mexico Indian Gaming Association.

Norgren, Jill. *The Cherokee Cases: The Confrontation of Law and Politics.* New York: McGraw Hill, 1996.

Nostrand, Richard L. *The Hispano Homeland.* Norman: University of Oklahoma Press, 1992.

O'Brien, Sharon. *American Indian Tribal Governments.* Norman: University of Oklahoma Press, 1993.

———. "The Government-Government and Trust Relationships: Conflicts and Inconsistencies." *American Indian Culture and Research Journal* 10 (1989): 57–80.

O'Connor, Karen. "The Rise of Conservative Interest Group Litigation." *Journal of Politics* 45 (1983): 479–89.

O'Connor, Karen, and Lee Epstein. "Amicus Curiae Participation in U.S. Supreme Court Litigation: An Appraisal of Hakman's 'Folklore.'" *Law and Society* 16 (1981): 311–20.

Oklahoma Tax Commission. *Oklahoma Tax Commission v. Citizen Band Potawatomi Indian Tribe of Oklahoma,* No. 89-1322. On Writ of Certiorari to the United States Court of Appeals for the Tenth Circuit. Brief for the Oklahoma Tax Commission. November 9, 1990.

———. *Oklahoma Tax Commission v. Graham,* No. 99-266. On Writ of Certiorari to the United States Court of Appeals for the Tenth Circuit. Brief for the Oklahoma Tax Commission. November 16, 1988.

————. *Oklahoma Tax Commission v. Sac and Fox Nation*, No. 92-259. On Writ of Certiorari to the United States Court of Appeals for the Tenth Circuit. Brief on the Merits By Petitioner. December 17, 1992.

————. *Oklahoma Tax Commission v. Chickasaw Nation*, No. 94-771. On Writ of Certiorari to the United States Court of Appeals for the Tenth Circuit. Brief of Petitioner. February 21, 1995.

————. "Oklahoma Tax Commission's Position on State Tax Law Compliance by Tribally Owned or Indian Owned Businesses." Paper presented at the Sovereignty Symposium II: "Divergent Points of View," Oklahoma City, May 30–June 1, 1989.

Olsen, Mancur, Jr. *The Logic of Collective Action*. Cambridge, Mass.: Harvard University Press, 1971.

Ornstein, Norman J., and Shirley Elder. *Interest Groups, Lobbying and Policymaking*. Washington, D.C.: Congressional Quarterly Press, 1978.

Pagano, Michael A., and Ann O. M. Bowman. "The State of American Federalism, 1992–1993." *Publius* 23 (1993): 1–22.

Parman, Donald L. *Indians and the American West in the Twentieth Century*. Bloomington: Indiana University Press, 1994.

Peters, B. Guy. "Insiders and Outsiders: The Politics of Pressure Group Influence on Bureaucracy." *Administration and Society* 9 (1977): 191–218.

Pipestem, F. Browning. "The Journey from *Ex parte Crow Dog* to *Littlechief*: A Survey of Tribal Civil and Criminal Jurisdiction in Western Oklahoma." *American Indian Law Review* 6 (1978): 1–80.

————. "The Mythology of the Oklahoma Indians Revisited: A Survey of the Legal Status of Indian Tribes in Oklahoma Ten Years Later." Paper presented at the first annual Sovereignty–Indian Law in the 1990s (A Training Session) conference, Oklahoma City, June 1–3, 1988.

Pipestem, F. Browning, G. William Rice. "The Mythology of the Oklahoma Indians: A Survey of the Legal Status of Indian Tribes in Oklahoma." *American Indian Law Review* 6 (1978): 259–328.

Pitchlynn, Gary S. Tribal/State Gaming Compacts: A Constitutional Challenge to IGRA. In *Sovereignty Symposium VII: "Full Faith and Credit," June 6–9, 1994*, by the Oklahoma Supreme Court, the Oklahoma Indian Affairs Commission, and the Sovereignty Symposium, Inc., 1994.

Pollack, Kenan. "Mashantucket Pequots: A Tribe That's Raking It In." *U.S. News & World Report*, January 15, 1996.

Pommersheim, Frank. "Tribal-State Relations: Hope for the Future?" *South Dakota Law Review* 36 (1991): 239–76.

Price, Catherine. *The Oglala People, 1841–1879: A Political History*. Lincoln: University of Nebraska Press, 1996.

Prucha, Francis Paul. *American Indian Policy in the Formative Years: The Indian Trade and Intercourse Acts, 1790–1834.* Cambridge, Mass.: Harvard University Press, 1962.

———. *American Indian Treaties: The History of a Political Anomaly.* Berkeley: University of California Press, 1995.

———. "Andrew Jackson's Indian Policy: A Reassessment." *Journal of American History* 56 (1969): 527–39.

———. *The Great Father: The United States Government and the American Indians,* abr. ed. Lincoln: University of Nebraska Press, 1986.

Quinn, William W., Jr. "Federal Acknowledgment of American Indian Tribes: The Historical Development of a Legal Concept." *American Journal of Legal History* 34 (1990): 331–64.

Reed, Alan, and Denise Fort. "The Fragmented Executive System." In *New Mexico Government,* 3d ed., edited by Paul L. Hain, F. Chris Garcia, and Gilbert K. St. Clair, 19–34. Albuquerque: University of New Mexico Press, 1994.

Reid, Harry. "Indian Gaming and the Law." In *Indian Gaming and the Law,* edited by William R. Eadington, 15–20. Reno: College of Business Administration, University of Nevada, Reno, 1990.

Remini, Robert V. *Andrew Jackson and the Course of American Freedom, 1822–1832.* Vol. 2. New York: Random House, 1981.

Ridgeway, Michael W. "The Potawatomi/Oklahoma Compact of 1992: Have Two Sovereigns Achieved a Meeting of the Minds?" *American Indian Law Review* 18 (1993): 515–37.

Ripley, Randall B. *Bureaucracy and Policy Implementation.* Homewood, Ill.: Dorsey Press, 1982.

Ripley, Randall B., and Grace A. Franklin. *Congress, the Bureaucracy, and Public Policy,* 3d ed. Homewood, Ill.: Dorsey Press, 1984.

Rogin, Michael Paul. *Ronald Reagan, the Movie, and Other Episodes in Political Demonology.* Berkeley: University of California Press, 1987.

Rose, I. Nelson. "The Indian Gaming Act and the Political Process." In *Indian Gaming and the Law,* edited by William R. Eadington, 3–14. Reno: College of Business Administration, University of Nevada, Reno, 1990.

Rosenthal, Alan. *The Third House: Lobbyists and Lobbying in the States.* Washington, D.C.: Congressional Quarterly Press, 1993.

Salisbury, Robert H. "An Exchange Theory of Interest Groups." *Midwest Journal of Political Science* 13 (1969): 1–32.

———. *Interests and institutions: Substance and Structure in American Politics.* Pittsburgh: University of Pittsburgh Press, 1992.

———. "Putting Interests Back into Interest Groups." In *Interest Group Politics,* 3d ed., edited by Allan J. Cigler and Burdett A. Loomis. Washington, D.C.: Congressional Quarterly Press, 1991.

Sando, Joe S. *Nee Hemish: A History of Jemez Pueblo.* Albuquerque: University of New Mexico Press, 1982.

———. *Pueblo Nations: Eight Centuries of Pueblo Indian History.* Santa Fe: Clear Light Publishers, 1992.

Santoni, Roland J. "The Indian Gaming Regulatory Act: How Did We Get Here? Where Are We Going?" *Creighton Law Review* 26 (1993): 387–447.

Sayer, John William. *Ghost Dancing the Law: The Wounded Knee Trials.* Cambridge, Mass.: Harvard University Press, 1997.

Schattschneider, E. E. *The Semisovereign People: A Realist's View of Democracy in America.* New York: Holt, Rinehart and Winston, 1960.

Schatzman, Leonard, and Anselm Strauss. *Field Research: Strategies for a Natural Sociology.* Englewood Cliffs, N.J.: Prentice Hall, 1973.

Scheppach, Raymond C. Statement of Raymond C. Scheppach Executive Director National Governors' Association before the Committee on Indian Affairs United States Senate on the Indian Gaming Regulatory Act Amendments Act of 1995, July 25, 1995. National Governors' Association, Washington, D.C.

Schlozman, Kay. *Organized Interests and American Democracy.* New York: Harper & Row, 1986.

Schlozman, Kay, and John Tierney. "More of the Same: Washington Pressure Group Activity in a Decade of Change." *Journal of Politics* 45 (1983): 351–78.

Segal, David. "Dances with Sharks: Why the Indian Gaming Experiment's Gone Bust." *Washington Monthly,* March 26–30, 1992.

Shannon, John, and James Kee. "The Rise of Competitive Federalism." *Public Budgeting and Finance* 9 (1988): 5–20.

Shapiro, Stephan M. "Amicus Briefs in the Supreme Court." *Litigation* 10 (1984): 21–24.

Shattuck, Petra, and Jill Norgen. *Partial Justice: Federal Indian Law in a Liberal Constitutional System.* Providence: Berg, 1993.

"Shouldn't Economic Development Also include Native Americans? *New Mexico Business Journal* (June 1995) (Lexis-Nexis).

Smith, Paul Chatt, and Robert Allen Warrior. *Like A Hurricane: The American Indian Movement from Alcatraz to Wounded Knee.* New York: New Press, 1996.

Sorkin, Alan L. *American Indians and Federal Aid.* Washington, D.C.: The Brookings Institution, 1971.

———. *The Urban American Indian.* Lexington, Mass.: Lexington Books, 1978.

Stipulation. *Pueblo of Santa Ana, et al. v. Kelly, et al.,* No. CIV 96 0002MV.

Stern, Kenneth S. *Loud Hawk: The United States versus the American Indian Movement.* Norman: University of Oklahoma Press, 1994.

Strickland, Rennard. "Genocide-at-Law: An Historic and Contemporary View of the Native American Experience." *University of Kansas Law Review* 34 (1986): 714–35.

———. "Indian Law and the Miner's Canary: The Signs of Poison Gas." *Cleveland State Law Review* 39 (1991): 483–504.

———. *The Indians of Oklahoma*. Norman: University of Oklahoma Press, 1980.

———. "The Puppet Princess: The Case for a Policy-oriented Framework for Understanding and Shaping American Indian Law." *Oregon Law Review* 63 (1983): 11–28.

———. "A Tale of Two Marshalls: Reflections on Indian Law and Policy, the Cherokee Cases and the Cruel Irony of Supreme Court Victories." *Oklahoma Law Review* 47 (1994): 111–26.

Svensson, Frances. "Liberal Democracy and Group Rights: The Legacy of Individualism and Its Impact on American Indian Tribes." *Political Studies* 27 (1979): 421–39.

Swanson, Eric J. "The Reservation Gaming Craze: Casino Gambling under the Indian Gaming and Regulatory Act of 1988." *Hamline Law Review* 15 (Spring 1992): 471–96.

Taylor, Theodore W. *The States and Their Indian Citizens*. Washington, D.C.: GPO, 1972.

Thompson, William, and Diana R. Dever. "Gambling and the Revitalization of Native American Sovereignty." Unpublished paper, n.d.

Thurber, James A. "Dynamics of Policy Subsystems." In *Interest Group Politics*, 3d ed., edited by Allan J. Cigler and Burdett A. Loomis, 319–44. Washington, D.C.: Congressional Quarterly Press, 1991.

"Tribal-State Compact." Paper presented at the Sovereignty Symposium V: "The Year of the Indian," Oklahoma City, June 9–11, 1990.

Truman, David F. *The Governmental Process: Political Interests and Public Opinion*. New York: Knopf, 1951.

Udall, Stewart L. "The Indian Gaming Act and the Political Process." In *Indian Gaming and the Law*, edited by William R. Eadington, 15–20. Reno: College of Business Administration, University of Nevada, Reno, 1990.

U.S. Attorney, District of New Mexico. News Release: Nine NM Gaming Tribes and U.S. Attorney Sign Stipulation to Amend Pending Court Action." January 18, 1996.

———. "News Release: U.S. Attorney Announces NM Gaming Tribes' Responses to Shutdown Plan Request." January 3, 1996.

———. "News Release: U.S. Attorney Sets Deadline for Tribes to Halt Gaming Operations." Albuquerque, December 14, 1995.

Valencia-Weber, Gloria. "Shrinking Indian Country: A State Offensive to Divest Tribal Sovereignty." *Connecticut Law Review* 27 (1995): 1281–1322.

Van Biema, David. "Bury My Heart in Committee." *Newsweek,* September 18, 1995.

Viola, Herman J. *Diplomats in Buckskin: A History of Indian Delegations in Washington City.* Bluffington, S.C.: Rivilo Books, 1995.

Walker, Jack. "The Origins and Maintenance of Interest Groups in America." *American Political Science Review* 77 (1983): 390–406.

Washburn, Wilcomb E. *Red Man's Land/White Man's Law,* 2d ed. Norman: University of Oklahoma Press, 1995.

Waters, Frank. *Masked Gods: Navaho and Pueblo Ceremonialism.* Athens, Ga.: Swallow Press, 1984.

Weissman, Joseph J. "Upping the Ante allowing Indian Tribes to Sue States in Federal Court under the Indian Gaming Regulatory Act." *George Washington Law Review* 62 (November 1993): 123–61.

Weyler, Rex. *Blood of the Land: The Government and Corporate War against the American Indian Movement.* New York: Everest House, 1982.

Wilkins, David E. "Breaking into the Intergovernmental Matrix: The Lumbee Tribe's Efforts to Secure Federal Acknowledgment." *Publius* 23 (1995): 123–42.

Wilkinson, Charles F. *American Indians, Time and the Law: Native Societies in a Modern Constitutional Democracy.* New Haven: Yale University Press, 1987.

Williams, Robert A. "The Algebra of Federal Indian Law: The Hard Trail of Decolonizing and Americanizing the White Man's Indian Jurisprudence." *Wisconsin Law Review* (1986): 219–99.

———. *The American Indian in Western Legal Thought: The Discourses of Conquest.* New York: Oxford University Press, 1990.

———. "Jefferson, the Norman Yoke, and American Indian Lands." *Arizona Law Review* 29 (1987): 165–94.

———. "The Medieval and Renaissance Origins of the Status of the American Indian in Western Legal Thought." *Southern California Law Review* 57 (1983): 1–99.

Williams, Walter, ed. *Indian Leadership.* Manhattan, Kan.: Sunflower University Press, 1984.

Wilmer, Franke. *Indian Gaming: Players and Stakes.* Billings: Local Government Center, Montana State University, 1994.

Wilmer, Franke, Michael E. Melody, and Margaret Maier Murdock. "Including Native American Perspectives in the Political Science Curriculum." *Political Science* (June 1994): 269–76.

Wilson, Thomas L. "Indian Gaming and Economic Development on the Reservation." *Michigan Bar Journal* (May 1989): 380–84.

Wolf, Sidney M. "Killing the New Buffalo: State Eleventh Amendment Defense to Enforcement of IGRA Indian Gaming Compacts." *Journal of Urban and Contemporary Law* 47 (1995): 51–119.

WPA. *New Mexico: A Guide to the Colorful State.* Compiled by Workers of
the Writers' Program of the Work Projects Administration in the
State of New Mexico. New York: Hastings House, 1953.

Wright, Muriel H. *A Guide to the Indian Tribes of Oklahoma.* Norman:
University of Oklahoma Press, 1986.

Wunder, John R. *"Retained by the People:" A History of American Indians
and the Bill of Rights.* New York: Oxford University Press, 1994.

Zeigler, L. Harmon. *Politics in the American States: A Comparative
Analysis,* 4th ed., edited by Virginia, Gary, Herbert Jacob, and
Kenneth N. Vines. Boston: Little, Brown, 1983.

CONGRESSIONAL DOCUMENTS

U.S. Congress. House. 1986. Committee on Interior and Insular
Affairs. *Establishing Federal Standards and Regulations for the Conduct
of Gaming Activities on Indian Reservations and Lands and for Other
Purposes: Report Together with Supplemental and Supporting Views.* 99th
Cong., 2d sess., 1986. Rept. 99-488.

———. *Indian Gaming Control Act: Hearing before the Committee on
Interior and Insular Affairs.* 98th Cong., 2d sess., 1984.

———. *Indian Gaming Regulatory Act: Hearing before the Committee on
Interior and Insular Affairs.* 100th Con., 1st sess., June 25, 1987.

U.S. Congress. House. Subcommittee on Native American Affairs of
the Committee on Natural Resources. *Oversight Hearing before the
Subcommittee of the Committee on Natural Resources on Implementation
of Public Law 100–497, the Indian Gaming Regulatory Act of 1988,
and Related Law Enforcement Issues.* 103d Cong., 1st sess., 1993.

U.S. Congress. Senate. Committee on Indian Affairs. *Amending the
Indian Gaming Regulatory Act, and For Other Purposes: Report to
Accompany S487.* 104th Cong., 2d sess., 1996. Rpt. 104-241.

U.S. Congress. Senate. Select Committee on Indian Affairs. *Estab-
lishing Federal Standards and Regulations for the Conduct of Gaming
Activities within Indian Country: Hearing before the Select Committee on
Indian Affairs.* 99th Cong., 2d sess., 1986.

———. *Gaming Activities on Indian Reservations and Lands: Hearing before
the Select Committee on Indian Affairs.* 100th Cong., 1st sess., 1987.

———. *Indian Gaming Regulatory Act: Report Together with Additional
Views.* 100th Cong., 2d sess., 1988. Rpt. 100-446.

U.S. Congress. Senate. Special Committee on Investigations of the
Select Committee on Indian Affairs. *Final Report and Legislative
Recommendations: A Report of the Special Committee on Investigations of
the Select Committee on Indian Affairs.* 101st Cong., 1st sess., 1989. S.
Rept. 101-216.

CASES

Bowman v. Lopez, U.S. Dist. Ct., Civ. A. No. 1391 (1948).

Brendale v. Confederated Tribes and Bands of the Yakima Indian Nation, 492 U.S. 408 (1989).

Bryan v. Itasca County, 426 U.S. 373 (1976).

Cabazon Band of Mission Indians v. City of Indio, 694 F.2d 634 (1982).

Cabazon Band of Mission Indians v. County of Riverside, 783 F.2d 900 (1986).

Cabazon Band of Mission Indians, et al. v. National Indian Gaming Commission, 827 F.Supp. 26 (1993).

Cabazon Band of Mission Indians, et al. v. National Indian Gaming Commission, 14 F.3d 633 (1994).

California v. Cabazon Band of Mission Indians, 480 U.S. 202 (1987).

Captain v. Ross, Case No. CIV-95-01 Miami Agency (1995).

Cherokee Nation v. Georgia, 30 U.S. 1 (1830).

Cheyenne River Sioux Tribe v. South Dakota, 3 F.3d 273 (1993).

Chickasaw Nation of Oklahoma v. Oklahoma Tax Commission, 31 F.3d 964 (1994).

Choctaw Nation, et al. v. Oklahoma, 397 U.S. 620 (1970).

Citation Bingo, Ltd. v. Otten, 1995 N.M. Lexis 426.

Citizen Band Potawatomi Indian Tribe of Oklahoma v. Green, 95 F.2d 179 (1993).

Cotton Petroleum Corporation v. New Mexico, 490 U.S. 163 (1989).

Duro v. Reina, 495 U.S. 676 (1990).

Elk v. Wilkins, 112 U.S. 94 (1884).

Ex parte Crow Dog, 109 U.S. 556 (1883).

Ex parte Young, 209 U.S. 123 (1908).

Harjo v. Kleppe, 420 F.Supp. 1110 (D.D.C. 1976).

Hotel Employees & Restaurant Employees International Union v. Davis. S074850 (1999).

Indian Country, U.S.A., Inc. v. Oklahoma Tax Commission, 829 F.2d 967 (1987).

Infinity Group, Inc. v. Manzagol, N.M. 632, 884 P.2d 523 (1994).

Johnson & Grahams Lessees v. McIntosh, 21 U.S. 543 (1823).

Kansas ex rel. Stephen v. Finney, 251 Kan. 559; 836 P.2d 1169 (1992).

Lone Wolf v. Hitchcock, 187 U.S. 553 (1903).

McClanahan v. Arizona State Tax Commission, 411 U.S. 164 (1973).

Merrion v. Jicarilla Apache Tribe, 455 U.S. 130 (1982).

Mescalero Apache Tribe v. New Mexico, No. CIV-92-0613-JC (D. N.M. 1992).

Montoya v. Bolack, 70 N.M. 196, 372 P.2s 387 (1962).

Muscogee (Creek) Nation v. Hodel, 851 F.2d 1439 (1988).

Narragansett Indian Tribe of Rhode Island v. Rhode Island, 1995 R.I. Lexis 267.

New Mexico ex rel. Clark v. Johnson, 1995 N.M. Lexis; 904 P.2d 11 (1995).

New Mexico v. Mescalero Apache Tribe, 462 U.S. 324 (1983).

New Mexico v. Aamodt, 537 F.2d 1102 (1976).

Oklahoma Tax Commission v. Graham, 489 U.S. 838 (1989).

Oklahoma Tax Commission v. Citizen Band Potawatomi Indian Tribe 111 S. Ct. 905 (1991).

Oklahoma Tax Commission v. Sac and Fox Nation, 508 U.S. 114 (1993).

Oklahoma Tax Commission v. Chickasaw Nation, 515 U.S. 450 (1995).

Oliphant v. Suquamish Indian Tribe, 435 U.S. 191 (1978).

Pennsylvania v. Union Gas Co., 496 U.S. 1 (1989).

Ponca Tribe of Oklahoma v. Oklahoma, 834 F.Supp. 1341 (1992).

Ponca Tribe of Oklahoma v. Oklahoma, 37 F.3d 1422 (1994).

Prince v. Board of Education of Central Consolidated Independent School District No. 22, 88 N.M. 548, 543 P.2d 1176 (1975).

Pueblo of Sandia v. King, No. CIV-92-076-JC D. N.M. (1992).

Ross v. Neff, 905 F.2d 1349 (1990).

Santa Clara Pueblo v. Martinez, 436 U.S. 49 (1978).

Seminole Tribe of Florida v. Butterworth, 491 F.Supp. 1015 (1980).

Seminole Tribe of Florida v. Butterworth, 658 F.2d 310 (1981).

Seminole Tribe of Florida v. Florida, No. 94-12, 1996 U.S. Lexis 2165 (1996).

Seminole Tribe of Florida v. Florida, 11 F.3d 1016 (1994).

Seneca-Cayuga Tribe of Oklahoma v. Oklahoma ex rel. Thompson, 874 F.2d 709 (1989).

Solem v. Bartlett, 465 U.S. 463 (1984).

Spokane Tribe of Indians v. Washington, 28 F.3d 991 (1994).

State v. George Tassels, 1 Dudley 229 (1830).

State ex rel. May v. Seneca-Cayuga Tribe of Oklahoma, 711 P.2d 77 (1985).

State v. Littlechief, 573 P.2d 263 (1978).

State v. Littlechief, No. 0-77-107, 573 P.2d 263 (1978).

Talton v. Mayes, 163 U.S. 376 (1896).

Trujillo v. Garley, U.S. Dist. Ct., Civ. A. No. 1353 (1948).

United Keetoowah Band of Cherokee Indians v. Oklahoma ex rel. Moss, D.C. No. 87-C-29-E (1987).

United Keetoowah Band of Cherokee Indians v. Oklahoma ex rel. Moss, 927 F.2d 1170 (1991).

United States v. Clapox, et al., 35 F. 575 (1888).

United States v Joseph, 94 U.S. 614 (1876).

United States v. Kagama, 118 U.S. 375 (1886).
United States v. Littlechief, No. 0-77-107, 573 P.2d 263 (1978).
United States v. McBratney, 104 U.S. 621 (1881).
United States v. Sandoval, 231 U.S. 28 (1913).
United States v. Wheeler, 435 U.S. 313 (1978).
Williams v. Lee, 358 U.S. 217 (1959).
Winters v. United States, 207 U.S. 564 (1908).
Worcester v. Georgia, 31 U.S. 515 (1832).

NEWSPAPERS

Albuquerque Journal
Albuquerque Tribune
Arizona Republic
Asbury Park Press
Cherokee Advocate
Chicago Tribune
Daily Oklahoman
Detroit News
Fresno Bee
Gallup Independent
Hartford Courant
Indian Country Today
Indian News Notes
Navajo Times
(Santa Fe) *New Mexican*
New York Times
Rio Grande Sun
Roll Call
Sac and Fox News
Sunday Oklahoman
Tulsa World
Wall Street Journal
Washington Post

Index

Navajo Nation, 34, 37, 39, 72, 74, 79–80, 82, 83, 84, 96, 101, 106, 118, 124, 174; New Mexico gaming referendum, 98, 99, 102
Nebraska, 33, 34
Nevada, 43, 44, 248, 251–52
New Echota, Treaty of (1835), 223, 224
New Federalism, 26
New Jersey, 43, 44
New Mexico, 4, 50, 70–75, 241; court decisions, 146–53; Indian gaming, battle for, 86–92, 235, 241; Indian gaming, legalization and regulation of, 245–47; Indian legislators, 94; Indian tribes in, 71–80; Indian voting rights, 83–86, 234; intertribal unity, 117–18, 172–74; Kelly's tribal confrontation, 154–57, 171–72, 240; tribal-Democratic party relations, 92–115; tribal-state conflict, 80–82, 115–28, 157–71, 174–75
New Mexico Coalition Against Gambling, 107, 113, 125, 126, 168
New Mexico ex rel. Clark v. Johnson (1995), 149–52, 162, 168, 175
New Mexico Indian Gaming Association (NMIGA), 70, 87, 91, 92, 106, 114, 118, 124, 126, 173, 174, 247
New Mexico Office of Indian Affairs, 88, 92, 106, 164
New Mexico Senate Select Committee on Gaming, 107, 111
New Mexico Supreme Court, 146–53
New York, 32
New York v. Attea, 225
Nez Perce Indians, 182
Nineteenth Amendment, 84
Nixon, Richard M., 26, 34, 37, 38, 78, 191
Non-Indian gaming interests, 104–10, 114, 116, 160, 230, 248

O'Connor, Sandra Day, 35, 52, 202
Office of Economic Opportunity (OEO), 38, 185
Office of Indian Affairs, 22, 23
Office of Special Trustee for the American Andians, 26
Off-track betting, 112, 203, 216, 217
Oglala Sioux Indians, 41–42
Oil resources, 81–82, 92, 183, 184
Oklahoma, 5, 25, 50, 241, 261; court decisions, 99, 222–25; elected and appointed officials of, 220–22; gaming in, 202–17, 240; history of, 180–83; Indian gaming, struggle for, 220–30, 235; Indian Gaming Association, 217–19; Indian tribes, 176–202, 244; political culture of, 220–21, 227, 228;

terminated tribes, restoration of, 34; tribal-state relations, 225–27; tribal uniqueness in, 219, 227
Oklahoma Highway Patrol, 197
Oklahoma Indian Gaming Association (OIGA), 217–19
Oklahoma Indian Gaming Commission, 218
Oklahoma Indian Welfare Act (OIWA) (1936), 184, 193
Oklahomans Against the Lottery, 204
Oklahomans for Indian Opportunity, 185
Oklahoma Tax Commission, 187, 199–202, 206–207, 224–26, 237, 242
Oklahoma Tribal Court Reports, 195
Oklahoma v. Littlechief (1978), 194, 196
Olguin, Michael, 165–66
Oliphant v. Suquamish Indian Tribe (1978), 27, 35
Oneida Nation, 160, 235
Oregon, 24, 33
Organic Act (1890), 182
Organized Crime Control Act (OCCA), 49–51
Osage Indians, 182–86
Osage Reservation, Okla., 190
Otoe-Missouri Indians, 261
Ottawa Indians, 34, 185
Owen, Robert L., 189

Pala Band, 249, 250, 251
Pari-mutuel betting, 86, 87, 163, 203, 210, 216, 221, 248
Pechanga Band, 252
Pecos, Regis, 88, 89, 165
Peoria Indians, 34, 182, 185
Pequot Indians, 235, 241
Permissive Lottery Law, 86, 89
Picuris Pueblo, 74, 158
Pipestem, F. Browning, 186, 190
Pitchlynn, Gary, 69, 213, 218, 219, 224, 239
Poarch Creek Indians, 224
Pojoaque Gaming, Inc., 95
Pojoaque Pueblo, 74, 91, 95, 96, 100, 106, 107, 109, 148, 155, 246
Political action committee (PAC), Oklahoma, 229
Political activism, 4, 6, 7, 39–42, 79, 233–35, 241; New Mexico, 70, 92–116, 127–28, 165, 175; Oklahoma, 185, 189, 227–29; and tribal attorneys, 238; voting rights, 83–86
Ponca Indians, 34, 91, 99, 196, 209, 211, 213, 219, 224, 225
Potawatomi Indians. *See* Citizen Band Potawatomi Indians
Power Bingo, 153